Contemporary Hum

Written by a former UN High Commissioner for Human Rights (2003–04), this book has been fully updated for a second edition and continues to provide a much needed, short and accessible introduction to the foundational human rights ideas of our times, and shows that every government is under international obligation to respect and uphold universal human rights.

Updates include:

- Discussion of the recent intellectual challenges to the international human rights movement.
- Examination of the establishment and functioning of the Human Rights Council and the Universal Review Process.
- Evaluation of the developments in the area of the responsibility to protect and continued efforts to implement the right to development.
- Inclusion of issues such as the push for compensation for slavery, experiments with democracy in a number of countries, and the decisions of international judicial and human rights organs on conceptual and protection issues.

This book will be of great interest to students and scholars of global institutions, international law, and human rights.

Bertrand G. Ramcharan, formerly Professor at the Graduate Institute of International and Development Studies, Geneva, is President of the nongovernmental organization UPR Info.

Global Institutions

Edited by Thomas G. Weiss
The CUNY Graduate Center, New York, USA
and Rorden Wilkinson
University of Sussex, Brighton, UK

About the series

The "Global Institutions Series" provides cutting-edge books about many aspects of what we know as "global governance." It emerges from our shared frustrations with the state of available knowledge—electronic and print-wise, for research and teaching—in the area. The series is designed as a resource for those interested in exploring issues of international organization and global governance. And since the first volumes appeared in 2005, we have taken significant strides toward filling conceptual gaps.

The series consists of three related "streams" distinguished by their blue, red, and green covers. The blue volumes, comprising the majority of the books in the series, provide user-friendly and short (usually no more than 50,000 words) but authoritative guides to major global and regional organizations, as well as key issues in the global governance of security, the environment, human rights, poverty, and humanitarian action among others. The books with red covers are designed to present original research and serve as extended and more specialized treatments of issues pertinent for advancing understanding about global governance. And the volumes with green covers—the most recent departure in the series—are comprehensive and accessible accounts of the major theoretical approaches to global governance and international organization.

The books in each of the streams are written by experts in the field, ranging from the most senior and respected authors to first-rate scholars at the beginning of their careers. In combination, the three components of the series—blue, red, and green—serve as key resources for faculty, students, and practitioners alike. The works in the blue and green streams have value as core and complementary readings in courses on, among other things, international organization, global governance, international law, international relations, and international political economy; the red volumes allow further reflection and investigation in these and related areas.

The books in the series also provide a segue to the foundation volume that offers the most comprehensive textbook treatment available dealing with all the major issues, approaches, institutions, and actors in contemporary global governance—our edited work *International Organization and Global Governance* (2014)—a volume to which many of the authors in the series have contributed essays.

Understanding global governance—past, present, and future—is far from a finished journey. The books in this series nonetheless represent significant steps toward a better way of conceiving contemporary problems and issues as well as, hopefully, doing something to improve world order. We value the feedback from our readers and their role in helping shape the on-going development of the series.

A complete list of titles appears at the end of this book. The most recent titles in the series are:

The Politics of International Organizations (2015)
edited by Patrick Weller and Xu Yi-chong

Global Poverty (2nd edition, 2015)
by David Hulme

Global Corporations in Global Governance (2015)
by Christopher May

The United Nations Centre on Transnational Corporations (2015)
by Khalil Hamdani and Lorraine Ruffing

The Challenges of Constructing Legitimacy in Peacebuilding (2015)
by Daisaku Higashi

The European Union and Environmental Governance (2015)
by Henrik Selin and Stacy D. VanDeveer

Rising Powers, Global Governance, and Global Ethics (2015)
edited by Jamie Gaskarth

Contemporary Human Rights Ideas

Second edition

Bertrand G. Ramcharan

LONDON AND NEW YORK

Second edition published 2015
by Routledge
2 Park Square, Milton Park, Abingdon, Oxon OX14 4RN

and by Routledge
711 Third Avenue, New York, NY 10017

Routledge is an imprint of the Taylor & Francis Group, an informa business

© 2015 Bertrand G. Ramcharan

The right of Bertrand G. Ramcharan to be identified as the author of this work has been asserted by him in accordance with the Copyright, Designs and Patent Act 1988.

All rights reserved. No part of this book may be reprinted or reproduced or utilised in any form or by any electronic, mechanical, or other means, now known or hereafter invented, including photocopying and recording, or in any information storage or retrieval system, without permission in writing from the publishers.

Trademark notice: Product or corporate names may be trademarks or registered trademarks, and are used only for identification and explanation without intent to infringe.

British Library Cataloguing in Publication Data
A catalogue record for this book is available from the British Library

Library of Congress Cataloging in Publication Data
Contemporary human rights ideas / Bertrand G Ramcharan. – 2nd edition.
   pages cm. – (Routledge global institutions series ; 102)
Includes bibliographical references and index.
   1. Human rights. 2. Human rights–International cooperation. I. Title.
   JC571.R353 2015
   323–dc23
           2014045174

ISBN: 978-1-138-80714-3 (hbk)
ISBN: 978-1-138-80716-7 (pbk)
ISBN: 978-1-315-75122-1 (ebk)

Typeset in Times New Roman
by Taylor & Francis Books

Contents

List of tables		viii
Foreword to the first edition		ix
Acknowledgments		xii
Abbreviations		xv
	Introduction	1
1	History: Shared heritage, common struggle	10
2	Human rights in the world community	33
3	International obligation	50
4	Universality	62
5	Equality	72
6	Democracy	84
7	Development	97
8	International cooperation and dialogue	114
9	Protection	134
10	Justice, remedy, and reparation	165
11	Conclusion	177
	Select bibliography	186
	Index	189
	Routledge Global Institutions Series	202

List of tables

1.1	The shared intellectual heritage of humanity in the development of ideas of law and justice	12
3.1	Acceptance and implementation of contemporary human rights ideas	51
7.1	World development and poverty indicators	106
9.1	The protection roles of international human rights institutions	144
9.2	The performance of the international protection system	146

Foreword to the first edition

It is with great pleasure that I write a foreword to this unique exposition and analysis of the system of international human rights. Reflecting the fundamental importance of the idea of human rights to effective international governance and international law, the legal discourse on human rights has been at the forefront of academic thought and on the UN agenda since the adoption of the Universal Declaration almost 60 years ago. This book by Professor Ramcharan is a most timely and valuable contribution to human rights scholarship and practice.

There can be few legal scholars better equipped to provide an account of contemporary human rights ideas than Professor Ramcharan. His widely acknowledged international expertise and leadership on the international law and practice of human rights have been instrumental in the success of the human rights movement. For over 30 years, Professor Ramcharan served at the United Nations where he worked at the Centre for Human Rights; headed the Speech-writing Service in the Office of the Secretary-General; served as Director with the UN peace negotiators/peace keepers in the Yugoslav conflict; served as Africa Director in the Department of Political Affairs; and most importantly, served as Assistant Secretary-General and Deputy High Commissioner for Human Rights for five years and then as Under-Secretary-General and High Commissioner for Human Rights for 14 months. The present work is the culmination of decades of reflection and practice in the international law of human rights. If nothing else, this alone sets the work apart from the rest of the extensive literature on international human rights.

In his book, Professor Ramcharan sets out the core ideas underpinning and characterizing human rights, and sets out an agenda for their advancement in the twenty-first century. With their roots in antiquity, human rights define the notion of world order and are crucial not only to governance and justice, but also to our global civilization as a whole.

The book traces the history of human rights development from the codes of Ancient Egypt and Mesopotamia to the human rights law of today. It addresses the empirical as well as philosophical basis for human rights in the respect for shared humanity in all major religions and philosophical traditions, and pays attention to the position of the individual in the community and the rights of groups and peoples.

This book advocates a world order with human rights at its base. It addresses the role human rights norms play in our globalized world and the implications they have for global security (human rights violations and the challenges of international protection). The book also addresses the idea of international obligation and sets out the sources of international human rights law, and also the idea of universality of human rights—as an idea, as a goal, and as a normative concept— with human societies cross-fertilizing and learning from each other, converging towards a great synthesis around binding international human right norms. Also analyzed are the ideas of equality in the UN Charter and the International Covenant on Civil and Political Rights and the work of the Human Rights Committee (non-discrimination and gender equality) and World Conferences devoted to women's rights and racial discrimination.

The book also looks at the idea of democracy and the principle of democratic legitimacy as one of the foundational principles of international human rights law and the contemporary world order. It traces the journey of the idea of development as a human right from the UN Charter to the International Covenant on Economic, Social, and Cultural Rights to the UN Declaration on the Right to Development to the Millennium Development Goals. The book also deals with the difficulties involved in the processes of international cooperation and dialogue on human rights. It highlights some of the salient issues concerning cooperation on different levels and gives a comprehensive account of the practice of human rights dialogues and their role in the promotion of democracy and the rule of law.

The book also focuses on the challenges of implementation. It examines the ideas of justice, remedy, and reparation, and the idea of protection of human rights on the national and international levels. It addresses the responsibility to protect, various types and degrees of protection, and the roles of the UN, its subsidiary bodies, and other international organizations in human rights protection. In advancing the idea of protection, Professor Ramcharan relies on the overlapping

Foreword to the first edition xi

bodies of international law: international human rights law, international humanitarian law, international refugee law, and international criminal law. The greatest value of this book is its foundation in the wealth of experience and information that the author has been uniquely well placed to make available to us. The result is a book that is at once a stock taking of human rights norms and a careful and lucid prognosis of the future of human rights and their protection by the world community. Few issues are more deserving of the attention of the world community as a matter of urgency. Professor Ramcharan's magisterial exposition and analysis of the ideas essential to realizing the promise of human rights is a massive step towards ensuring that human rights theory and protection remain a matter of the highest priority on the world community's agenda.

Judge Abdool Koroma
Judge of the International Court of Justice

Acknowledgments

This book draws on a lifetime of work and reflection on human rights ideas, and there are many people to thank. I should start with the editors of this series, Professor Thomas Weiss and Professor Rorden Wilkinson, for inviting me to offer this volume and for supporting me with their comments and encouragement. I would also like to thank their associates, including Janet Reilly, Danielle Zach, and Nancy Okada. Professor Ben Rivlin, emeritus director of the Ralph Bunch Institute for International Studies, and Dr James S. Sutterlin of Yale University have been mentors for many a year.

Alison Rose helped me tighten the text and make it more presentable to a general audience. I am grateful to her. Professor Robin Ramcharan offered helpful comments and support in developing and finalizing the book. Dr Lily Ramcharan also provided invaluable support.

There is an intellectual debt to many people going back over several years. Professor Paul Taylor and Professor David Johnson of the London School of Economics and Political Science set me on the course to an understanding of international relations, international organizations, and international law. Professors Karel Vasak and Stephen Marks, then of the International Institute of Human Rights in Strasbourg, helped launch me on the journey of rights at the United Nations, and have provided friendship and encouragement ever since.

Three decades and more of human rights colleagues in the United Nations and in regional and nongovernmental organizations provided inspiration and encouragement. Professor John Humphrey, Dr Mark Schreiber, Professor Theo van Boven, and Dr Kurt Herndl, all former heads of the UN human rights program, provided leadership and helped develop a strategy in the pursuit of human rights. Dr Egon Schwelb, Dr Kamleshwar Das, Dr Edward Lawson, and Dr Kwado Nyamekye, all former deputy directors of the UN Division/Center of Human Rights, provided inspiration by their example and their commitment. Mary Robinson and Sergio Vieira de Mello, both UN High Commissioners for Human Rights, provided leadership and offered room to develop initiatives.

In my more than three decades at the UN, I have been fortunate to have served under secretaries-general who provided space to develop human rights approaches. As speechwriter to Secretary-General Pérez de Cuéllar, I made inputs into developing human rights policy. In doing groundwork and an early drafting of *Agenda for Peace* under Secretary-General Boutros Boutros-Ghali, I had the opportunity to learn from that dynamic scholar/practitioner. Secretary-General Kofi Annan led the international community on the human rights cause in a dramatic way. I was privileged to have been Deputy High Commissioner and High Commissioner under his courageous leadership.

My colleagues and friends Jacob Moller, Enayat Houshmand, and William Hogg have been sterling human rights partners. Philippe Le Blanc has encouraged and supported me ever since I first met him at the International Institute of Human Rights. Andreas Mavrommatis has provided inspiration through example and leadership. Tapio Kanninen's faith in the United Nations has been comforting. Ambassador Peter Maurer has been a dynamic partner and leader.

My former assistants, Judith Edrich, Aline Cousineau, Elise Smith, Barbara Boynton, Christine Dumonal, Alice Weber, Lydia Bawar, Adelia Ocampo, Janet Cummins, Janet Weiler, Margaret Ben Mansour, and Jean-Paul M'Bengue, gave me their friendship and support in a human rights journey of three and a half decades at the United Nations.

My former colleagues in the UN Office of the High Commissioner for Human Rights inspired me to stay on the high ground when it came to defending human rights. Colleagues in the nongovernmental world, such as Margo Picken and Felice Gaer, also provided sterling examples and encouraged me to walk the high road. Chris Kruger of the European Commission of Human Rights, Peter Leuprecht of the Council of Europe's Human Rights Directorate, and Christina Cerna of the Inter-American Commission on Human Rights provided inspiration and friendship in the journey of human rights.

Two people whom I count amongst the most devoted human rights thinkers and practitioners in the world have inspired me by their lifes' work: Michael McCormack and Merle Mendonca, co-founders of the Guyana Human Rights Association and international champions of human rights.

My friends Professor Roger Clark, Professor Bert Lockwood, Professor David Weisbrodt, Professor and Judge Ronald St J. Macdonald, and Ambassador Dan Livermore gave me friendship and intellectual support of a special kind.

Some of the ideas discussed in this book were offered in a graduate course at Columbia University in 1988. I am grateful to Dr Paul Martin, director of the Institute for Human Rights at Columbia, for inviting me to teach the course and for being a friend and a partner over the ten years I taught human rights at Columbia and in the years since. Professors Oscar Schachter and Louis Henkin of Columbia were inspirational mentors for a lifetime.

My students and colleagues at the Geneva Graduate Institute of International and Development Studies have provided challenges, questioning, and inspiration that helped sharpen the ideas in the book, especially the idea of protection, to which I gave special emphasis in my courses.

In presenting the human rights ideas discussed in this book, I have drawn on their essence in the world of scholarship and therefore have many intellectual debts. In some instances I have, however, struck out on submissions of my own. These are based on the convictions of a professional lifetime of work and reflection in human rights. I believe deeply, for example, that societies have cross-fertilized and learned from one another. Although the idea of human rights has seen great intellectual fermentation in Western philosophy and practice since the Magna Carta of 1215, this intellectual activity drew on earlier ideas of law, justice, and humanity from ancient civilizations. Justice is undoubtedly the fundamental basis and yardstick for determining the content and implementation of human rights. The quest for justice in Babylon, China, India, Egypt, wider Mesopotamia, Persia, and Sumeria long predated that drive in Western civilization. We all owe an intellectual debt to those early thinkers who set us on the course to justice and respect for humanity that now forms part of the intellectual patrimony of humankind. We should also thank the global human rights champions of the twentieth century. Ours is now a truly global cause.

Bertrand Ramcharan
Professor of Human Rights
Graduate Institute of International and Development Studies
Geneva, 31 July 2007

Abbreviations

APRM	African Peer Review Mechanism
ASEAN	Association of Southeast Asian Nations
AU	African Union (formerly OAU)
BPG	UN Basic Principles and Guidelines on the Right to a Remedy and Reparation for Victims of Gross Violations of International Human Rights Law and Serious Violations of International Humanitarian Law
CAAC	children and armed conflict
CHR	Commission on Human Rights (United Nations) (replaced by the Human Rights Council)
CSCE	Conference on Security and Co-operation in Europe
ECHR	European Court of Human Rights
ECOSOC	Economic and Social Council (United Nations)
GA	General Assembly (United Nations)
HC	humanitarian coordinator
HRC	Human Rights Council (United Nations)
ICC	International Criminal Court
ICCPR	International Covenant on Civil and Political Rights
ICESCR	International Covenant on Economic, Social and Cultural Rights
ICJ	International Court of Justice
ICRC	International Committee of the Red Cross
IDEA	International Institute for Democracy and Electoral Assistance
ILO	International Labour Organization
IPU	Inter-Parliamentary Union
ISF	Iraqi Security Forces
ISIL	Islamic State in Iraq and the Levant
ISIS	Islamic State in Iraq and Syria
MDGs	Millennium Development Goals (United Nations)

MOU	memorandum of understanding
NAM	Non-Aligned Movement
NEPAD	New Partnership for Africa's Development
NGO	nongovernmental organization
OAS	Organization of American States
OAU	Organization of African Unity
ODA	official development assistance
OHCHR	Office of the High Commissioner for Human Rights
OSCE	Organization for Security and Co-operation in Europe
RC	resident coordinator
SRSG	special representative of the secretary-general
UDHR	Universal Declaration of Human Rights
UN	United Nations
UNAMI	United Nations Assistance Mission for Iraq
UNDP	United Nations Development Programme
UNESCO	United Nations Educational, Scientific and Cultural Organization
UNHCR	United Nations High Commissioner for Refugees
UNICEF	United Nations Children's Fund
UNSC	United Nations Security Council
UPR	Universal Periodic Review

Introduction

> We consider certain fundamental values to be essential to international relations in the twenty-first century. These include: freedom, equality, solidarity, tolerance, respect for nature, shared responsibility.
>
> (Millennium Declaration)

Massive human rights violations are characteristic of a world in deep crisis. Universal respect for human rights could lead to a chain reaction that would help solve many of the world's ills. This book examines the key human rights ideas that could help start this chain reaction.

Ours is a world that is wounded and tormented by environmental degradation,[1] conflicts, strife, poverty, discrimination, terrorism, and atrocities committed by state and non-state actors on innocent human beings, millions of whom have fled their national borders.[2] For large swaths of humankind, life is indeed miserable, nasty, brutish, and short. Often it is no less than hellish, when individuals are tortured, made to disappear, arbitrarily executed, trafficked into slavery or prostitution, or suffer from honor killings. All of these, and more, have occurred at the start of the twenty-first century. Protection—nationally, regionally, and internationally—is sparse.[3]

The human rights idea, faithfully implemented, can help ameliorate the human condition and lay the foundation for a more peaceful, prosperous, and equitable future. However, there are vigorous debates over human rights; debates that were at the heart of the ideological confrontation during the Cold War and now feature in a political confrontation between countries of the developed North and the developing South, between countries of the Western and non-Western worlds, and in the face of frontal assaults by fundamentalist and terrorist groups. Arguments over universal values and supposedly divergent cultural tenets in countries with differing religious or philosophical persuasions are also thrown into this maelstrom. Oftentimes, this is simply opportunistic, as the representatives of repressive governments seek to counter criticism by asserting that human rights are alien values. Sometimes, though, this is due to genuine misunderstanding about the degree of consensus that exists over universal human values—what is described in this book as the rolling history of the global development of human rights in which different societies have learned about law, justice, and human rights from each other. This crystallized in an historic consensus in 1948 with the adoption of the Universal Declaration of Human Rights (UDHR) and its reconfirmation in 1993 at the World Conference on Human Rights.

More recently, in the UN Millennium Declaration, leaders from all countries in the world re-endorsed shared values for the twenty-first century, including freedom and equality. This declaration draws directly from ancient trends in human history, as will be shown later.

Indeed, the human rights idea has run together and remains intertwined with the destiny of humankind.[4] In *Freedom in the Ancient World*,[5] Herbert Muller traced the development of the idea of law in societies from across the globe, as well as the use of law to protect freedom and human rights. Law has been traced to ancient scripts such as the Codex Ur-Nammu, the Sumerian Codex, the Babylonian Codex Lipit-Ishtar, Codex Eshnunna, and the Code of Hammurabi, significantly predating the development of the idea of law in Western civilizations.[6] The ideas of law and justice were not Western ideas in their inception. Rather they are part of the patrimony of humankind, and different civilizations have contributed to them.[7]

This is also the case with human rights. Admittedly, in the second millennium of the common era, there was a great deal of fermentation and debate over the idea of natural or human rights in Europe. However, elements of the rights idea, such as law and justice, can be traced to ancient civilizations, such as ancient Egypt, India, Mesopotamia, Sumeria, and Persia. The famous decree of Cyrus issued in 539 BCE after his conquest of Babylon, provided for the protection of human rights. When accepting the Nobel Peace Prize in December 2003, Shirin Ebadi invoked Cyrus's laws, urging that "[t]he Charter of Cyrus the Great should be studied in the history of human rights."[8]

Cyrus's Charter declared:

I undertake to honor the religion and custom of all nations under my kingdom; I shall never impose my kingdom to any nation,
I shall not allow anyone to oppress another;
I shall not allow anyone to dispossess others' property by force or take it without consideration or satisfaction of the owner;

I shall not allow anyone to use forced or unpaid labor;
Everybody is free to choose any religion he believes in;
Everybody is responsible for himself;
I shall not allow any man or woman to be sold as a slave ... This custom shall be totally abolished throughout the world.[9]

Yet, a millennium later, millions of Africans would be enslaved, and genocide would be committed. Colonialism, segregation, and apartheid would all be committed in the name of Western civilization.

All societies have seen struggles for what is now known as human rights, and the seeds of the human rights idea are scattered in different parts of the world. Some experts have traced instances of workers' and women's rights to ancient Egypt. Elements of humanitarian law have been traced to practices in Africa and Asia.[10] Societies have cross-fertilized and shared ideas, and some societies have taken ideas further in different historical epochs. It is a matter of historical record that the Greek philosophers owed debts to Babylon and Egypt.[11] The philosophies of Socrates, Plato, and Aristotle drew and built on intellectual strands in ancient civilizations. The development of human rights is a rolling process, and ideas have been developed across different lands. Now, these ideas are further expanded within the framework of international human rights law that took root with the establishment of the United Nations.[12]

In the history of the human rights idea across the globe, there are two interrelated strands: law, struggle, and policy, on the one hand, and philosophical reflections, on the other. Ancient texts such as the Code of Hammurabi, the Charter of Cyrus, and the Law of Manu are examples of statements of law and policy from authoritative sources. The Magna Carta, one of the foundation documents of the Western human rights tradition, emerged from struggle and political negotiations. A historian of the charter commented that it:

> was a product of intermittent negotiations which lasted for at least six months. It was the culmination of hard bargaining and skilful manoeuvring. Perhaps it registered too the weariness of the negotiators in the face of the intractable character of the king, the intransigence of some of his opponents and the hard facts of English administration.[13]

When writing the history of the idea of human rights in Western thought, Kenneth Minogue pointed out that, although the idea of natural rights was a topic of political discussion during the Civil War of the 1640s in England, "most political discussion in England tended to be conducted in historical and legal terms rather than philosophical."[14]

This has been the case with all of the great declarations of human rights. Grievances led to claims that were articulated in the form of asserted rights and then fought over or negotiated, with the outcome being distillations of rights in political statements or agreed outcome documents. Political struggles and negotiations drew, in part, on philosophical ideas, and some philosophers were partisans in political struggles. This combination of struggle and philosophy is seen in the elaboration of the English Declaration of Rights,[15] the American Declaration of Independence,[16] and the French Declaration of the Rights of Man and the Citizen.[17] Struggles, negotiations, and philosophical debates intertwined to produce these and subsequent human rights statements, including the celebrated UDHR.

The idea of human rights has thus served as a moral and political banner for people fighting for progress, equity, and justice, who have used a combination of pragmatic and philosophical arguments.[18] The struggle for human rights was a major feature of the twentieth century and remains so in the twenty-first century. It would not be too extravagant to claim that the future of human progress depends on human rights as defined and elaborated at the United Nations (UN).

Here, human rights means rights contained in consensual international instruments promulgated by the UN, whether they be civil and political rights or economic, social, and cultural rights. The UN has never classified rights into generations, and thus this term is not used here. Rights cannot be separated into generational categories except as academic classifications for the purposes of teaching or research.

There are raging debates over human rights ideas concerning issues such as universality and relativism. There are debates in the UN and elsewhere regarding the responsibility to protect and governments' arguments against the dangers of interventionism. Many countries emphasize their sovereignty over the international protection of human rights. Nevertheless, the vindication of human rights is vital for human progress and ameliorating the human condition, and, political fireworks aside, there is a widespread international consensus on a solid core of human rights ideas, which are entrenched in contemporary international law. In all instances, once the debates are pushed aside, the realities of the landscape remain. The Millennium Declaration, cited at the opening of this introduction, brings out the centrality of human rights in the aspirations of humankind for the twenty-first century.

The clarification of the core human rights ideas can help develop cooperative strategies to advance human rights in the twenty-first century. This book seeks to set out the essence of the law regarding the topics discussed. Governments have an obligation to implement the norms of international law dealing with human rights to which they have freely consented. Governmental compliance with international human rights obligations is a necessity. The fact that many governments do not live up to those obligations does not diminish their legal force. The task, rather, is to work for faithful compliance. The fact that laws are violated does not negate their validity. The case is the same with international human rights law.

Taking the idea of human rights as a point of departure, this study examines key constituent strands that help move the global human rights mission forward. It begins with an historical discussion of the idea of rights and then examines the role of human rights in the contemporary world order. As this study will illustrate, human rights define the notion of world order, are crucial to governance, are the value framework for our global civilization, provide indispensable anchors for a globalizing world, must be protected from violations through preventive strategies, and lead to the quest for justice. In addition, human rights call for new strategies, particularly in the areas of education and the prevention of gross and criminal violations, and serve as an international policy framework for humanity's aspirations for a world of progress in freedom.

The book then examines governments' international obligations to uphold binding human rights norms, based on the premise that there is an international legal order that stipulates that governments are legally bound to uphold certain human rights. In the first place, every UN member state has legal obligations under the UN Charter, particularly Articles 1, 55, and 56. Member states' key legal obligations under the charter have passed into international customary law, under which there are certain norms of international public policy from which no state may legally deviate. These are the peremptory norms of public international law or, in technical parlance, *jus cogens* norms.[19]

In addition to the UN Charter as a world constitutional document[20] and international customary law, governments have freely subscribed to human rights obligations under international treaties. Treaties are thus a source of legal obligation to uphold human rights. Finally, international law recognizes general principles of law that are common to the principal legal systems of the world as a source of law. It may be possible to ground a binding legal obligation to uphold human rights in such a general principle of law.

Human rights thus often represent hard legal obligations binding on governments—not abstract or vague notions. In *The Economist* magazine, a global leader sought to deny that economic and social rights are human rights.[21] This is an issue to be determined in accordance with the rules of international law governing whether a particular right is a human right. 163 states have ratified the International Covenant on Economic, Social and Cultural Rights (ICESCR), and thereby have undertaken binding legal obligations. Under international law, these are human rights.

After discussing the international obligation to uphold human rights, this text looks at the idea of universality, which is the notion that all human beings are equally entitled to basic human rights, such as the rights not to be arbitrarily killed, enslaved, or tortured. Evidence will be presented that convincingly establishes that the authoritative bodies of the world community have declared and reconfirmed the universally valid and binding international human rights of every human being.

Accompanying universality is the great idea of equality, which is examined in key instruments such as the UN Charter and the International Covenant on Civil and Political Rights (ICCPR), as well as major world conferences on the quest for racial and gender equality. Although enshrined in key international legal instruments, equality is still a distant reality for large parts of humankind, especially women.

The idea of democracy is considered next. According to the UDHR, governments' authority is derived from the will of the people, which should be determined in freely held periodic elections under adult suffrage. It will be shown that the right to democratic governance has crystallized in the international legal order. The book will also examine efforts to centralize the right to democracy and examine practical programs of assistance and support for free and fair elections.

Building on universality, equality, and democracy, an important new idea that has emerged at the UN—the notion of development as a human right—is also examined. This idea is a simple but powerful one, namely that governments and regional and international institutions should endeavor to provide all individuals with decent life chances and the opportunity to realize their potential. Ongoing efforts to put this idea into application will be also investigated.

In this journey of human rights ideas, the idea of international cooperation and dialogue for the universal realization of human rights is also explored. The duty to cooperate is grounded in the UN Charter, the UN Declaration on Principles of International Law Concerning Friendly Relations and Cooperation among States (1970), and key human rights instruments, including pertinent General Assembly (GA) resolutions and those of the former Commission on Human Rights (CHR), now succeeded by the Human Rights Council (HRC). The practice of human rights dialogue in a number of contexts is also discussed, and it will be shown that the purpose of such dialogues is to promote and protect internationally recognized human rights. Thereafter, the idea of the protection of human rights is also discussed. This examination submits that protection has preventive, curative, and remedial or compensatory dimensions. The GA's recognition of a responsibility to protect is also reviewed, with an eye on both the deficiencies and challenges of international protection. Next, this study looks at efforts to strengthen national protection systems and at the organs and instrumentalities of protection at the international level.

Finally, the ideas of justice, redress, and reparation for the victims of human rights violations are explored. The idea of justice as an arbiter of other values is discussed, with reference to the quest for justice for victims of human rights violations, including the concept of transitional justice, as well as the ideas of redress and reparation in the light of the UN Basic Principles and Guidelines, which were adopted in 2006 by the GA on the basis of work within the former CHR and the Economic and Social Council (ECOSOC). The key provisions of these guidelines are also set out, which provide, in essence, a synthesis of the core parts of the contemporary international law on human rights. The guidelines provide a superb encapsulation of the thrust of the human rights idea in the contemporary world and a fitting conclusion to this work.

The *raison d'être* of this book is a simple one: Over the long history of humanity, with the contribution of different peoples and leaders, we have arrived at the twenty-first century with a solid set of human rights ideas and international norms. Let us insist that governments must uphold and defend these human rights.

Notes

1 W. Paul Gormley, *Human Rights and Environment: The Need for International Cooperation* (Leyden, the Netherlands: A.W. Sijthoff, 1976).
2 See for example, Niklaus Steiner, Mark Gibney and Gil Loescher, eds, *Problems of Protection: The UNHCR, Refugees, and Human Rights* (New York and London: Routledge, 2003); and Thomas G. Weiss and David A. Korn, *Internal Displacement: Conceptualization and its Consequences* (London and New York: Routledge, 2006).
3 See generally, Julie Mertus, *The United Nations and Human Rights: A Guide for a New Era* (London and New York: Routledge, 2005).
4 See generally, UNESCO, *Birthright of Man*, a selection of texts prepared under the direction of Jeanne Hirsch (New York: UNIPUB, 1969).

8 Introduction

5 Herbert Muller, *Freedom in the Ancient World* (London: Secker and Warburg, 1961).
6 Russ ver Steeg, *Law in the Ancient World* (Durham, N.C.: Carolina Academic Press, 2002). The author lists additional ancient codes such as the Middle Assyrian Laws and the Hittite Laws circa 1000 BCE, the neo-Babylonian Laws, the Covenant Code, the Deuteronomic Code of Syria–Palestine, the Drakon, the Gortyn Code, and the Twelve Tables of Greece/Rome. See his table, "Distribution of legal sources."
7 See generally, Bernard Grun, *The Timetables of History: A Horizontal Linkage of People and Events* (New York: Simon and Schuster, 1982).
8 Shirin Ebadi, "In the Name of the God of Creation and Wisdom," acceptance speech for Nobel Peace Prize, 2003, www.nobelprize.org.
9 Text available in A. Hajipour, "Human Rights Charter of Cyrus," 30 May 2006, at www.iran-law.com.
10 See for example, Emmanuel Bello, *African Customary Humanitarian Law* (Geneva, Switzerland: ICRC, 1980). According to Bello, in certain parts of Africa, some tribes "took pride in according respect and human rights to women, children and old persons." See also Taslim Olawale Elias, *Africa and the Development of International Law* (Leiden, the Netherlands: A.W. Sijthoff, 1972).
11 See Cheikh Anta Diop, *The African Origins of Civilization: Myth or Reality* (Chicago, Ill.: Lawrence Hill Books, 1967).
12 See Thomas Buergenthal, "The Normative and Institutional Evolution of International Human Rights," *Human Rights Quarterly* 19, no. 1 (1997): 703–25.
13 James Clark Holt, *Magna Carta* (Cambridge: Cambridge University Press, 1992), 6.
14 Walter Laqueur and Barnett Rubin, eds, *The Human Rights Reader*, 2nd edn (New York: Meridian Books, 1989), 6. One could see the element of political bargaining in *Federalist Paper No. 84*. The Bill of Rights is now celebrated in the United States, but the original constitution did not include a bill of rights. Some used this as an argument against ratification. Alexander Hamilton, making the case for ratification, marshaled arguments against the need for a bill of rights. See Alexander Hamilton, James Madison, and John Jay, *The Federalist Papers, with an Introduction and Commentary by Gary Wills* (New York: Bantam Books, 1982), 434.
15 See Lois Schwoerer, *The Declaration of Rights, 1689* (Baltimore, Md.: Johns Hopkins University Press, 1981). See also Bernard Schwartz, *The Roots of Freedom: A Constitutional History of England* (New York: Hill and Wang, 1967).
16 Michael J. Meyer and William A. Parent, eds., *The Constitution of Rights: Human Dignity and American Values* (Ithaca, NY and London: Cornell University Press, 1992).
17 See Pierre Agrillet, *La bataille des droits de l'homme* (The struggle for human rights) (Ville de Vaux Le Pénil, France, 1987).
18 See generally Edmund S. Morgan, *Inventing the People. The Rise of Popular Sovereignty in England and America* (New York: W.W. Norton & Company, 1988).
19 See Article 53, the Vienna Convention on the Law of Treaties, 1969. See generally "*Jus Cogens*" in Ian Brownlie, *Principles of Public International Law*, 6th edn (Oxford: Oxford University Press, 2003), 488–90.

20 See Ronald St J. Macdonald and Douglas M. Johnston, eds, *Towards World Constitutionalism: Issues in the Legal Ordering of the World Community* (Leiden, the Netherlands: Martinus Nijhoff, 2005).
21 See "Stand Up for Your Rights ..." *The Economist*, 22 March 2007. *The Economist* argues that "food, jobs and housing are certainly necessities but no useful purpose is served by calling them 'rights'." It adds: "it is hardly an accident that the countries keenest to use the language of social and economic rights tend to be those that show least respect for rights of the traditional sort."

1 History
Shared heritage, common struggle

- Law and justice: the common heritage of humanity
- Respect for shared humanity in the major religious and philosophical traditions
- The place of the individual in the community and the rights of groups and peoples
- The common struggle for human rights
- Positive rights
- Natural rights
- The public policy function of human rights
- The contemporary role of international consensus and legislation
- Conclusion

> Each time a man stands up for an ideal, or acts to improve the lot of others, or strikes out against injustice, he sends forth a tiny ripple of hope, and crossing each other from a million different centers of energy and daring, those ripples build a current that can sweep down the mightiest walls of oppression and resistance.
> (Robert Kennedy, 1966[1])

This chapter looks at historical aspects of the development of human rights and at the global quest for their implementation and vindication. The following strands are discussed: the shared heritage of humanity in the development of the ideas of law and justice; major religions' emphasis on respect for shared humanity; the place of the individual in the community and the rights of groups and peoples; philosophical debates that have accompanied the evolution of rights; the idea of the individual's positive rights; the idea of natural rights; the role of struggle and policy in the development of rights; and the role of international consensus and legislation in the contemporary concept of rights captured in the UDHR's opening article: "All human beings are born free and equal in dignity and rights. They are endowed with reason and conscience and should act towards one another in a spirit of brotherhood."[2]

Law and justice: the common heritage of humanity[3]

To understand and appreciate the contemporary concepts of law and rights, it is essential to have a sense of the common heritage of humanity in the development of these concepts (see Table 1.1). In *Freedom in the Ancient World*, the historian Herbert J. Muller noted that although ancient men scarcely believed that freedom and justice were one and inseparable as is now commonplace, "there has always been a real connection between them beginning with the necessity of law for any effective freedom. Law codes, written or unwritten, confer some rights in the very act of specifying obligations and penalties."[4]

While these codes mainly imposed constraints, they also protected the individual against uncustomary or arbitrary constraints: "Early civilizations made positive advances towards such ideals in particular through the efforts of kings to protect ordinary men against the abuses of power and privilege."[5]

Ancient Egypt, Muller assessed, foreshadowed democratic principles of justice when a god declared—in respect of the rights of the deceased—that he had made every man like his fellow man, made the great flood waters of the Nile for the benefit of the poor man and the great man alike, and given all men equal access to the kingdom of the dead. Even if Egypt never achieved this ideal of equality, "at least the next world was thrown open to common men."[6]

The priests of the Middle Kingdom, scholars noted, were cognizant of the tendency toward recognizing the equality of all men. A declaration of the Sun God in the following excerpt from one of the "Coffin Texts" brought this out dramatically:

> I made the four winds that every man might breathe thereof like his father in his time ... I made the great inundation that the poor man might have rights therein like the great man ... I made every man like his fellow. I did not command that they do evil, but it was their hearts that violated what I had said ... I made their hearts to cease from forgetting the West in order that divine offerings might be given to the gods of the nomes ... I brought into being the four gods from my sword, while men are the tears of my eyes.[7]

Table 1.1 The shared intellectual heritage of humanity in the development of ideas of law and justice

BCE	
4241	First dated year in history
3500–3001	Earliest known writing, Sumerian cuneiform
2500–2001	The first libraries in Egypt; in Egyptian literature, lamentations and skepticism about meaning of life
2000–1501	Egyptian alphabet of 24 signs
	Mesopotamian Codex Ur-Nammu
	Babylonian Codex Lipit-Ishtar, Codex Eshnunna
	Hammurabi, King of Babylon, sets laws of kingdom in order; Code of Hammurabi is first of all legal systems
1500–1001	Middle Assyrian laws
	Hittite laws
	Hymns of the Rigveda (Vedic religion assigns different powers to the separate deities of the heavens, the air, and the earth)
	Gilgamesh epic
	Moses receives the Ten Commandments on Mount Sinai
1000–901	Pantheistic religion develops in India (Brahmanism and Atmanism) teaching identity of self, transmigration of soul; caste system
	In China, rational philosophy gains over mysticism
900–801	*Iliad* and *Odyssey*; leather scrolls with translations of Old Babylonian texts into Aramaic and Greek
	The earliest Jewish prophets
800–601	Laws of Lycurgus at Sparta
	Indian Vedas completed (a collection of religious, philosophical, and educational writings). In India, Brahmanic religion defines six stages of the transmigration of the soul
	First written laws of Athens by Draco
	Anaximander of Miletus, Greek philosopher (611–546)
	Zoroaster, founder of Persian religion (631–653)
	Lao-tse, Chinese philosopher, b. 604
600–501	Mayan civilization in Mexico

History: shared heritage, common struggle

BCE	
	During the Babylonian Captivity of the Jews, many books of the Old Testament, based on word of mouth tradition, are first written down in Hebrew
	Cyrus II, the Great of Persia (553–529) established Persian empire; in 536, he frees Jews from Babylonian captivity and aids their return to Israel
	Solon's laws promulgated in Athens
	Anaximenes and Pythagoras, Greek philosophers
	Mahavira Jina founds Jainism in India; first known rebel against caste system
	Kung Fu-tse (Confucius), Chinese philosopher
	Siddhartha Gautama, Buddha, founder of Buddhism
	Xenophanes founds school of philosophy
	Parmenides, Greek philosopher*
500–451	Neo-Babylonian Laws
	Covenant Code
	Deuteronomic code
	Beginning of historical writing in Greece
	Ramayana, ancient Hindu poem (c.500)
	Empedocles and Protagoras, Greek philosophers
	Herodotus, father of Greek history
	Heraclitus, Greek philosopher
	Socrates, Athenian philosopher (470 to 399)
	Democritus, Greek philosopher
	Ezra, Hebrew scribe, goes to Jerusalem to restore the laws of Moses (458)
450–401	The Decemvirs codify Roman laws in a form known as the Twelve Tables (450)
	The Torah becomes the moral essence of the Jewish state
	Plato (427–347)
	Thucydides, Greek historian (424)
400–351	Aristotle, Greek philosopher (384–322)
350–301	The Indian epic, Mahabharata being written
250–201	Asoka, the Indian emperor, erects columns 40 feet high inscribed with his laws (c.250)

14 *History: shared heritage, common struggle*

BCE	
CE	
401–450	St Augustine's *City of God* (411)
529	Justinian's Code of Civil Laws
570	Mohammed, founder of Islam
598	Probably the first English school at Canterbury
640	Arabs find famous Alexandria library with 300,000 papyrus scrolls

The information in this table is excerpted from two sources: the highly acclaimed work *The Timetables of History: A Horizontal Linkage of People and Events* by Bernard Grun, based on Werner Stein's *Kulturfahrplan* (New York: Simon and Schuster, 1982); and Russ ver Steeg, *Law in the Ancient World* (Durham, N.C.: Carolina Academic Press, 2002).

Note: * *The Timetables of History*, cited above, comments: "In Confucius, Buddha, Zoroaster, Lao-tse, the Jewish prophets, the Greek poets, artists, philosophers and scientists, the sixth century BC reaches a zenith of human wisdom and achievement."

In Mesopotamia, the idea grew that justice was man's right, not merely a royal favor, and that the gods themselves had approved this right. The ancient Sumerians were the first to formulate law codes; one of the earliest was that of Lipit-Ishtar, who ruled in the first half of the nineteenth century BCE.[8] The code includes an invocation of the principle of justice: "If a man cut down a tree in the garden of (another) man, he shall pay one-half mina of silver."[9]

The Code of Hammurabi, which is preserved on a large black stone, contains 282 clauses. It sought to protect the interests of the state and those who served it. The invocation of justice is at the very outset of the code. In the prologue, Hammurabi announced that the gods had sent "me, Hammurabi, the obedient, God-fearing prince to make manifest justice in the land, to destroy the wicked and the evil-doer, that the strong harm not the weak."[10] Maintaining the principle of justice, the prologue proudly continued: "when Marduk sent me to rule over men, to give the protection of right to the land, I did right and righteousness … and brought about the well being of the oppressed." It went on:

> In my bosom I carried the peoples of the land of Sumer and Akkad,
> They prospered under my protection,
> I have governed them in peace;
> I have sheltered them in my strength,
> In order that the strong might not oppress the weak,
> That justice might be dealt the orphan and the widow …
> I wrote my precious words on my stela,

> And in the presence of my statute as the king of justice,
> I set it up in order to administer the laws of the land,
> To prescribe the ordinances of the land,
> To give justice to the oppressed ...
> Let any oppressed man who has a cause
> Come into the presence of my statue as king of justice
> And then read my inscribed stela ...
> May he understand his case,
> May he set his mind at ease ...
> In the days to come for all time
> Let the king who appears in the land observe
> The words of justice which I wrote in my stela ...
> Let him not scorn my statutes.[11]

The epilogue recalled "laws of justice which Hammurabi the wise king established, a righteous law and pious statute did he teach the land."[12]

In his human rights charter, Cyrus the Great declared that he would not allow anyone to oppress another person, and he would not allow any man or woman to be sold as a slave. One notes the universalist perspective of these pronouncements.

In ancient India, codes such as the Laws of Manu also invoked the principle of justice when they affirmed that "justice being violated, destroys; justice being preserved, preserves; therefore, justice must not be violated lest violated justice destroy us ... The only friend who follows men even after death is justice."[13]

Although many of these ancient examples present concepts of equality and justice, it is clear that they were not just and equitable throughout. To the contrary, some of their provisions were quite objectionable, but, nevertheless, they bring out two vital points: first, the common heritage of humanity in the development of the idea of law to regulate human conduct; and second, the affirmations of the ideal of justice. The development and perfection of the law is a process that continues today across the globe and at the international level. It took champions such as Blackstone, Sir Edward Coke, and others to develop English law. Napoleon initiated the famous Napoleonic Codes in France. Even in contemporary times, great jurists still strive to make the law more just. The same can be said of the international human rights regime. The quest for law and justice is an integral part of humanity's pursuit of a better world. The concepts of law and justice are indeed part of the shared heritage of humanity.

Respect for shared humanity in the major religious and philosophical traditions

Although emphasis on the language of rights was part of the Western tradition, ideas akin to rights may be found in many religions going back centuries before the first great Western human rights statement, the Magna Carta of 1215. A book entitled *Religious Diversity and Human Rights*, published in 1996, examined precisely this issue. After discussing Buddhism, Christianity, Confucianism, Hinduism, Islam, and Judaism, the study found that space was generally made for, or claimed by, the individual within a holistic order in all of the above religions, and there was also a fundamental concern for the value of individual lives. In the realm of religious practice, individual determinations and choices often abounded.[14] According to the book, there was a profound and complex connection between the metaphysical ideas central to traditions and their particular conceptions of the individual and individual dignity.[15] Further, the book continued, one of the functions of human rights norms was to regulate the ways in which people coming from different traditions, ideologies and cultures may deal with each other: "The basic contribution to the shaping of our norms for the treatment of others comes from our religious traditions."[16]

A monograph on the role of religion and culture in the development of human rights in Sri Lanka, published by the Sri Lanka Foundation in 1982, summarized the findings of five working groups that examined the links between religion and human rights in Buddhism, Hinduism, Islam, and Christianity, the last being considered in separate groups on Catholicism and Christianity in general. According to the working groups, in all five major religious groups:

> Fundamental human rights are inalienable and have a valid basis for the meaningful consideration of human rights in the universal love of man and animal and the respect for every thing that exists, both animate and inanimate, including the environment. While the differences have their distinct religious perceptions and philosophical explanations of the universe, of human relationships and of development, of motivations and of ultimate destiny, the religious and cultural traditions of the five major religions uphold in common certain basic moral and ethical values for the promotion of which man must be enabled to exercise his rights and perform his duties in a mutuality of relationships. Among these values held in common are human dignity and worth, equality, freedom, love and compassion, truth, justice, brotherhood and charity.[17]

History: shared heritage, common struggle 17

In his book, *The Evolution of International Human Rights: Visions Seen*, Paul Gordon Laurens provided snapshots of human rights-related thought in the principal religions. Hinduism, he noted, was one of the world's oldest religions, dating back some 3,000 years. Hindu scriptures:

> address the existence of good and evil, wisdom, the necessity for moral behavior and especially the importance of duty ... and good conduct ... towards others suffering in need ... All human life, despite the vast differences among individuals, is considered sacred, to be loved and respected without distinction as to family member or stranger, friend or enemy.[18]

Hinduism's doctrine of non-violence was also very much in the stream of dignity and humanity: one should not cause pain to any living being at any time through the actions of one's mind, speech, or body.[19]

Buddhism advocated the principles of universal brotherhood and equality. One of the great advocates in our times, the Dalai Lama, urged that one show kindness, love, and respect for all humanity and an understanding of one another's fundamental humanity; respect one another's rights, and share one another's sufferings and problems.[20]

Confucian philosophy emphasized the importance of an ethical life on earth as well as harmony and cooperation from all persons, honoring their duty and responsibility toward others. It also emphasized goodness, benevolence, love, and human-heartedness.[21]

Islam emphasized the common humanity and equality of all of humankind. The *Quran* emphasized the role of justice, the sanctity of life, personal safety, freedom, mercy, compassion, and respect for all human beings.[22]

An assessment of the positive contributions of Christianity and Judaism offered by Edward James Schuster held that: "[D]espite obvious abuses of power and authority, Judaism and Christianity furnished the principles, guidelines and inspiration in support of human rights."[23] Judaism, Laurens noted, emphasized the shared fatherhood of God for all people and the fundamental importance of the creation of human beings as members of one family and as individuals endowed with worth.[24] Isaiah called on all believers to let the oppressed go free, to share their bread with the hungry, and to bring the homeless and poor into their homes.[25] In Christianity, Jesus taught the value of all human beings in the sight of God, and advocated love and compassion as well as charity, healing the sick, feeding the hungry, welcoming the stranger, and caring for the oppressed.[26]

According to Schuster, the positive contributions of both religions are: affirmation of the unique value and dignity of the human person; ethical norms of justice and equity to govern interpersonal relations; condemnations of injustice and offenses against man; norms for just government and institutions; social justice as an extension of individual rights; and supremacy and integrity of the conscience as ultimate arbiter of right and wrong.[27]

From the foregoing, which are mere samples, it is clear that the great religions and philosophical systems all emphasize the common humanity and dignity of every person. The UDHR, with its declaration that all human beings are born free and equal in dignity and rights, can be traced to these early streams.

The place of the individual in the community and the rights of groups and peoples

All great religious and philosophical systems view the individual in his or her relationship with the community. While preparing to draft the UDHR, the UN Educational, Scientific and Cultural Organization (UNESCO) asked leading thinkers and statesmen to share their insights on rights and what might be included in the declaration. In his response, Mahatma Gandhi pointed out that, in India, emphasis had been placed, historically, on the individual's duties to the community.[28]

This phenomenon is found in other religious and philosophical systems. Looking back historically, John Locke, who is associated with the theory of natural rights, considered that the law of nature, which conferred natural rights, imposed duties as well.[29] Locke regarded the performance of these duties as the source of the individual's right to order his actions and dispose of his possessions and person as he thought fit. He also saw their non-performance as adequate reason for withdrawal of that right. He wrote:

> That all men may be restrained from invading others' rights, and from doing hurt to one another, and the law of Nature be observed, ... the execution of the law of Nature is in that state put into every man's hands, whereby everyone has a right to punish the transgressors of that law to such a degree as may hinder its violation. For the law of Nature would, as all other laws that concern men in this world, be in vain, if there were nobody that in the state of Nature had a power to execute that law, and thereby preserve the innocent and restrain offenders.[30]

When African nations proceeded to draft the African Charter of Human and People's Rights, it was emphasized that the beneficial relationship of the individual, the group, and the community added to the catalogue of African rights alongside rights recognized in international law.

It was in recognition of tenets such as these that Article 29 of the UDHR affirmed that all people have duties to the community in which the free and full development of his or her personality is also possible. In the exercise of rights and freedoms, all people shall be subject to limitations only as determined by law for the purpose of securing the recognition and respect for the rights and freedoms of others and meeting the just requirements of morality, public order, and general welfare in a democratic society.

The UN Charter, the International Covenants on Human Rights, and the Declaration on Decolonization[31] subsequently recognized the right to self-determination. The International Covenant on Civil and Political Rights (ICCPR) recognized the rights of minorities to practice their rights in community with other members of their group, to enjoy their own culture, to profess and practice their own religion, and to use their own language.

Today, indigenous peoples claim rights as a group and the UN adopted a Declaration on the Rights of Indigenous Peoples in 2007.

The common struggle for human rights

In *Rights from Wrongs*, Alan Dershowitz asked "Where do rights come from?" and challenged the approach to rights taken by classic natural law and classic legal positivism.[32] He suggested a third way—an experiential approach based on nurture rather than nature. According to Dershowitz, based on experience with wrongs, rights can be designed to prevent (or at least slow down) the recurrence of such wrongs. In his view, humanity's collective experience with injustice constitutes a fruitful foundation on which to build a theory of rights.

It is more realistic, he argued, to build a theory of rights on the agreed-upon wrongs of the past that we want to avoid repeating, rather than to build a theory of rights based on idealized conceptions of the perfect society. Moreover, a theory of rights as an experiential reaction to wrongs is more empirical, observable and debatable, and less dependent on faith, metaphor and myth than theories premised on sources external to human experience. According to Dershowitz, this theory of rights is more democratic and less elitist than divine or natural law theories.

Dershowitz continues that if rights are the product of human lawmaking, they are subject to modification, even abrogation, by the same source that devised them in the first place. However, a fundamental right should be more difficult to change than a mere legislative preference. He considers that human equality should be an important foundation for any theory of rights, but argues that it is an invention rather than a discovery. Decent human beings invented the counter-intuitive right to equal treatment to avoid recurrence of the wrongs of unequal opportunity—wrongs now recognized as immoral.

This experiential approach indeed explains the origins of many internationally recognized rights of the contemporary world order. Nonetheless, it is important to hold on to the ideas of equal rights inhering in the individual as a matter of his or her birthright. If laws break down, these notions of inherent, equal, and inalienable rights can provide the philosophical and legal bases for appeals to justice.

Positive rights

In a well-known work on this subject, Maurice Cranston asked the question "What does it mean to say that all men have rights?" In response, he suggested that there is, first of all, a sense in which to have a right is to have something that is conceded and enforced by the law of the realm. He termed these positive rights, which are recognized by positive law—the law of states. There is also, he suggested, a second meaning of the word "right," which differs from a positive right and is closer to the idea of deserts or justice. He termed these moral rights. Cranston offered the following distinctions between legal rights and moral rights: "First, a positive right is necessarily enforceable; if it is not enforced, it cannot be a positive right. A moral right is not necessarily enforced. Some moral rights are enforced and some are not." It is also possible to discern positive rights by reading laws that have been enacted, examining books, or going to a court and asking a judge. There is no similar authority to consult regarding moral rights.

Moving from rights per se to human rights, Cranston asked: "Are they some kind of positive right or some kind of moral right, something men actually have or something men ought to have?" Using UDHR provisions as examples, he claimed that the declaration's sponsors intended to specify something that everyone ought to have and drew the conclusion that "the rights they named were moral rights." To say that human rights are moral rights, he explained, is not to deny that they are positive rights as well as moral rights for many people. Where human rights are upheld by positive law, human rights are both moral and positive rights.

Regarding the distinction between human rights and other kinds of moral rights, Cranston suggested that human rights have that quality because they are universal. Many moral rights belong to particular people because of a particular situation: the rights of a landowner, for example, or the rights of an editor, a clergyman, judge, or stationmaster. These rights arise from these particular positions and are intimately linked to the duties required for the positions. However, human rights do not derive from a particular situation; they belong to a person simply because he is human.[33]

How does one determine the existence of a positive right in law? H.L.A. Hart offered the following view:

1 A statement of the form "X has a right" is true if the following conditions are satisfied:

   a there is in existence a legal system;
   b under a rule or rules of the system some other person Y is, in the events which have happened, obliged to do or abstain from some action;
   c this obligation is made by law dependent on the choice of either X or some person authorized to act on his behalf so that either Y is bound to do or abstain from some action only if X (or some authorized person) so chooses or alternatively only until X (or such person) chooses otherwise.

2 A statement of the form "X has a right" is used to draw a conclusion of law in a particular case which falls under such rules.[34]

This is one of the classical statements of legal positivism that asserts that individuals have legal rights only insofar as they have been created by explicit rules. It rejects the idea that individuals or groups can have rights in adjudication other than those provided in the collection of explicit rules that compose a community's laws.

Dworkin has argued, however, that this is an inadequate conceptual theory of law. According to Dworkin, when lawyers reason about legal rights and obligations, particularly in those difficult cases when problems with concepts seem most acute, they make use of standards that do not function as rules, but operate differently as principles, policies, and other sorts of standards. Individuals may have legal rights other than those created by explicit rules; that is, they may have rights to specific adjudicative decisions based on principles even in difficult cases when no explicit rule requires a decision either way.[35] This raises the question of whether there may be a basis to establish legal rights additional to those mentioned by Hart. For the purposes of this study, a further exploration of this aspect of the issue is not required. It suffices to note that Hart describes the way most legal systems operate in practice, including international law.

Natural rights

The idea of natural law has been the subject of a long debate among Western philosophers since the ancient Greeks. In ancient Greece, debate flowed from the law of the gods as well as the idea of justice, which had already been advocated in Mesopotamia well before the Greeks began their philosophical reflections.

For the Stoics, to live in accord with nature meant, first, to live as part of a moral world order and, second, to develop fully a human endowment that was fundamentally rational and social. Therefore:

> [J]ustice and law, upon which the social life depends, exist by nature and not by convention. They are natural not only in the sense that an inborn social impulse has brought men together, but also in the more important sense that the development of reason, which is the specifically human capacity, issues inevitably in a life according to justice and law.[36]

A fundamental Stoic principle was "the existence of a universal and world-wide law, which is one with reason both in nature and in human nature and which ... knits together in a common social bond every being which possesses reason, whether god or man."[37]

The Romans had their national law, the *jus civile*, which was binding on nationals, the *jus gentium*, the law common to all nations, and the *jus naturale*, the law established by nature. Roman natural law also emphasized the laws of God. Cicero advocated that there was one eternal and immutable law applicable to all peoples at all times, and God was the source of that law. The Romans considered that one could resort to natural law to find the answers to legal questions that could not be answered by looking in a legal provision.

In the Middle Ages, the Catholic doctrine of natural law rested in a belief in a law of God above all human laws. Saint Augustine considered that the enacted law that violated the law of God was invalid in principle. He formulated the doctrine according to which participation in God's thought and creative work was imposed as a moral and obligatory end. Natural law was the formulation of this moral order.[38]

Saint Thomas Aquinas maintained that the legal rules of society only possessed the quality of law if they conformed with correct divine reason. Their validity was thus derived from eternal principles of law. If a law deviated from the injunction of reason, it did not deserve the qualification of being a law.

In the tradition of Enlightenment thinkers, the great Dutch jurist Hugo Grotius made a clear break from natural law or higher justice derived from the holy scriptures and the will of God. Instead, he offered a conception of natural law based on reason:

> [T]he law of nature ... is unchangeable—even in the sense that it cannot be changed by God. Measureless as is the power of God, nevertheless it can be said that there are certain things over which that power does not extend; for things of which this is said are spoken only, having no sense corresponding with reality and being mutually contradictory. Just as even God, then, cannot cause that two times two should not make four, so he cannot cause that which is intrinsically evil be not evil.[39]

Hobbes made the transition from the laws of nature to natural rights, formulating the theory of a social contract between human beings in a state of nature and a sovereign. He advanced the following concept of natural rights: the "right of nature is the liberty each man hath, to use his own power, as he will himself for the preservation of his own nature; that is to say, of his own life, and consequently of doing anything which, in his own judgment, and reason, he shall conceive to be the aptest means there unto."[40] According to Hobbes, human beings had given overwhelming power to the sovereign through their contract with him, but if the state of nature prevailed, humans had the right to defend themselves and advance his or her interests. In the words of Michael Freeden, "Hobbes detached the concept of natural right from that of natural law."[41]

John Locke further developed Hobbes's idea of a contract with the sovereign, presenting it as a social contract according to which the sovereign rules with the consent of the governed. If that consent is withdrawn, the sovereign no longer has the right to rule. Unlike Hobbes, Locke regarded natural rights as derivative from natural law. He sought to counter the Stuart notion of the divine right of kings and replace it with a notion of the natural rights of man, particularly the rights to life, liberty, and property. He considered that all sovereigns owed their power to the original social contracts made at the beginning of history. Consent was their only title to rule:

> The liberty of man in society is to be under no other legislative power but that established by consent in the commonwealth, nor under the dominion of any will, or restraint of any law but what that legislation shall enact, according to the trust put in it.

Freedom for man under government is not for everyone to do as he lists but to have a standing rule to live by, common to everyone of that society and ... by the legislative power erected in it; to have a liberty, to follow his own will in all things where the Rule prescribes not and not to be subject to the inconstant, uncertain, arbitrary will of another man.

Locke continued:

[W]henever the legislators endeavor to take away or destroy the property of the people, or to reduce them to slavery under arbitrary power, they put themselves into a state of war with the people, who are thereupon absolved from any further obedience, and are left to the common refuge, which God hath provided for all men against force and violence—resistance.[42]

Jean-Jacques Rousseau also advanced the theory of the social contract in *The Social Contract*, written in 1792. He considered the contract an agreement entered into by the various members of the community in an original state of nature in which all men enjoy equal rights. This agreement—whereby all members of society subordinated themselves to the general will (*la volonté générale*)—created the "sovereign." The general will was synonymous with the will of the majority since all were equal, and the general will was synonymous with the law.[43]

The doctrine of natural rights would break onto the American and the international scene in a dramatic way with the American Declaration of Independence, of 4 July 1776, which argued for "unalienable rights of the individual." The Virginia Declaration of Rights of that same year had also made the case for eternal, inviolable human rights.

The French Declaration of the Rights of Man and the Citizen of 1789 internationalized natural rights for individuals by claiming them not only for Frenchmen but for all human beings. The declaration affirmed the principle of sovereignty of the people: the principle of legality, namely that restrictions on citizens' freedom of action could only be established by law—the principle of the distribution of powers, fair justice, and various inviolable rights to freedom.

The dramatic effect of the American Declaration of Independence and the French declaration was that philosophical arguments in favor of natural rights had passed into national policy documents—with international significance in the case of the French declaration. The assertion of natural rights in the United States and France sparked a major philosophical debate involving, among others, Edmund Burke,

Thomas Paine, and Jeremy Bentham. In his *Reflections on the Revolution in France*, Burke considered that natural rights were not real rights. Real rights were prescriptive "and entailed inheritance derived to us from our forefathers ... without any reference whatever to any other more General or prior right."[44] Burke attacked the foundations of the rights of man by denying that man possessed any rights and by asserting that men should be subservient to the will of their rulers.

Burke's attack on the French declaration drew a powerfully argued response from Paine in his *Rights of Man*. Paine argued that people had fought for their basic rights in the French Revolution and for justice from oppressive masters. In defending the uprising of the French people against their monarch, he pointed out that this revolution had not been against the individual who personified the monarch but, rather, the French nation had revolted against the system of the monarchy, which was founded on oppression and despotism. Paine retraced man's origin and the origin of his rights. By being born, he said, man entered into society with certain natural rights, defined as follows:

> Natural Rights are those which appertain to man in right of his existence. Of this kind are the intellectual rights, or rights of the mind, and also rights of acting as an individual for his own comfort or happiness, which are not injurious to the natural rights of others. Civil rights are those which appertain to man in the right of his being a member of society. Every civil right has for its foundation some natural right pre-existing in the individual, but to the enjoyment of which his individual power is not, in all cases, sufficiently competent. Of this kind are all those which relate to security and protection.[45]

Jeremy Bentham also fiercely attacked the concept of natural and imprescriptible rights as rhetorical nonsense or, as he put it, nonsense upon stilts. He considered the theory of natural law as arbitrary.[46] Bentham thought that rights did not exist outside government; they could not be absolute without gross contradiction, and their imprescriptibility removed them entirely from the sphere of law and thus human direction for the purpose of reform. Their subjects and upholders were unspecified; they were based on an unsustainable belief in human equality. He considered that no declaration such as the French one "under any such name, or with any such design, should have been attempted."[47]

Instead of natural law, Bentham offered a doctrine of social utility. He held it to be "a sacred truth" that "the greatest happiness of the greatest number is the foundation of morals and legislation." He expanded on his theory of utility as follows:

> It is the principle of *utility*, accurately apprehended and steadily applied, that affords the only clue to guide a man through these straits. It is for that, if any, and for that alone to furnish a decision which neither party shall dare in theory to disavow. It is something to reconcile men even in *theory*. They are at least *something* nearer to an effectual union than when at variance as well as in respect of theory as practice.[48]

Bentham's theory of utility would be taken up by John Stuart Mill, Herbert Spencer, and others.

Immanuel Kant, for his part, was of the view that the system of rights, viewed as a scientific system of doctrines, is divided into natural and positive rights. Natural right rested on pure rational principles *a priori*; a positive or statutory right proceeded from a legislator's will. The system of rights might again be regarded in reference to the implied powers of dealing morally with others as bound by obligations, that is, as furnishing a legal title of action in relation to them. Thus viewed, the system was divided into innate right and acquired right. Innate right was the right that belonged to everyone by nature independent of all juridical acts of experience. Acquired right was founded on such juridical acts. Innate right might also be called the "internal mine and thine" for external right must always be required.[49]

Kant's presentation of natural rights, coexisting alongside positive rights, would eventually be upheld in national and international laws and practice. The philosopher Mortimer Adler summarized the situation admirably in a book that was written on the bicentennial of the American Constitution.

Adler, an editor of the *Encyclopaedia Britannica* and a great popularizer of philosophy, reviewed the American Declaration of Independence, the American Constitution, and the Gettysburg Address, and listed the following human rights ideas: equality, inalienable rights (or human rights), pursuit of happiness, civil rights (to secure human rights), the consent of the governed, the dissent of the governed, justice, domestic tranquility (or civil peace), common defense (or national security), general welfare, and blessings of liberty.[50]

According to Adler, human equality consisted in the fact that no human being is more or less human than another because all have the same specific nature by virtue of belonging to the same species. If all humans have the same nature, it cannot be denied that they are all equal: no one has more or less than another.[51]

Adler further argued that the inalienability of inherent natural or human rights consisted in rights that are not *ab initio* conferred on persons by man-made laws and so cannot be rendered null and void by man-made laws: "If all human beings are equal by virtue of their having the same nature, and if they possess certain rights by virtue of their having that nature then it follows that they are all equally endowed with those rights."[52] Among these rights are life, liberty, and the pursuit of happiness. The primary right is the right to happiness, which is based on the moral obligation of human beings to make good lives for ourselves.[53]

For Adler, the protection of human rights is one of government's key purposes. The violation of such rights or the neglect of them is a manifest injustice. For human beings living in organized societies under civil governments, rights are conferred on them by the laws of the state or its constitution. These are usually called civil rights, legal rights, or constitutional rights. If justly conceived, they are intended to uphold inalienable rights.[54]

Political liberty comes into existence with the establishment of constitutional government and its creation of citizenship under a system where human beings are governed with their own consent—in contrast to those subject to arbitrary power. Self-government means being governed with one's consent and also having a voice in government. Political liberty is secured by enfranchisement[55] and consists in the freedom to do as one pleases, to carry out in action the choices one has freely made, with the understanding that the exercise of personal liberty is regulated by just law.[56]

Economic rights, like political rights, Adler continued, are rights to goods that every human being needs to lead a decent human life and to succeed in the pursuit of happiness. The right to life involves more than security of life and limb; it is a right not merely to subsist but to live well.[57] The basic economic right is the right to a decent livelihood by whatever means it can be honestly obtained.[58] Economic rights are secured by means of income-producing property and the economic equivalents of property and by a combination of the first two.[59]

During the twentieth century, the institutions of the international community, influenced by reasoning such as those adduced by Adler and with past injustices in mind, have distilled, recognized, and proclaimed a broad range of human rights under the categories of inalienable rights, civil and political rights, and economic, social, and cultural rights. This process has led some experts, as shown earlier in the case of Dershowitz, to proffer an empirical explanation of rights. Amartya Sen has offered an appealing additional explanation.

The public policy function of human rights

Amartya Sen gives an added, valuable insight into the nature and origins of rights. He argues that human rights are best seen, foundationally, as commitments in social ethics. This is comparable to but very different from accepting utilitarian reasoning. Sen states:

> In this sense, the viability of human rights is linked with what John Rawls has called "public reasoning" ... This view of human rights in terms of social ethics and public reasoning contrasts with seeing human rights in primarily legal terms, either as consequences of humane legislation, or as precursors of legal rights. Human rights may well be reflected in legislation, and may also inspire legislation, but this is a further fact, rather than a defining characteristic of human rights themselves.[60]

Human rights thus perform aspirational roles in the contemporary world community and help provide a policy framework for international cooperation. The right to development, the right to peace, and the right to a clean and safe environment are examples of this. Opinions may differ as to whether these have concretized into hard legal rights, but authoritative organs of the international community, as well as other regional bodies, have declared them rights in order to consecrate major public policy goals of the international community. The language of rights is thus used to support key public policy goals, elevating their status to one of rights.

The contemporary role of international consensus and legislation

The process of recognizing, declaring, or proclaiming rights at the national and international levels is essentially a normative one. To determine the existence of a right, one must enquire into whether it has been authoritatively recognized by a competent organ. In international law, human rights may be grounded in an international convention, an international declaration, international customary law, and the general principles of law recognized by nations. In addition, it can be determined by reference to judicial decisions and the academic work of experts. International law recognizes ordinary legal rights and human rights. Human rights possess one or more of certain qualitative characteristics: appurtenance to the human person or group; universality; essentiality to human life, security, survival, dignity, liberty, equality; essentiality for international order; essentiality in the conscience of humankind; and essentiality to protect vulnerable groups.

The stock of human rights evolves over time. While some rights are eternal, some old ones may be modified, and new rights may be created. There are ongoing processes of discovery, recognition, enlargement, enrichment and refining, and adaptation and updating.

Conclusion

The idea of human rights is one of the pillars of the contemporary world order. In the words of one of the leading scholars on the subject, this is the age of rights.[61] The World Conference on Human Rights couched it in terms of the spirit of our age, the realities of our time, capturing the longing of all human beings for a world of human rights under the rule of law and democratic governance.

The human rights idea is powerful in its simplicity and its thrust. It is that all human beings, wherever they are, enjoy certain fundamental, inalienable rights stemming from their humanity, which have been recognized and enunciated by the authoritative organs of the international community, most notably the General Assembly of the United Nations. Whatever the historical, philosophical, political, economic, or sociological factors that contributed to this,[62] the international legal system is the source of obligation regarding human rights in the contemporary world. Additional or higher levels of rights may be provided in national legal systems, but they may never reduce the content of rights defined in international law.

Human rights have emerged through centuries of struggle across the globe for the recognition and protection of rights. Claims of human rights have been influenced by religious or other beliefs, political activists, philosophers' reasonings, and people's movements protesting injustice. In this process, human rights are articulated, distilled, and recognized by authoritative national, regional, or international organs, with pre-eminence now enjoyed by international organs within the sphere of international law. The basis of human rights is thus partly empirical, partly philosophical.

Notes

1 Brian MacArthur, ed., *The Penguin Book of Twentieth Century Speeches* (London: Penguin Books), vii.

30 *History: shared heritage, common struggle*

2 Article 1, UDHR.
3 On the concept of law, see Philip Wiener, *Dictionary of the History of Ideas*, vol. III (New York: Charles Scribner's Sons, 1973), 1–12; Russ ver Steeg, *Law in the Ancient World* (Durham, N.C.: Carolina Academic Press, 2002). See also Cheikh Anta Diop, *The African Origins of Civilization: Myth or Reality* (Chicago, Ill.: Lawrence Hill Books, 1967).
4 H.J. Muller, *Freedom in the Ancient World* (London: Secker and Warburg, 1962), 58.
5 Muller, *Freedom in the Ancient World*, 58.
6 Muller, *Freedom in the Ancient World*, 58–59.
7 Bailey Diffie and Aaron Noland, eds, *Selected Readings in the History of Civilization* (New York: Department of History, City College of New York, 1981), 10.
8 Diffie and Noland, *Selected Readings*, 24–25.
9 Diffie and Noland, *Selected Readings*, 24.
10 Diffie and Noland, *Selected Readings*, 59.
11 "Epilogue, Code of Hammurabi," in Diffie and Noland, *Selected Readings*, 28.
12 *Code of Hammurabi*, at www.wsu.edu/~dee/MESO/Code.
13 Articles 15 and 17, Chapter VII, *Laws of Manu*, trans. George Buhler, at www.sacred-texts.com/sbe/index.htm.
14 Irene Bloom, J. Paul Martin, and Wayne L. Proudfoot, eds, "Introduction," in *Religious Diversity and Human Rights* (New York: Columbia University Press, 1996), 4.
15 Bloom et al., "Introduction," 4.
16 Bloom et al., "Introduction," 6.
17 Sri Lanka Foundation, *Religion and Culture in the Development of Human Rights in Sri Lanka*, Monograph Series 4 (Colombo, Sri Lanka: SLF, 1982), x.
18 Paul Laurens, *The Evolution of International Human Rights: Visions Seen* (Philadelphia: University of Pennsylvania Press, 2003), 5. See also Charles Alexdrowicz, "Kutiliyan Principles and the Law of Nations," *British Yearbook of International Law* 41 (1965/66): 301–20; Gerald Draper, "The Contribution of the Emperor Asoka Maurya to the Development of the Humanitarian Ideal in Warfare," *International Review of the Red Cross* 77, no. 305 (1995): 192–206; L.R. Penna, "Traditional Asian: An Indian View," *Australian Yearbook of International Law* 9: 168–206; Kadayan Ramachandra Ramabhadra Sastry, "Hinduism and International Law," *Collected Courses of the Hague Academy of International Law* 1, no. 117 (1966): 507–614; Manoj Kumar Sinha, "Hinduism and International Humanitarian Law," *International Review of the Red Cross* 87, no. 858 (June 2005): 285–94.
19 Laurens, *The Evolution of International Human Rights*, 5.
20 Laurens, *The Evolution of International Human Rights*, 6.
21 Laurens, *The Evolution of International Human Rights*, 7. See also Stephen Angle, *Human Rights and Chinese Thought: A Cross Cultural Inquiry* (Cambridge: Cambridge University Press, 2002).
22 Laurens, *The Evolution of International Human Rights*, 8. See also Mashood Baderin, *International Human Rights and Islamic Law* (Oxford: Oxford University Press, 2003); James Cocayne, "Islam and International Humanitarian Law: From a Clash to a Conversation Between

Civilizations," *International Review of the Red Cross* 84, no. 847 (September 2002): 597–625; and Abdul Aziz Said, "Human Rights in Islamic Perspectives," in *Human Rights: Cultural and Ideological Perspectives*, eds Adanabtua Pollis and Peter Schwab (New York: Praeger Publishers, 1979).
23 Edward James Schuster, *Human Rights Today: Evolution or Revolution* (New York: Philosophical Library, 1982), 62.
24 Laurens, *The Evolution of International Human Rights*, 5–6.
25 Laurens, *The Evolution of International Human Rights*, 6. See also Norman Solomon, "Judaism and the Ethics of War," *International Review of the Red Cross* 84, no. 858 (June 2005): 295–309.
26 Laurens, *The Evolution of International Human Rights*, 7. See also Allen O. Miller, ed., *Christian Declaration on Human Rights* (Grand Rapids, Mich.: William B. Eerdmans, 1977).
27 Schuster, *Human Rights Today*, 62–63.
28 See UNESCO, *Human Rights, Comments and Interpretations*. A symposium edited by UNESCO, introduced by Jacques Maritain, submission by Mahatma Gandhi (Paris: UNESCO, 1950).
29 See A. John Simmons, *The Lockean Theory of Rights* (Princeton, N.J.: Princeton University Press, 1992).
30 Locke, quoted in Willmoore Kendall, *John Locke and the Doctrine of Majority Rule* (Urbana: University of Illinois Press, 1969), 68–69.
31 General Assembly resolution 1514.
32 Alan Dershowitz, *Rights from Wrongs: A Secular Theory of the Origins of Rights* (Cambridge, Mass.: Basic Books, 2005).
33 Maurice Cranston, *What are Human Rights?* (London: Bodley Head, 1973), 4–7.
34 H.L.A. Hart, *Definition and Theory of Jurisprudence: An Inaugural Lecture Delivered Before Oxford University on 30 May 1953* (Oxford: Clarendon Press, 1953), 16–17.
35 Ronald Dworkin, *Taking Rights Seriously* (Cambridge, Mass.: Harvard University Press, 1977).
36 See G.H. Sabine and S.B. Smith, trans., "Introduction," *Cicero on the Commonwealth* (Indianapolis, Ind.: Bobbs-Merill Company, 1976), 22.
37 Sabine and Smith, "Introduction," 22.
38 See Philip Wiener, "Natural Law and Natural Rights," in *Dictionary of the History of Ideas*, vol. III (New York: Charles Scribner's Sons, 1973), 13–27.
39 Hugo Grotius, *De Jure Belli Ac Pacis*, trans. Francis W. Kelsey (Oxford: The Carnegie Endowment for International Peace, Classics of International Law, 1925), Book I, Chapter I, Part X, para. 5.
40 Michael Freeden, *Rights* (Milton Keynes: Open University Press, 1991), 12–13.
41 Freeden, *Rights*, 13.
42 See Maurice Cranston, "John Locke and Government by Consent," in *Political Ideas: From Machiavelli to the Present*, ed. David Thomson (New York: Basic Books, 1966), 64–78.
43 Jean-Jacques Rousseau, *The Social Contract* (London: Penguin Books, 2006).
44 Edmund Burke, *Reflections on the Revolution in France*, ed. Conor Cruise O'Brien (Harmondsworth: Penguin, 1969), 119.
45 Thomas Paine, *Rights of Man* (New York: Penguin Books, 1984), 68.

46 Philip Wiener, "Natural Law and Natural Rights," 22.
47 Michael Freeden, *Rights*, 18.
48 Jeremy Bentham, "A Fragment on Government," in *Introduction to Jurisprudence with Selected Texts*, ed. Dennis Lloyd, 2nd edn (London: Stephens and Sons, 1965), 127.
49 Immanuel Kant, "Division of the Science of Right," in *Great Treasury of Western Thought*, eds Mortimer Adler and Charles van Doren (New York and London: R.R. Bowker Company, 1977), 872.
50 Mortimer Adler, *We Hold These Truths* (New York and London: Macmillan, 1987), 29–30.
51 Adler, *We Hold These Truths*, 43.
52 Adler, *We Hold These Truths*, 47.
53 Adler, *We Hold These Truths*, 59.
54 Adler, *We Hold These Truths*, 48.
55 Adler, *We Hold These Truths*, 124.
56 Adler, *We Hold These Truths*, 126.
57 Adler, *We Hold These Truths*, 148.
58 Adler, *We Hold These Truths*, 149.
59 Adler, *We Hold These Truths*, 151–52.
60 Amartya Sen, "Human Rights and Development," in *Development as a Human Right*, eds. Bard Andreassen and Stephen Marks (Cambridge, Mass.: Harvard University Press, 2006), 3.
61 Louis Henkin, *The Age of Rights* (New York: Columbia University Press, 1990).
62 See Lynn Hunt, *Inventing Human Rights: A History* (New York and London: W.W. Norton & Company, 2007).

2 Human rights in the world community

- Human rights and world order
- Human rights and governance
- Human rights, our global civilization, and globalization
- Human rights violations and the challenges of international protection
- The Human Rights Council
- Conclusion

> The promotion and protection of all human rights and fundamental freedoms must be considered as a priority objective of the United Nations in accordance with its Purposes and Principles ... The promotion and protection of all human rights is a legitimate concern of the International Community.
>
> (Vienna Declaration, paragraph 4)

This century finds the world convulsed and confused, with principles and a framework for world order, but with disorder, conflicts, terrorism, chaos, and rampant violations of human rights across the globe. Great masses of the world's population live in misery. The international economic system favors the strong over the weak. The fear of terrorism stalks the world. After the decolonization successes of the twentieth century, many governments of the newly independent countries are particularly sensitive about perceived dangers of external interferences in their internal affairs. Many now insist that organizations such as the United Nations should engage in dialogue and cooperation, rather than criticize human rights violations. Powerful permanent members of the UN Security Council (UNSC) also advocate this line.[1] For example, this is the mantra at the HRC. Yet, without standing up for principle in the face of violations, without integrating respect for human rights in strategies for peace, development, and progress, it is difficult to see how the international community can make headway in ameliorating the plight of humanity.

The World Conference on Human Rights, held in 1993, recorded the formal consensus of the international community on the priority of human rights in international cooperation and the legitimate role of the international community in protecting human rights. Nonetheless, this consensus has not yet found its way into actual practice. How can this be done? What is the way forward?

The human rights idea can perform many vital roles in the world community. Human rights should give meaning to the concept of world order. Governance must be grounded in human rights precepts. Peace and security should be defined and achieved through respect for human rights. Human rights provide the international framework of public policy for our global civilization. A globalizing world must be inspired by and respectful of international human rights norms. The responsibility to protect is a basic norm of contemporary international law. The principle of justice is given meaning by international human rights norms. The challenge of the twenty-first century is to realize the potential of the human rights idea in practice. This chapter examines these and related roles—potential and actual—of the human rights idea in the world community.

Human rights and world order

The notion of world order must be conceived with the idea of human rights as its base, with the insistence that any policies, practices, or institutions that violate human rights are antithetical to the notion of world order.[2] Addressing the UN Commission on Human Rights on 2 February 1981, Theodor van Boven stated:

> Gross violations of human rights which occur in various parts of the world scandalize any notion of world order. For if we believe in the equality and interdependence of all human beings and if we believe in the duty of solidarity in the realization of human rights, we cannot rest content when human rights are being flagrantly violated in any part of the world. Nevertheless … our methods for tackling violations of human rights are still in their infancy and are often inadequate to deal with the problems faced.[3]

The world order must seek to advance the human rights norms included in the UDHR. Human security must be conceived and pursued in terms of human rights. A contemporary challenge is the issue of global terrorism. That there is a threat is clear; that it must be countered is accepted. However, security must be pursued while safeguarding respect for human rights. Judicial or independent monitoring of counter-terrorism measures is needed; instruction in human rights for security personnel is important.

Migration will also have a great bearing on the future world order. Migration involves people, who have basic human rights. Human rights must be brought to the fore when considering the migratory movements of people. How relevant is the Convention on the Rights of Migrants and their families? What policy, normative, and institutional framework is required from the point of view of human rights and migration?

Human rights must be central to the work of the principal organs of the contemporary world order, including the UNSC, the GA, ECOSOC, and other specialized agencies and regional organizations. While the UNSC is primarily dedicated to maintaining international peace and security, it cannot fail to act in situations of gross violations of human rights that threaten security or contribute to breaches of it.[4] It would be helpful for the UNSC to consider and adopt a presidential statement on human rights and the maintenance of international peace and security. The GA also needs to adopt a policy statement on human rights challenges of the future. Former Secretary-General Boutros Boutros-Ghali prepared and issued *An Agenda for Peace, An Agenda for Development*, and *An Agenda for Democratization*. To date, there has been no UN agenda for human rights, and the GA should commission such a report in the near future. The 70th anniversary of the UDHR would be a fitting time to do so.

ECOSOC was established to coordinate economic, social, humanitarian, and human rights policies and strategies to advance economic, social, and cultural rights. It does little in the human rights field, and it is difficult to discern its human rights policy. This is a shortcoming that needs to be urgently remedied.

Every specialized agency of the UN and all regional and sub-regional organizations should have a human rights policy statement to help centralize the role of human rights in the future world order. Unfortunately, because many governments are defensive about human rights, these organizations tend to shy away from human rights issues, but constructive engagement on human rights issues should be unobjectionable to governments acting in good faith.

Gross violations of human rights often lead to conflict. Hence there should be human rights risk analysis in countries to warn of impending danger and to head it off. Preventive human rights strategies are beginning to receive attention, but they should be given greater prominence in policies and strategies of early warning and preventive diplomacy.

The International Commission on Intervention and State Sovereignty, which launched the concept of the responsibility to protect, was firm in its view that prevention is the single most important dimension of the responsibility to protect: prevention options should always be exhausted before intervention is contemplated, and more commitment and resources must be devoted to it. The exercise of the responsibility to prevent and react should always involve less intrusive and coercive measures being considered before more coercive and intrusive ones are applied.

A preventive orientation should also characterize the HRC. (Prevention here means detecting potential gross violations before they occur and acting to head them off in cooperation with regional and other partners.) The prevention of genocide is a case in point.

There is now greater understanding of the importance of negotiating peace on the basis of respect for human rights and justice. Thus it has also become accepted wisdom that all peacekeeping operations should have human rights components. Further, the UN has established the Peacebuilding Commission, and peace building must be pursued on the foundations of human rights.

Human rights and governance[5]

The conception of the UDHR, the ICCPR, and the ICESCR is that governments and governance shall have the pursuit of the core civil and political and economic, social, and cultural rights as their *raison d'être*. The structure of government should be based on human rights values, notably, the will of the people shall be the basis of authority, to use the words of the UDHR. However, even in democracies, governance is rarely monitored from the point of view of basic human rights. Although nongovernmental organizations (NGOs) do this to a limited degree, this issue deserves more attention. National human rights institutions might help in this kind of monitoring, and the High Commissioner for Human Rights might be able to contribute to human rights monitoring of international governance.[6]

One way to strengthen the role of human rights in governance is to build on each country's national protection system since the protection of human rights should take place at the country level. The national protection system is, therefore, one of the most important means for realizing human rights.

A national protection system has six dimensions.

Constitutional dimension

A country's constitutional structure depends on the sovereign choice of its people. However, three issues require particular attention and scrutiny from the perspectives of international human rights law: the structure's fundamental human rights guarantees, its judicial institutions, and its national institutions to protect human rights.

Fundamental human rights guarantees in the constitution or the bill of rights should not be less but may be more than what is provided for in international human rights law. Each country should be able to illustrate that it has done two things: first, that it has methodically compared the provisions of its fundamental human rights guarantees and those in the principal international human rights instruments; second, that rights guaranteed in international customary law, particularly *jus cogens* norms, are among its constitutional human rights guarantees.

Legislative dimension

International law gives states discretion about whether treaties they have adopted are directly applicable in their legal systems or whether these treaties are reflected in national legislation. Whichever route a country chooses, it must ensure that its national laws correspond to its legal commitments under international human rights law or treaties. National parliaments should exercise oversight over whether this obligation has been met and, where action is required, make legislative changes or enactments as required. Human rights treaties often make suggestions for legislative updating, and national parliaments should require regular reports from their executive about the recommendations of the human rights treaty bodies. There is a role for parliamentary oversight over governmental compliance with international human rights obligations, and each parliament should establish a human rights committee to perform this role.

Judicial dimension

The judicial dimension requires that courts be independent and effective. (There are UN declarations and statements on the meaning of judicial independence and effectiveness.) As already indicated, international law allows governments to decide whether to make a treaty directly applicable in its legal system or enact legislation incorporating the treaty's obligations. However, international human rights norms of *jus cogens* status and human rights norms that have the status of international customary law should be directly applicable in national courts.

International law requires all states to provide adequate guarantees against human rights violations. This responsibility falls, in the first place, on the national judiciary. International law can provide remedies if there is a failure to protect.

Judges and legal practitioners must be provided with access to the key decisions of international human rights bodies in local languages so they are aware of them and can draw upon them. International human rights organizations and NGOs may assist with this, but national ministries of justice must also pay attention to this matter.

Institutional dimension

Experience has shown that, in addition to the courts, institutions such as national human rights commissions, national human rights commissioners, or ombudspersons can be quite helpful in advancing and protecting human rights. International law does not make such institutions mandatory but, as a matter of policy, a country should periodically assess its institutional arrangements to examine whether national human rights bodies could help protect human rights.

National human rights institutions could perform key tasks such as seeking an amicable settlement of human rights grievances through conciliation or binding decisions; informing the complainant of his or her rights and of available means of redress and promoting access to such redress; hearing complaints or referring them to a competent authority; and making recommendations to the competent authorities, including proposals to amend laws, regulations, or administrative practices that obstruct the free exercise of rights.

Monitoring dimension

The responsibility to protect and to prevent demands that every country monitor itself to detect situations of distress and to address them before they erupt into human rights violations or conflict. This calls for independent bodies that systematically watch out for such distress situations and draw attention to them. A national human rights commission could be given the mandate to do this. In multiethnic countries, special arrangements may be required. However, the concept of self-monitoring is a vital part of a national protection system.

Educational dimension

Human rights education has a key role to play in combating discrimination and advancing universal values of respect and tolerance, and education on human rights should be provided in primary and secondary schools and higher institutions of learning. The HRC should take the lead in encouraging human rights education in schools, universities, and other educational institutions in local languages. This is an immense task on which there is a great deal to be done. Working together with UNESCO and UNICEF (the UN Children's Fund), the HRC should make this a priority issue for consideration.

There is need for an international convention on human rights education, going beyond the UN Declaration,[7] which would have three simple goals: all countries should provide to teachers—at all levels—a manual, in the local language, on teaching human rights. Unfortunately this does not happen in many places.

The UN should provide all judges with a basic manual, in the local language, containing the key international human rights norms and the key international human rights jurisprudence.

Human rights, our global civilization, and globalization[8]

We are living in times of great contestation across cultures. Debates abound about so-called clashing civilizations, dialogue among civilizations, fundamentalist movements, and extremism and terrorist threats. Human rights are not a religion—religious space is a private matter for individual belief and conscience. Human rights norms provide policies of public order—both internationally and nationally. While leaving belief or conscience to the individual, governments and related institutions are required to uphold and apply the international human rights norms that have been developed through consensus at the UN.

From this perspective, human rights norms become the basis of dialogue between societies and peoples. Inter-religious dialogue concerns the private sphere of belief or conscience. Fostering dialogue among societies and peoples requires the pursuit of cooperation. However, when it comes to the international public order, there must be respect for international law and the international law of human rights. There must be further work on this notion of human rights norms as underpinning global civilization. The time has come for a high-level panel of experts to produce and issue a report on the human rights threads that knit different peoples and cultures across the globe. UNESCO could commission and issue such a report.

Globalization, which has been underway for centuries, involves the spread of trade, communications, people, ideas, culture, and values. It has positive attributes, but economic globalization can make it more difficult for smaller countries to survive and prosper. Therefore, there must be an international policy framework on the future of globalization and the way it impacts on the lives of people worldwide.

In the twentieth century, the human rights idea was itself globalized. The idea of the universality of human rights, namely that all human beings have and should enjoy basic human rights, is a key tenet of our world. From a human rights perspective, there must be an insistence that globalization does not lead to departures from human rights norms. How can this be achieved? There must be close scrutiny of how globalization impacts on efforts to uphold human rights—civil and political, as well as economic, social, and cultural. There is a massive academic and research challenge here.[9]

Globalization is not free of the pull of politics and nor are human rights. Countries seek to advance their interests, and globalization is not necessarily altruistic. The human rights idea proceeds from a different intellectual and policy point of departure, namely, that all people are entitled to a social and international order in which the rights in the UDHR can be achieved across the globe.

Economic and communications globalization will undoubtedly progress, but will the globalization of human rights values progress likewise? The evidence so far gives cause for concern and points to the need to strengthen the international policy and legal framework.

Some argue that growth and development will advance political and economic freedom. Others argue that globalization brings economic benefits, and the challenge is to see that these benefits are shared by all. However, should economic freedom further marginalize and impoverish vast numbers of the world's population? The human rights answer to this is a firm no. The UDHR must influence the future of globalization. Systems of governance and economic and social activities must aim to realize basic human rights. The synthesis of globalization and human rights would be the pursuit of human rights strategies of governance. Governments and business organizations should also have the realization of the basic rights contained in the UDHR as their priority objective. The key civil and political rights are mandatory and immediate: no one should torture or enslave another human being. Some of the economic and social rights are to be realized progressively provided that there is no discrimination in the allocation of available resources.

Human rights strategies of governance apply not only to governments but to all organs of society, including corporations. It should be the shared mission of all to advance the basic rights, and none, including corporations, should be guilty of violating them. The UN Global Compact with business seeks to encourage corporations to contribute to human rights causes. A related but somewhat different approach was advanced in the former UN Sub-Commission on the Promotion and Protection of Human Rights, namely that there should be a human rights code of conduct for corporations. The "Ruggie Principles" took a softer approach on this issue.[10]

How can one ensure respect for human rights in a globalizing world? A key point of departure is that all governments should commit themselves to abide by the core international human rights conventions. This requires, as discussed earlier, adequate and effective national human rights protection systems in all countries. UN human rights work should increasingly emphasize the importance of effective national protection systems in each country.

It is also crucial to identify and take urgent corrective measures in respect of the plight of the vulnerable and the extremely poor. The international community should bring two concepts to the fore, namely, gross violations of economic and social rights and the concept of preventable poverty. There are many situations where more efficient and equitable governance could prevent extreme poverty. This would be a way of giving practical relevance to human rights for the poor and the vulnerable.

From this, it follows that the push for better governance must be a basic tenet of our globalizing world. Better governance involves constitutional democracy, participatory governance, and the rule of law grounded in international human rights law. In short, international human rights law must be the indispensable legal and policy framework for a globalizing world, and the responsibility to protect must be shared by all.

Human rights violations and the challenges of international protection

Thus far, framework issues when it comes to the place of human rights in our world community have been addressed. However, there are also reality issues: human rights are violated massively in many parts of the world.

Gross violations of human rights, alas, continue to be rampant worldwide. In early 2014, the Office of the UN High Commissioner for Human Rights (OHCHR) issued its annual publication, "United Nations Special Procedures: Facts and Figures 2013." The Special Procedures of the HRC are, in the words of the publication, independent human rights experts mandated to report and advise on human rights from either a thematic or a country-specific perspective: "The system of Special Procedures is a central element of United Nations human rights machinery and covers all sets of rights, civil, cultural, economic, political and social."[11] All together, there were 51 in 2013, thematic and country based.

Thematic special procedures involve documenting and reporting on a broad range of gross human rights violations worldwide, including: arbitrary detention; sale of children, child prostitution and child pornography; enforced or involuntary disappearances; extrajudicial, summary or arbitrary executions; the right to food; freedom of peaceful assembly and of association; freedom of religion or belief; the right to health; the right of human rights defenders; independence of judges and lawyers; indigenous peoples; internally displaced persons; the human rights of migrants; minority issues; lack of reparations and guarantees on non-recurrence; racism, racial discrimination, xenophobia and related intolerance; violations of human rights while countering terrorism; trafficking in persons, especially women and children; violence against women; and discrimination against women in law and in practice. In addition to other thematic special procedures, there were also country-based mandate holders on 14 countries.

The publication listed numerous reports these procedures had submitted to the HRC, including on their visits to countries and on their urgent action intercessions in cases of emergency. Taken together, the reports of the procedures amount to a veritable world report cataloguing shocking human rights violations. Most of them have been doing this annually for several years. Serious violations of human rights, in 2014, were being committed in peacetime as well as during armed conflicts.

Every five minutes a child dies as the result of violence. According to a groundbreaking 2014 report from UNICEF UK, a third of children who were victims of violence were likely to develop long-lasting symptoms of post-traumatic stress disorder. Those living in poverty were more likely to be victims of violence wherever they live in the world. Over 70 percent of child deaths due to violence each day are the result of interpersonal violence, rather than conflict.[12]

In October 2014, three UN special procedure mandate holders issued a statement calling for a concerted global response to fight the transnational scourge of trafficking in persons. All over the world, they said, child trafficking—often connected to the sale and sexual exploitation of children—was on the rise as a proportion of all human trafficking. Indeed, detected cases of child trafficking represented 27 percent of human trafficking. In recent years the increase has been greater for girls: two out of every three child victims are young girls. They pleaded:

Trafficking is a grave violation of human rights, yet it remains pervasive because its eradication requires coordinated efforts to address its root causes across multiple sectors. It is of paramount importance that countries of origin, transit, and destination, work together to tackle poverty, inequality, discrimination, and other factors causing vulnerability.[13]

UN High Commissioner for Human Rights Zeid Ra'ad Al Hussein, in his opening statement to the HRC in September 2014, underlined that there was no justification ever for the degrading, the debasing or the exploitation of other human beings—on whatever basis: nationality, race, ethnicity, religion, gender, sexual orientation, disability, age, or caste. "Yet today," he stated, "the international news ... is still filled with the sobbing of victims, of the oppressed, of the poor alongside the remains and the ashes of the killed. This remains a most pathetic stain on humanity's record of achievement."[14]

In recent months, he continued, OHCHR's concerns had been numerous. They had included severe acts of discrimination in many regions, widespread violations of economic and social rights due to failures of governance and other concerns; apparent violations of human rights in the context of counter-terrorism; sexual violence; attacks motivated by stereotypes and hatred of many kinds; over-incarceration; the death penalty, and many other issues.

In Syria, he noted, more than 190,000 identified persons had been killed between March 2011 and April 2014. More than 3 million Syrians had fled their country and 6.5 million were internally displaced—in other words, almost half the people in the country had fled their homes. This ancient civilization had devolved into a "slaughterhouse" where children were tortured in front of their parents or executed in public amid wanton killing and destruction. He stated that the so-called Islamic State in Iraq and the Levant (ISIL), also known as the Islamic State in Iraq and Syria (ISIS), which then controlled large swaths of northern Iraq and eastern Syria, had demonstrated "absolute and deliberate disregard for human rights. The scale of its use of brute violence against ethnic and religious groups is unprecedented in recent times." The high commissioner also reported to the HRC on shocking violations of human rights in several other conflicts.

In September 2014, OHCHR and the UN Assistance Mission for Iraq (UNAMI) jointly published a "Report on the Protection of Civilians in Armed Conflict in Iraq: 6 July–10 September 2014." It recorded that the conflict between the Iraqi Security Forces (ISF) and affiliated forces on the one hand, and ISIL and associated armed forces on the other, had continued to take a heavy toll on civilians: "Gross human rights abuses and acts of violence of an increasingly sectarian nature, committed by armed forces, have exacerbated the effect on civilians and contributed to the deterioration in the human rights situation and the rule of law, in many parts of the conflict."[15]

The report noted accusations of serious violations of international humanitarian law and gross abuses of human rights perpetrated by ISIL and associated groups, with an apparent systematic and widespread character. These had included attacks directly targeting civilians and civilian infrastructure, executions and other targeted killings of civilians, abduction, rape and other forms of sexual and physical violence perpetrated against women and children, forced recruitment of children, destruction or desecration of places of religious or cultural significance, wanton destruction and looting of property, and denial of fundamental freedoms.

Members of Iraq's diverse ethnic and religious communities, including Turkmen, Shabak, Christians, Yezidi, Sabaeans, Kaka'e, Faili Kurds, and Arab Shi'a had particularly been affected by the situation. ISIL and associated groups had intentionally and systematically targeted these communities for gross human rights abuses, at times aimed at destroying, suppressing, or cleansing them from areas under their control. They had also murdered captured soldiers and other security forces or government personnel. Many of these violations and abuses may amount to war crimes or crimes against humanity.

The report also noted accusations of serious violations of international humanitarian law and gross violations or abuses of international human rights law by ISF and affiliated armed groups. These included air strikes and shelling, as well as conduct of particular military operations and attacks that might have violated the principles of distinction and proportionality under international humanitarian law. Armed groups affiliated to or supporting the government had also carried out targeted killings, including of captured fighters from ISIL and associated groups, and abductions of civilians.

If these horror stories were being committed during armed conflict, others were being committed by governments and others in peacetime. Arbitrary execution, torture, enforced or involuntary disappearance, arbitrary detention, and violence against women and children were rampant worldwide. Amnesty International's annual report for 2013 said that the rights of millions of people who had escaped conflict and persecution, or migrated to seek work and a better life for themselves and their families, had been abused.[16] Governments around the world, Amnesty complained, were showing more interest in protecting their national borders than the rights of their citizens or the rights of those seeking refuge or opportunities within those borders.

Other developments highlighted included:

- specific restrictions on free speech documented in at least 101 countries, and torture and ill treatment in at least 112;
- half of humanity remained second-class citizens in the realization of their rights, as numerous states had failed to address gender-based abuse. Soldiers and armed groups had committed rape in many countries, and women and girls pregnant through rape or whose pregnancy threatened their health or life were denied access to safe abortions in many countries;
- across Africa, conflict, poverty, and abuses by security forces and armed groups had exposed the weakness of regional and international human rights mechanisms;
- in the Americas, prosecutions in some countries had marked important advances towards justice for past violations, but the inter-American human rights system had come under criticism by several governments;
- freedom of expression had come under fire across the Asia-Pacific region, with state oppression in many countries;
- in Europe and Central Asia, accountability for crimes committed in rendition programs had been elusive. In the Balkans, the likelihood of justice had receded for some victims of the 1990s war crimes; and
- in the Middle East and North Africa, countries where autocratic rulers had been ousted had seen greater media freedom and expanding opportunities for civil society, but setbacks too had been seen, with challenges to freedom of expression on religious or moral grounds. Across the region, human rights and political activists had continued to face repression, including imprisonment and torture in custody.

In Human Rights Watch's "World Report 2014," Executive Director Kenneth Roth, in the foreword, reflecting on the "Rights Struggles of 2013," highlighted three main themes: in Syria, the slaughter of civilians had continued with only a weak international response, straining the responsibility to protect.[17] Elsewhere, governments were engaged in what Roth called "abusive majoritarianism," that is to say, expressing outward commitment to democracy while in reality using the real or perceived preferences of the majority to limit dissent and suppress minorities. In the United States, new disclosures about the use of dragnet surveillance and targeted drone killings had fuelled debate about the tactics of counter-terrorism.

How are we to protect people from such atrocities? Human rights NGOs are on the front line here. At the UN, special rapporteurs, working groups of the HRC, and the UN high commissioner for human rights are the leading actors. The HRC is mandated to promote and protect human rights and help prevent human rights violations. As a very minimum, the HRC should seek to develop strategies at the national, regional, and international levels to prevent gross violations of human rights. Surely preventive strategies can attract a global consensus.

The establishment of the International Criminal Tribunals for the former Yugoslavia and on Rwanda were major breakthroughs in the pursuit of international criminal justice. The International Criminal Court (ICC) is undoubtedly a landmark institution. The concept of rendering justice to those who have suffered grievous violations of human rights is a foundation concept of the world community, which must be pursued in imaginative ways in places such as Syria. This is discussed more fully below.

The Human Rights Council

The HRC is expected to act on the basis of the human rights norms in the UN Charter, the UDHR, and human rights treaties. It is expected to advance the implementation of these treaties in cooperation with the human rights treaty bodies, which should also participate in the council.

At the World Summit in 2005, world leaders rightly called for the HRC to address situations of gross violations of human rights, including economic and social rights as well as civil and political rights. The HRC should develop an emphasis on prevention. It should strengthen the system of special procedures—rapporteurs and working groups working against torture, arbitrary executions, disappearances, arbitrary detention, violence against women and children, and other blots on our civilization.

The HRC must work closely with civil society and assure optimal participation for human rights NGOs. It should also enhance its public policy or the parliamentary role.

The HRC should also work in closer partnership than the Human Rights Commission did in its later years with regional human rights bodies such as the African Commission and Court on Human Rights, the European Court of Human Rights (ECHR), and the Inter-American Commission and Court of Human Rights.

The HRC should take the lead in encouraging human rights education in the schools, universities, and other educational institutions of every country. This is an immense task. Working together with UNESCO and UNICEF, the HRC should make this a priority issue for consideration.

Three principles should guide future international efforts for the universal protection of human rights: the principles of respect, of protection, and of confidence building. Mutual respect is a way of advancing with dialogue. Dialogue, however, must be influenced by the principle of protection. Respect and protection require that we build up confidence in our methods of protection. A patient process is required to establish international consensus on the core methods of protection, which must be prompt, adequate, and effective.

Conclusion

This chapter has intended to give a sense of the centrality of human rights in the world community and elucidate some aspects of this relationship. It has argued that the notion of world order must be conceived with human rights prominently in view, and has also sought to make the case for greater reflection of this in the work of the Security Council, the General Assembly, ECOSOC, and the agencies of the UN system. It presented the concept of the national protection system and argued that this should feature prominently in ideas and strategies of governance. Further, a national human rights protection system has constitutional, legislative, judicial, educational, institutional, and monitoring dimensions.

In a globalizing world, international human rights must provide the anchors for justice; this chapter presented poignant evidence of gross violations of human rights prevalent in the world. It noted the significance of the International Criminal Court and looked to future leadership from the HRC in protecting human rights. The council would do well to heed the following plea of Ugandan President Godfrey Binaisa, when he addressed the General Assembly in 1979, following eight years of injustice under the reign of Idi Amin Dada:

> [O]ur people naturally looked to the United Nations for solidarity and support in their struggle against the fascist dictatorship. For eight years they cried out in the wilderness for help; unfortunately, their cries seemed to have fallen on deaf ears ... The Uganda situation is merely one example of a very serious global problem involving extensive violations of human rights. The increasing

number of refugees and displaced persons is sufficient testimony to the gravity of the situation ... For how long will the United Nations remain silent while Governments represented within this Organization continue to perpetrate atrocities against their own people? Governments come and go, but the peoples of the world remain a permanent constituency of the United Nations. It was for the well-being of the peoples of the world that the United Nations were founded in the first instance. Indeed, it is for their welfare that the United Nations must continue to work. It would be unfortunate if this Organization were reduced to a club of governments afraid to speak out boldly for the rights of the citizens of the world.[18]

Notes

1 See Jared Genser and Bruno Ugarte, eds, *The United Nations Security Council in the Age of Human Rights* (Cambridge: Cambridge University Press, 2014).
2 See Myres McDougal, Harold Laswell, and Lung-chu Chen, *Human Rights and World Public Order: The Basic Policies of an International Law of Human Dignity* (New Haven, Conn.: Yale University Press, 1979). See also Michael Reisman and Burns Weston, eds., *Toward World Order and Human Dignity* (New York: The Free Press, 1976).
3 Theo van Boven, *People Matter: Views on International Human Rights Policy* (Amsterdam, the Netherlands: Muelenhoff, 1982), 72.
4 See Bertrand G. Ramcharan, *The Security Council and Human Rights* (Dordrecht, the Netherlands: Martinus Nijhoff, 2003).
5 See Hans Otto Sano, *Human Rights and Good Governance: Building Bridges* (The Hague, the Netherlands: Martinus Nijhoff, 2002).
6 See *Report of the UN Seminar on Good Governance Practices for the Promotion of Human Rights, 2004* (UN Doc. E/CN.4/2005/97). See, generally, Joseph Nye, Jr and John Donahue, eds, *Governance in a Globalizing World* (Washington, DC: Brookings Institution Press, 2000).
7 General Assembly, "United Nations Declaration on Human Rights Education and Training," resolution 66/137, 19 December 2011.
8 See Jean-Marc Coicaud, Michael W. Doyle, and Anne-Marie Gardner, *The Globalization of Human Rights* (Tokyo and New York: The United Nations University Press, 2003).
9 See for example, Robert McCorquodale, "Globalization and Human Rights," *Human Rights Quarterly* 21, no. 3 (1999): 735–66.
10 See the *Guiding Principles on Business and Human Rights* (New York and Geneva: United Nations, 2011), at www.ohchr.org/documents/publications/GuidingprinciplesBusinesshr_en.pdf.
11 OHCHR, "United Nations Special Procedures: Facts and Figures 2013," February 2014, 1.

12 UNICEF UK, "Violence Report 2014," at www.unicef.org.uk/UNICEFs-Work/What-we-do/violence/Violence-report.
13 OHCHR, "Poverty, Inequality, Discrimination—Let's Stop Human Trafficking at the Roots,"18 October 2014, at www.ohchr.org/EN/NewsEvents/Pages/DisplayNews.aspx?NewsID=15182&LangID=E.
14 OHCHR, Statement of the High Commissioner, 8 September 2014.
15 Office of the High Commissioner for Human Rights and UNAMI, "Report on the Protection of Civilians in Armed Conflict in Iraq: 6 July–10 September 2014," 2014, I, www.ohchr.org/documents/countries/iq/unami_ohchr_poc_report_final_6july_10september2014.pdf.
16 Amnesty International, "Amnesty International Report 2013: The State of the World's Human Rights," 23 May 2013, www.amnesty.org/en/annual-report/2013.
17 Human Rights Watch, "World Report 2014: Events of 2013," www.hrw.org/world-report/2014.
18 Quoted in Theo van Boven, *People Matter: Views on International Human Rights Policy* (Amsterdam, the Netherlands: Muelenhoff, 1982), 61.

3 International obligation

- The United Nations Charter
- International customary law
- Human rights treaties
- General principles of law and international declarations or guidelines
- Conclusion

> The World Conference on Human Rights reaffirms the solemn commitment of all States to fulfill their obligations to promote universal respect for, and observance and protection of, all human rights and fundamental freedoms for all in accordance with the Charter of the United Nations, other instruments relating to human rights and international law.
>
> (Vienna Declaration, paragraph 1)

The idea of international obligation helps people in their everyday lives. Sandra Lovelace was one such person. In her tribe in Canada, a man who married outside the tribe retained his communal rights on the reservation. However, if a woman did this, she lost her communal rights. Tribal leaders wished to retain this system, and the government of Canada, in accordance with internal legislation, was obliged to respect their wishes. Lovelace took her case to the Canadian Supreme Court, which upheld the internal legislation. She then brought a case to the Human Rights Committee under the Optional Protocol to the ICCPR. The committee held that Sandra Lovelace had been denied the right to enjoy her culture within her community. It based its findings on Article 27 of the covenant. Canada accordingly changed its laws.[1]

The idea of international obligation is a simple but decisive one, namely that states have international obligations under the UN

Table 3.1 Acceptance and implementation of contemporary human rights ideas

	Formal international agreement	Actual degree of consensus	Degree of implementation worldwide
Universality	*****	***	**
Equality	*****	***	**
Democracy	****	***	**
Development	*****	***	**
International cooperation and dialogue	*****	****	***
Protection	***	***	*
Justice, remedy, and reparation	***	***	*

Note: Five-star system, five stars being the highest in each category.

Charter and international law to uphold the human rights norms to which they are accountable (see Table 3.1). The reasoning is as follows: states exist and function in their international relations on the basis of international law. International law determines whether a state is a state, whether it has legitimacy, and what is permissible or impermissible conduct. Over the centuries, international customary law has developed. These are norms that have emerged through the practice of the great majority of states accompanied by the belief that the norm in question is obligatory and has attained the status of a legal norm in international law. As illustrated below, the norm interdicting slavery emerged as a norm of international customary law.

In addition to norms that have emerged through international customary law, states conclude treaties that, when signed and ratified, contain binding obligations under international law. The normal process is signature followed by ratification. Signature is usually an indication of a future intention to be bound. Ratification is the solemn act performed by the prescribed authority within the state by virtue of which it solidifies its earlier intention to be bound. If a state has not signed a treaty within the prescribed period, it may deposit what is known as an instrument of accession that equally binds it to uphold the terms of the treaty under international law.

If an applicable norm may not be identified under international customary law or in a binding treaty, one may look at what are termed general principles of law that are common to the principal legal systems of the world. This is a way of ensuring that there are no gaps in international law when it comes to determining lawful or unlawful behavior.

These three sources of law are reflected in the statute of the International Court of Justice (ICJ), which empowers the court to apply international conventions establishing rules expressly recognized by the state or states in question; international custom, as evidence of a general practice accepted as law; and the general principles of law recognized by "civilized nations."[2] These are sometimes called the law-creating sources. The ICJ's statute also refers to two law-determining agencies, namely judicial decisions and the teachings of the most highly qualified publicists. Thus, if someone is looking for the answer to a legal question and cannot find a clear answer in one of the three sources, one may look to see what judges and leading authors have said about the subject. This may be used as guidance in deciding cases.

No state can opt out of a norm once it has attained the status of international customary law. Only practice by the overwhelming majority of states can modify a pre-existing norm of international customary law. Some treaties allow participating states to enter reservations to certain provisions. Some treaties allow participating states to withdraw by giving requisite notice. In addition, some treaties allow temporary suspension of certain provisions in times of emergency, provided that the emergency has been publicly declared and is proportional to the threat faced. However, there are some provisions that may not be suspended even in such public emergencies. For example, Article 4 of the ICCPR makes it illegal to torture another human being in any circumstances.

The World Court has recognized the existence of peremptory norms of international law or norms of international public policy that take precedence over all other norms of international law.[3] In other words, they are binding on all states regardless of their internal structure or other commitments. The duty to protect the environment could be an example of such a peremptory norm of international law.

Some argue that the UN Charter represents international constitutional law, thereby according it special status in international law.[4] This argument has particular relevance when it comes to assessing the obligations of member states to respect, protect, and ensure human rights under the charter and the UDHR.

From the above, it may be seen that human rights norms, like other international legal norms, may have their origins in international customary law, human rights treaties, or legal principles shared by the main legal systems of the world. The Second American Restatement of the Foreign Relations Law of the United States is considered a highly authoritative summary of the current state of international law. (This document was produced by a distinguished group of American international lawyers, including the late Louis Henkin, the well-known human rights lawyer.) The restatement explains states' obligations to respect human rights as follows:

> A state is obliged to respect the human rights of persons subject to its jurisdiction that it has undertaken to respect by international agreements; that states generally are bound to respect as a matter of customary international law; and that it is required to respect under general principles of law common to the major legal systems of the world.[5]

Before a discussion of states' obligations under the three sources of international law, this study will examine the UN Charter, the international constitutional document of the world.

The United Nations Charter

The UN Charter's preamble expressed people's determination to reaffirm faith in fundamental human rights, the dignity and worth of the human person, and the equal rights of men and women and nations. The UN's purposes include achieving international cooperation to solve international economic, social, cultural, or humanitarian problems, and promoting and encouraging respect for human rights and fundamental freedoms. The UN was to be a center for harmonizing nations' actions in attaining these ends.[6]

All UN members pledge to fulfill their obligations required by the charter.[7] Articles 55 and 56 elaborate on this duty. According to Article 55, the UN promotes universal respect for and observance of human rights and fundamental freedoms for all, without distinction as to race, sex, language, or religion. Under Article 56, members pledge to take joint and separate action in cooperation with the organization to achieve the purposes under Article 55. Together, the two articles represent the binding legal obligations on member states, which are spelled out in more detail in the UDHR.

In determining a state's international obligations to uphold human rights, the first port of call is thus the UN Charter, with the UDHR as an elaboration of its human rights provisions. The second port of call is international customary law.

International customary law

The Second American Restatement of the Foreign Relations Law includes a succinct statement on states' human rights obligations under international customary law:

> A state violates international customary law if, as a matter of state policy, it practices, encourages, or condones: genocide; slavery or slave trade; the murder or causing the disappearance of individuals; torture or other cruel, inhuman or degrading treatment or punishment; prolonged arbitrary detention; systematic racial discrimination; or, a consistent pattern of gross violations of internationally recognized human rights.[8]

This list was drawn up three decades ago. In the light of subsequent experiences, ethnic cleansing could be added to the list of prohibited acts under international customary law.

Human rights treaties

Under the League of Nations, the practice began of concluding treaties to protect people from slavery and slavery-like practices and to protect minorities. This practice has continued under the UN, and dozens of international treaties have now been accepted by states and are legally binding. The most widely accepted treaty is the Convention on the Rights of the Child, which is binding on 194 states. Other major treaties are the International Convention on the Elimination of All Forms of Racial Discrimination, the International Convention on the Elimination of All Forms of Discrimination Against Women, the ICCPR, the ICESCR, the International Convention against Torture, and the International Convention on the Human Rights of Migrant Workers and their Families. All of these treaties, except the one addressing migrant workers, have been widely ratified.[9] More recently, in 2006, the UN General Assembly adopted a new Convention on the Rights of Persons with Disabilities and a Convention on the Protection of All Persons from Enforced Disappearance. *Human Rights: A Compilation of International Instruments*, published in 2002,[10] lists 94 instruments, not including those from regional organizations such as the Organization of American States, the Council of Europe, the Organization of African Unity (OAU, now the African Union—AU) and the Conference on Security and Co-operation in Europe. Since this publication was issued, more instruments have been adopted at the UN, including the Convention against Enforced and Involuntary Disappearances.

Stated summarily, the international covenants on human rights, the conventions against racial discrimination and gender discrimination, the Convention on the Rights of the Child, the Convention against Torture, the Convention on the Rights of Migrants and their Families, and similar conventions contain norms by which states parties have consented to be bound. Depending on the treaty, they have also agreed to submit reports periodically, engage in a dialogue with the body established under each treaty, consider advice and recommendations of the treaty body, and generally make the treaty provisions part of their national order in law and in practice. Some states have also accepted to be bound by petitions procedures or even by state-to-state complaints procedures.

The feature that is unique about the regime of human rights treaties is that they have been freely accepted by the ratifying or adhering governments. They are, therefore, the most solid consensual bases on which to build national, regional, and international human rights work in the twenty-first century.

There is a practical inference to be drawn from this conclusion, namely that the bulk of the resources of the UN and regional organizations should be deployed to support implementing human rights treaties. The ultimate rationale of the human rights treaty regime is to provide the basis for building effective national protection systems. The human rights treaty regime often provides a solid basis for dealing with new problems or threats, such as global terrorism, even if they have to be supplemented to address such new issues.

What are the legal consequences of a state becoming a party to such a convention? The Human Rights Committee, which functions under the ICCPR, has adopted a series of general comments spelling out states' obligations. General Comment no. 31/80, of 29 March 2004, addresses the obligations of states that are parties to a human rights treaty. The principles contained in General Comment no. 31, although based on the covenant, reflect the general obligations of a state party to a human rights treaty.

The Human Rights Committee recalled states' legal obligations, under Article 2 of the covenant, under which, among other things, each state party to the covenant undertakes to respect and ensure the rights recognized in the document to all individuals within its territory and subject to its jurisdiction. The Human Rights Committee observed that while Article 2 is couched in terms of the state obligations toward individuals as right holders, every state party has a legal interest in other state parties' performance of their obligations. This follows from the fact that the rules concerning a person's basic rights are *erga omnes* (or universal) obligations and that, as indicated in the covenant's preamble, the UN Charter includes the obligation to promote universal respect for and observance of human rights and fundamental freedoms.

The committee noted that a general obligation is imposed on states parties to respect the covenant rights and ensure them for all individuals in their territory and subject to their jurisdiction. Pursuant to Article 26 of the Vienna Convention on the Law of Treaties, states parties must give effect to their obligations under the covenant in good faith.

The covenant's obligations are binding on every state party. All branches of government (executive, legislative, and judicial), and other public or governmental authorities engage the responsibility of the state party. This understanding flows directly from Article 27 of the Vienna Convention on the Law of Treaties, according to which a state party may not invoke the provisions of its internal law to justify its failure to perform a treaty.

The obligation to respect and ensure the rights recognized in the covenant has immediate effect for all states parties. Reservations to Article 2 would be incompatible with the covenant. The legal obligation under Article 2(1) is both negative and positive in nature. States parties must refrain from violating the rights recognized by the covenant, and any restrictions on those rights must be permissible under the covenant's relevant provisions. Where such restrictions are made, states must demonstrate their necessity and only take measures that are proportionate to pursuing legitimate aims to ensure continuous and effective protection of covenant rights. Restrictions may not be applied or invoked in a manner that would impair the essence of a covenant right.

According to Article 2, states parties should adopt legislative, judicial, administrative, educational, and other appropriate measures to fulfill their legal obligations. The committee believes that it is important to raise awareness about the covenant not only among public officials but also among the population at large.

The positive obligations on states parties to ensure covenant rights will only be discharged if individuals are protected by the state—not just against violations of covenant rights by its agents but also against acts committed by private persons or entities that would impair the enjoyment of covenant rights insofar as they are amenable to application between private persons or entities. There may be circumstances in which a failure to ensure covenant rights as required by Article 2 would give rise to violations by states parties of those rights as a result of states parties permitting or failing to take appropriate measures or to exercise due diligence to prevent, punish, investigate, or redress the harm caused by such acts by private persons or entities.

The beneficiaries of the rights recognized by the covenant are individuals. Although (with the exception of Article 1—the right of self-determination), the covenant does not mention the rights of legal persons or similar entities or collectivities, many of the rights it recognizes may be enjoyed in community with others.

Article 2(1) requires states parties to respect and ensure covenant rights to all persons who may be within their territory and to all persons subject to their jurisdiction. This means that a state party must respect and ensure the rights laid down in the covenant to anyone within the power or effective control of that state party even if not on the state's territory. The enjoyment of covenant rights is not limited to citizens of states parties but must also be available to all individuals, regardless of nationality or statelessness, such as asylum seekers, refugees, migrant workers, and other persons on the territory or subject to the state's jurisdiction. This principle also applies to those within the power or effective control of the forces of a state party acting outside its territory, regardless of the circumstances in which such power or effective control was obtained, such as forces constituting a national contingent of an international peacekeeping or peace-enforcement operation.

The covenant also applies to situations of armed conflict to which the rules of international humanitarian law are applicable. While more specific rules of international humanitarian law may be relevant to interpret covenant rights, both spheres of law are complementary and are not mutually exclusive.

Article 2 entails an obligation not to extradite, deport, expel, or otherwise remove a person from his/her territory where there are substantial grounds for believing that a real risk of irreparable harm—either in the country to which removal is to be effected or in any country to which the person may be removed—exists.

Article 2(2) requires states parties to take steps necessary to give effect to the covenant rights in the domestic order. Thus, unless the covenant rights are already protected in domestic law or practices, states parties must change their domestic laws and practices to ensure conformity with the covenant. Where domestic law and the covenant contradict each other, Article 2 requires that the domestic law or practice be changed to meet the standards required by the covenant.

Article 2 allows a state party to pursue this according to its own domestic constitutional structure and does not require that the covenant be directly applicable in the courts by incorporating the covenant into national laws. The committee takes the view, however, that covenant guarantees may receive enhanced protection in those states where the covenant is part of the domestic legal order. In those states where the covenant is not part of the domestic legal order, states parties were invited to consider incorporating the covenant into domestic law.

Article 2's requirement that states take steps to give effect to covenant rights is unqualified and of immediate effect. A failure to comply with this obligation cannot be justified by referring to political, social, cultural, or economic considerations within the state.

In addition to protecting covenant rights, Article 2(3) stipulates that states parties must ensure that individuals have accessible and effective remedies to vindicate those rights. Such remedies should be appropriately adapted to take account of the special vulnerability of certain people such as children. The committee attaches importance to states parties establishing appropriate judicial and administrative mechanisms to address claims of rights violations under domestic law.

The Human Rights Committee noted that the judiciary can ensure the enjoyment of covenant rights in many different ways, including direct applicability of the covenant, application of comparable constitutional or other legal provisions, or the interpretive effect of the covenant in the application of national law. In particular, administrative mechanisms are required to give effect to the general obligation to investigate allegations of violations promptly, thoroughly, and effectively through independent and impartial bodies. National human rights institutions, endowed with appropriate powers, can contribute to this end. A failure by a state party to investigate allegations of violations could give rise to a separate breach of the covenant. Cessation of an ongoing violation is an essential element of the right to an effective remedy.

Article 2(3) requires that states parties make reparation to individuals whose covenant rights have been violated. Without such reparation, the obligation to provide an effective remedy, which is central to Article 2(3), is not discharged. In addition to the reparation required by Articles 9 and 14, the committee considers that the covenant requires appropriate compensation more generally. Further, the committee has noted that reparation can involve restitution, rehabilitation, and other measures, such as public apologies, public memorials, guarantees of non-repetition and changes in relevant laws and practices, and the bringing to justice of the perpetrators of human rights violations.[11]

In general, the covenant would be defeated without an obligation to take measures to prevent its recurred violation. Accordingly, in its consideration of individual petitions, the committee frequently includes the need for measures in its views (decisions), beyond a victim-specific remedy, to avoid recurrence of violations. Such measures may require changes in the state party's laws or practices.

Where investigations reveal violations of rights, states parties must ensure that those responsible are brought to justice. As with failure to investigate, failure to bring perpetrators of violations to justice could also be a separate breach of the covenant. These obligations arise notably regarding those violations recognized as criminal under domestic or international law, such as torture and similar cruel, inhuman, and degrading treatment (Article 7), summary and arbitrary killing (Article 6), and enforced disappearance (Articles 6, 7, and 9). Indeed, the problem of impunity for these violations may contribute to the recurrence of violations. When committed as part of a widespread or systematic attack on a civilian population, these violations are crimes against humanity (Article 7 of the Rome Statute of the ICC).

Accordingly, where public officials have violated covenant rights, states parties may not relieve perpetrators from personal responsibility. Furthermore, there is no official status that allows someone to be immune from legal responsibility for such violations. Other impediments to establishing legal responsibility should also be removed, such as the defense of obedience to superior orders or unreasonably short periods of statutory limitation. States parties should also assist each other in bringing to justice persons suspected of violating the covenant.

The committee further took the view that the right to an effective remedy may require states parties to provide for and implement provisional or interim measures to avoid continuing violations and to endeavor to repair—at the earliest possible opportunity—any harm that may have been caused by such violations.

General Comment no. 31 is a magisterial summary of the idea of international obligation under international human rights treaties. It represents, in many respects, the heart of international human rights law. Its principles are applicable, subject to textual variations, to human rights treaties in general.

General principles of law and international declarations or guidelines

As mentioned earlier, if an international decision-making body is called on to decide a human rights case, and there is no clear norm of international customary law or in a human rights treaty, there may be recourse to general principles of law common to the principal legal systems.

In the Chorzow Factory case, the World Court remarked "that it is a principle of international law, and even a general conception of law, that any breach of an engagement involves an obligation to make reparation."[12] In his authoritative *Principles of Public International Law*, the late Ian Brownlie discusses considerations of humanity[13] as part of the general principles of law and notes that, in recent years, the UN Charter provisions concerning protection of human rights and fundamental freedoms and references to the charter principles have been used as a more concrete basis of considerations of humanity, "for example in matters of racial discrimination and self-determination."[14]

General legal principles may be deduced from the numerous declarations, bodies of principles, or guidelines adopted at the UN. The *Compilation of International Instruments* contains several such instruments. In theory, a declaration, body of principle, or guideline may not be legally binding to begin with, but a particular provision could mutate into a rule of international customary law. Or it would be perfectly normal to look to such provisions when seeking to identify a general legal principle. The declarations, bodies of principle, or guidelines are usually adopted by consensus and therefore reflect a good synthesis of the thinking of governments and civil society on a particular issue.

Conclusion

The international obligation to uphold human rights has a great deal of specificity. All states are members of the UN and subject to the charter's human rights obligations. International customary law is applicable to all states, and there are solid human rights norms that must be complied with. Nearly every state has committed to one or more of the principal human rights treaties. Their legal obligations were clarified by the Human Rights Committee in General Comment no. 31 which related to the ICCPR, but whose principles are applicable to human rights treaties. As a residual source of obligation, there may be recourse to general principles of law including the principle of humanity.

The conclusion to be drawn from this discussion of international obligation is that all states have human rights obligations under the UN Charter, international customary law, treaties, and general principles of law, including the principle of humanity. Unlike at earlier times in history, there is no longer a question as to whether a state has a legal obligation to uphold human rights. Rather, the question, purely and simply, is whether it is fulfilling its international obligation to respect, protect, and ensure internationally recognized human rights.

Implementation and accountability are the challenges of our time, but human rights are defined and universal.

In a resolution adopted on 9 April 2014, on strengthening and enhancing the effective functioning of the human rights treaty body system, the General Assembly underlined "the obligation that States have to promote and protect human rights and to carry out the responsibilities that they have undertaken under international law, especially the Charter, as well as various international instruments in the field of human rights, including under international human rights."[15] The idea of international obligation thus received the strongest reaffirmation by the most representative organ of the international community.

Notes

1 *Sandra Lovelace v. Canada* (Communication no. 24/1977), views adopted 30 July 1981, Report of the Human Rights Committee, *GAOR* 36, Supplement no. 40 (A/36/40), 166–75.
2 Article 38(1), *Statute of the International Court of Justice*.
3 See *Barcelona Traction Light and Power Co. Ltd*, International Court of Justice, 5 February 1970, *ICJ Reports* (1970): 1.
4 See Ronald St John Macdonald and Douglas Johnston, *Towards World Constitutionalism: Issues in the Legal Ordering of the World Community* (Boston, Mass. and Leiden, the Netherlands: Martinus Nijhoff Publishers, 2005).
5 American Law Institute, *Restatement of the Law. The Foreign Relations Law of the United States*, vol. 2 (St Paul, Minn.: American Law Institute, 1987), Articles 701 and 702.
6 Article 1, UN Charter.
7 Article 2, UN Charter.
8 Article 702, *Restatement of the Law. The Foreign Relations Law of the United States*.
9 For the latest state of ratifications, see www.ohchr.org.
10 OHCHR, *Human Rights: A Compilation of International Instruments* (New York and Geneva: United Nations, 2002), www.ohchr.org/documents/publications/compilation2en.pdf.
11 See Chapter 10 for more on this.
12 *Chorzow Factory* (Merits), *PCIJ*, series A, nos. 17 and 29. See generally, Ian Brownlie, *Principles of Public International Law*, 6th edn (Oxford: Oxford University Press, 2003), 15–18.
13 In the "Corfu Channel Case," *ICJ Reports* (1949), the World Court invoked "elementary considerations of humanity, even more exacting in peace than in war." See also *Nicaragua v. United States, ICJ Reports* (1986), 112–14.
14 Brownlie, *Principles of Public International Law*, 27.
15 UN General Assembly, "Strengthening and Enhancing the Effective Functioning of the Human Rights Treaty Body System," UN doc. A/RES/68/268, 9 April 2014.

4 Universality

- Universality as an idea
- Universality as a goal
- Universality as a normative concept
- The democratic test of universality
- The bases of universality
- Challenges of implementation
- Conclusion

> The universal nature of these rights and freedoms is beyond question.
> (Vienna Declaration, paragraph 1)

> We resolve ... to respect fully and uphold the Universal Declaration of Human Rights; to strive for the full protection and promotion in all our countries of civil, political, economic, social and cultural rights for all.
> (Millennium Declaration, paragraph 25)

During his tenure, UN Secretary-General Kofi Annan had to contend with assertions by some African leaders that international human rights norms were foreign impositions and did not correspond to African culture and realities. He met these challenges head on during an address to the OAU summit in Harare on 2 June 1997. He declared:

> [L]et us dedicate ourselves to a new doctrine for African politics: where democracy has been usurped let us do what ever is in our power to restore it to its rightful owners, the people.
> Verbal condemnation, though necessary and desirable, is not sufficient. We must also ostracize and isolate putschists.
> The success of Africa's third wave depends equally on respect for fundamental human rights. The conflicts which have disfigured our

continent have all too often, been accompanied by massive human rights violations.

Africa can no longer tolerate and accept as *faits accomplis*, coups against elected governments, and the illegal seizure of power by military cliques. I am aware of the fact that some view this concern as a luxury of the rich countries for which Africa is not ready. I know that others treat it as an imposition, if not a plot, by the industrialized west. I find these thoughts truly demeaning, demeaning of the yearning for human dignity that resides in every African heart.

Do not African mothers weep when their sons or daughters are killed or maimed by agents of repressive rule? Are not African fathers saddened when their children are unjustly jailed or tortured? Is not Africa as a whole impoverished when even one of its brilliant voices is silenced?

We cannot afford to lose one life, spare one idea, relinquish one hope, if we are to succeed on our chosen course. So I say this to you, my brothers and sisters, that human rights are African rights, and I call upon you to ensure that all Africans are able fully to enjoy them.

Let us work together and with the United Nations to develop good governance and respect for the rule of law. When we succeed, Africa will have taken a great step forward.[1]

In politics and academia, great debates continue to rage over the universality of human rights.[2] Some contend that human rights are not universal, arguing rather for cultural relativism in applying human rights norms. Some have argued for the primacy of religious tenets over international human rights norms. As will be demonstrated here, these arguments are flawed.

The thread running through this book is one of human societies cross-fertilizing and learning from one another, converging toward a great synthesis around binding international human rights norms. Viewed from this perspective, the universality of rights has been authoritatively affirmed in the international community, and there is a formal consensus on universality.

The universality of human rights must be vigorously upheld. It rests on the idea that there is a minimum body of basic human rights that belongs to every human being regardless of his or her country of origin or philosophical, religious, or other beliefs. Regional or national charters may add to the universal body of human rights but may not detract from them.

The validity of the universality of human rights is not lessened by the fact that, in practice, human rights are violated in many parts of the world. However, rights exist even if they are breached, and the challenge is to work for their implementation and protection. This chapter discusses universality as an idea, a goal, a normative concept, its democratic test, the basis of universality, and problems of implementation.

Universality as an idea

As illustrated in previous chapters, the concept of human rights has developed over the centuries and has roots in all of the major world religions. In turn, these principles have been codified in international legal instruments, namely the UDHR. Since its declaration in 1948, the UDHR has been re-endorsed in international and regional treaties and in authoritative policy pronouncements by governments and people in Africa, the Americas, Asia, and Europe. This certainly underscores the universality of human rights.

Some years ago, the late Senator José Diokno of the Philippines summarily dispatched spurious arguments about cultural diversity that diminished universality:

> Two justifications for authoritarianism in Asian developing countries are currently fashionable ... One is that Asian societies are authoritarian and paternalistic and so need governments that are also authoritarian and paternalistic; that Asia's hungry masses are too concerned with filling their stomachs to concern themselves with civil liberties and political freedoms; that the Asian conception of freedom differs from that of the West; that, in short, Asians are not fit for human rights.
>
> Another is that developing countries must sacrifice freedom temporarily to achieve the rapid economic development that their exploding populations and rising expectations demand; in short, that governments must be authoritarian to promote development.
>
> Well, the first justification is racist nonsense. And I will say no more than that. The second is a lie: authoritarianism is not needed for development; what it is needed for is to maintain the status quo.
>
> Regardless ... of what dictators and social scientists may say, we Asians know that the loss of freedom does not lead to a better life. On the contrary, we know that life cannot become better—it cannot even be good—unless people are free.[3]

Universality as a goal

If human beings have so many things in common, is it strange to want to preserve these common characteristics and to reach out in mutual support and cooperation? Can we protect the environment or keep the air clean unless we do so together? Is it wrong to say that every human being should have an equal opportunity to develop his or her potential? Is universality then not valid as a goal for common aspirations?

The idea that all human beings in the twenty-first century possess, as part of their birthright, a core of inalienable rights is not disputed. What is sometimes debated is the content of particular rights and the need for change. This is a legitimate debate. The international human rights treaties inspired by the UDHR contain amendment procedures that could deal with claims for modernization or updating. The UDHR, however, stands on its own as an historic, inspirational document. The universality of core human rights is quite compatible with cultural diversity, and the argument of cultural diversity should not challenge the core universal human rights but, rather, might influence the mode and manner of their application in particular societies. One can, for example, proclaim freedom of religion or belief, while leaving it to each person to choose a religion or belief. The notion of good faith in applying universal human rights norms comes into the picture here.

The existence of duties does not negate the universality of human rights. Rather, as is explicitly recognized in Article 29 of the UDHR, everyone has duties to his or her community. That same article further states that one may be subject only to such limitations as are determined by law in the exercise of rights and freedoms. Such limitations may only be for the purpose of securing due recognition and respect for the rights and freedoms of others and of meeting the requirements of morality, public order, and general welfare.

Universality as a normative concept

In the history of the international community, has it not been found necessary to postulate universal norms? Have the norms not been useful? Is not the very notion of international law grounded in the concept of a law applicable to all communities—at least in respect of imperative norms of public policy (*jus cogens*) and international customary law? Would order be possible in the international community without a system of norms of universal applicability and validity? The answer can only be in the negative. That being the case, is it not entirely natural and proper that the stock of norms of international law would also include norms of universal human rights?

By the very act of joining the organization, all UN member states commit to the principle of universality contained in the charter and the UDHR. The commitment to universality is itself universal. When the Commission on Human Rights began drafting the UDHR in 1947, Charles Malik of Lebanon urged that the commission base itself on the following four principles:

1 the human person is more important than the racial, national, or other group to which he may belong;
2 the human person's most sacred and inviolable possessions are in his mind and his conscience, enabling him to perceive the truth, choose freely, and to exist;
3 any social pressure on the part of the state, religion, or race involving the automatic consent of the human person is reprehensible; and
4 the social group to which the individual belongs may, like the human person himself, be wrong or right. The person alone is the judge.[4]

The spirit animating the drafting committee members is inspiring to read, even nearly 70 years later. At an early drafting session, René Cassin proposed that two or three fundamental principles be incorporated in the outline:

1 the unity of the human race or family;
2 the idea that every human being has a right to be treated like every other human being; and
3 the concept of solidarity and fraternity among men.[5]

Hernán Santa Cruz of Chile opined that the drafting committee must draw up a charter of human rights, giving it not only legal but real human content. He further suggested that this charter should be a spiritual guide for humanity, enumerating the rights that must be respected everywhere.[6]

The UDHR's opening article was significantly influenced by Asia. During the second session of the drafting committee, on 5 December 1947, Carlos Romulo of the Philippines proposed to redraft Article 1 as discussed in the first session in June 1947 on the basis of Cassin's draft proposal. In response, the chairman invited the French and Philippines representatives to submit a new text of the article. At the ninth meeting of the drafting committee, on 10 December 1947, Romulo proposed the following text: "All men are brothers. Being endowed by nature with reason and conscience, they are born free and possess equal dignity and rights."[7]

Following further discussion, the following text proposed by the Philippines and France was adopted: "All men are born free and equal in dignity and rights. They are endowed with reason and conscience and should act towards one another like brothers."[8] With some subsequent polishing, the following is what was adopted as the UDHR's opening article: "All human beings are born free and equal in dignity and rights. They are endowed with reason and conscience and should act towards one another in a spirit of brotherhood."

The Egyptian representative, Osman Obeid, made a case for including a mention of individuals' duties as a corollary to his or her rights. He made the following stirring plea for justice for the peoples of the world: "The principles of human rights should be set forth in clear terms. The peoples of the world would greet with enthusiasm the first action taken by the United Nations to enforce redressment of wrongs."[9]

Representatives from Africa, Asia, the Americas, and Europe thus influenced the drafting of the UDHR. In the drafting process, detailed draft declarations were submitted by Chile, Cuba, and Panama. In compiling materials from all over the globe to aid in drafting the declaration, the secretariat drew on the constitutions and legislation of 55 countries from Africa, Asia, Latin America, and Eastern Europe. Only 14 were from Western countries.[10]

Developing countries also were actively involved. The Philippines proposed an article stating that everyone had the right to participate in their government, both directly or indirectly, through elections that are periodic, free, and conducted by secret ballot.[11] The Panamanian representative proposed an article declaring that the state has a duty to maintain comprehensive arrangements to promote health, prevent sickness and accident, and provide medical care and compensation for the loss of livelihood.[12]

Malik argued that social and economic rights and the problem of discrimination were very important and should form part of the instrument.[13] P.C. Chang of China called for a document that would accord with the spirit and atmosphere of the post-war era and argued that the document should reflect freedom from want.[14] India tabled a draft declaration that included the following statement: "Every human being has the right of equality, without distinction of race, sex, language, religion, nationality or political belief."[15]

This is a mere sampling of the defining contributions of the representatives from Africa, Asia, and Latin America in drafting the UDHR. At the World Conference on Human Rights in 1993, the representatives, assembled from around the world, reaffirmed the universality of human rights in the most emphatic terms.

68 Universality

The UDHR has inspired regional instruments to protect human rights throughout the globe, all of which have reaffirmed its precepts. This may be seen in the constitution of the OAU (now the African Union), the African Charter on Human and People's Rights, the Arab Charter on Human Rights, the Cairo Islamic Declaration on Human Rights, the LAWASIA Statement of Basic Principles of Human Rights, the American Convention on Human Rights, the European Convention on Human Rights, and the Association of Southeast Asian Nations (ASEAN) Human Rights Declaration. These endorsements of the UDHR bear witness to its universal status.[16]

The democratic test of universality

There is an irrefutable democratic test that confirms the concept of the universality of rights. It is a simple matter. Just ask any human being: Would you like to live or be killed arbitrarily? Would you like to be tortured or enslaved? Would you like to live free or be in prison? Would you like to be in bondage? Would you like to have a say in how you are governed? The democratic test of universality is the basis for its strongest affirmation.[17]

The bases of universality

The bases of the universality of human rights are: 1) all human beings claim their inherent human rights; 2) the common humanity of all human beings and the inherency of rights; 3) the formal affirmation and reaffirmation of human rights in consensual processes of authoritative decision-making bodies such as the GA and world conferences on human rights.

There may, indeed, be discussion about whether every internationally proclaimed human right is universal or if global consensus is lacking regarding a particular asserted right. There is, for example, a lively debate about the right to change one's religion or belief. This right was included in the UDHR but not in the ICCPR, and was finessed in the 1992 Declaration on Freedom of Religion or Belief. Where a particular human right is contested by one or more government or group, the matter must be assessed by referring to the tests of inherency and consensus.

When a right is contested, recourse may be had to the principle of inherency, namely that one should enjoy certain rights from the very nature of common humanity. The example of the right to change one's religion or belief may be cited. One can understand religions or laws prohibiting religious proselytizing or forbidding campaigns to convince people to change religions. However, if an individual decides to change her or his religion or belief, how can this be forbidden by any religion or law? The universality of the right to change one's religion or belief would therefore rest in the principle of inherency.

There are repeated instances of the reaffirmation of consensus over the universality of human rights in authoritative forums of the international community such as the Vienna World Conference on Human Rights, the Millennium Declaration, and the outcome document of the Summit of World Leaders in 2005.

The Vienna conference reaffirmed all states' solemn commitment to fulfill their obligations to promote universal respect for, observance of, and protection of all human rights and fundamental freedoms in accordance with the UN Charter, other instruments relating to human rights, and international law. In ringing terms, it proclaimed that: "The universal nature of these rights and freedoms is beyond question."[18]

The Millennium Declaration reaffirmed the UN's commitment to the charter's purposes and principles, "which have proved timeless and universal. Indeed, their relevance and capacity to inspire have increased, as nations and peoples have become increasingly interconnected and interdependent." It pledged: "We resolve ... to respect fully and uphold the Universal Declaration of Human Rights; to strive for the full protection and promotion in all our countries of civil, political, economic, social and cultural rights for all."[19]

The GA considered certain fundamental values essential to international relations in the twenty-first century. These included freedom, equality, solidarity, tolerance, respect for nature, and shared responsibility.[20]

The Summit of World Leaders in 2005 reaffirmed the centrality of human rights in the UN's work and endorsed the responsibility to protect.[21] The world leaders declared their readiness to refer genocide, ethnic cleansing, crimes against humanity, and war crimes to the UNSC.

Challenges of implementation

It has been argued that the universality of human rights is belied by the fact that these rights are not respected in practice or are grossly violated in large parts of the world. Lack of implementation is certainly a feature of our contemporary world. So are gross violations of human rights. But this is not an argument against universality. In national legal systems, the validity of laws is not belied by the fact that many are breached. This is an issue of law and order and protection.

An individual's rights are not taken away because they are not respected or are violated. This is a challenge of universal implementation and protection that the entire international human rights movement is striving to address.

Conclusion

To reiterate, there is a simple test of universality. If any human being were asked whether she or he would like to be free from arbitrary and summary execution, torture, arbitrary arrest and detention, enforced or involuntary disappearance, and persecution on grounds of religion or belief, there can be no doubt that every human being would answer in the positive. From this, we may conclude that there is a basic set of fundamental human rights that all human beings would claim, affirm, and defend.

Notes

1. United Nations, "Secretary-General Calls for Efforts to Unleash African 'Third Wave' Based on Democracy, Human Rights and Sustainable Development," ECOSOCDEV, Geninfo, 11, 1 (2 June 1992).
2. See generally, William Theodore de Bary, *Asian Values and Human Rights. A Confucian Communitarian Perspective* (Cambridge, Mass.: Harvard University Press, 1998); Joanne Bauer and Daniel Bell, *The East Asian Challenge for Human Rights* (Cambridge: Cambridge University Press, 1999); Jack Donnelly, *Universal Human Rights in Theory and Practice* (Ithaca, NY and London: Cornell University Press, 1989); Peter Van Ness, ed., *Debating Human Rights* (London: Routledge, 1999).
3. José Diokno, Amnesty International 1978 Sean MacBride Human Rights Lecture (AI Index: ICM 01/11/78), 8.
4. Commission on Human Rights, E/CN.4/SR.14, 3–4.
5. Commission on Human Rights, E/CN.4/SR.2, 2.
6. Commission on Human Rights, 3.
7. Commission on Human Rights, E/CN.4/AC.2/SR.9, 21.
8. Commission on Human Rights.
9. Commission on Human Rights, E/CN.4/SR.8, 3.
10. Some of the countries were Afghanistan, Argentina, Belorussian Soviet Socialist Republic (SSR), Bolivia, Brazil, Chile, China, Colombia, Costa Rica, Cuba, Czechoslovakia, Dominican Republic, Ecuador, Egypt, El Salvador, Ethiopia, Guatemala, Haiti, Honduras, India, Iran, Iraq, Lebanon, Liberia, Mexico, Nicaragua, Panama, Paraguay, Peru, Philippines, Poland, Saudi Arabia, Syria, Turkey, Ukraine SSR, USSR, Union of South Africa, Uruguay, Venezuela, and Yugoslavia. Only 14 were from Western countries: Australia, Belgium, Canada, Denmark, France, Greece, Iceland, Luxembourg, Netherlands, New Zealand, Norway, Sweden, the UK, and the United States.

11 Commission on Human Rights, E/CN.4/AC.2/SR.7, 7.
12 Commission on Human Rights, E/CN.4/AC.2/SR.8, 11.
13 Commission on Human Rights, E/CN.4/AC.3/SR.5, 3.
14 Commission on Human Rights, E/CN.4/SR.4, 6.
15 Commission on Human Rights, E/CN.4/11.
16 On this, see Bertrand G. Ramcharan, "The Universality of Human Rights," *Review of the International Commission of Jurists*, nos. 58–59 (December 1997): 86–104. See also Dato Param Cumaraswamy, "The Universal Declaration of Human Rights—Is it Universal?" *Review of the International Commission of Jurists*, nos. 58–59 (December 1997): 118–23.
17 See the author's comments on universality in *Universality of Human Rights in a Pluralistic World*, proceedings of a colloquy organized by the Council of Europe in cooperation with the International Institute of Human Rights, Strasbourg, France, 17–19 April 1989 (Council of Europe/N.P. Engel Publisher, 1990), 24–27.
18 *Vienna Declaration* (1993), para. 1.
19 *UN Millennium Declaration*, UNGA resolution 55/2 (18 September 2000), para. 25.
20 *UN Millennium Declaration*, para. 6.
21 *Report of the Commission on Intervention and State Sovereignty* (Ottawa, Canada: International Development Research Centre, 2001).

5 Equality

- The idea of equality in the UN Charter and the ICCPR
- Equal enjoyment of enumerated rights
- Non-discrimination
- Discrimination versus distinction
- Affirmative action
- General Comment 18/37 of the Human Rights Committee (non-discrimination)
- General Comment 4/13 of the Human Rights Committee (gender equality)
- The Beijing World Conference on Women's Rights (1995)
- The Durban World Conference Against Racism, Racial Discrimination, Xenophobia and Related Intolerance (2001)
- Conclusion

> Respect of Human Rights and for fundamental freedoms without distinction of any kind is a fundamental rule of international human rights law.
> (Vienna Declaration, paragraph 15)

> The human rights of women should form an integral part of the United Nations human rights activities, including the promotion of all human rights instruments relating to women.
> (Vienna Declaration, paragraph 18)

An earlier chapter described how Canada's international obligation brought relief to Sandra Lovelace. Similarly, the concept of equality in international human rights law brought relief to the women of Mauritius. According to the laws of that country, if a man married a woman outside Mauritius, his wife was entitled to his nationality. A Mauritian woman, however, who married a non-national could not pass on her nationality to her husband. A group of Mauritian women brought a class action case before the Human Rights Committee. The committee ruled that the law was discriminatory on grounds of gender, and the government of Mauritius changed the law.[1]

The idea that every human being should be treated equally under the law and should be given equal access to opportunities is an article of faith of the UN and a bedrock principle of international human rights law. Seventy years since the UN was established, the international community has registered important progress in developing norms to buttress the principle of equality and pursue programs to promote this equality. Discrimination on grounds of race and gender has been given prominence, and elaborate programs of action have been adopted to counter such discrimination.

The pursuit of equality and non-discrimination, however, is not a simple matter. In practice, complex issues of principle and reconciliation arise. These must be resolved in light of the fundamental meaning of equality. The following seeks to present the pith and substance of the idea of equality. First, the drafting history of this idea in the UN Charter and the ICCPR will be examined. General comments of the Human Rights Committee on non-discrimination and gender equality will also be considered, as well as the challenges facing the implementation of equality that emerged at the 1995 World Conference on the Rights of Women and the 2001 World Conference on Racism and Racial Discrimination. The chapter seeks to elucidate the idea of equality on the basis of principle and practice.

The idea of equality in the UN Charter and the ICCPR

The inherent dignity and the "equal and inalienable rights of all members of the human family" were recognized in the UDHR's opening lines as the "foundation of freedom, justice and peace in the world." The claim to equality, the late Sir Hersch Lauterpacht held, "is in a substantial sense the most fundamental of the rights of man. It occupies the first place in most written constitutions. It is the starting point of all other liberties."[2]

The bedrock nature of the principles of equality and non-discrimination in international human rights law were admirably brought out in an address by the head of the Federal Political Department of Switzerland at the opening of the World Conference to Combat Racism and Racial Discrimination on 14 August 1978:

> Of all human rights, the right to equality is one of the most important. It is linked to the concepts of liberty and justice, and is

manifested through the observance of two fundamental complementary principles of international law. The first of these principles, that "all human beings are born free and equal in dignity and rights," appears in the 1948 Universal Declaration of Human Rights; the second, the principle of nondiscrimination, has been solemnly reaffirmed in Article 1 of the Charter of the United Nations. It is upon those two principles that all the instruments on human rights adopted since 1945 are based ... The prohibition of discrimination has become a norm of positive law, as has been recognized by the International Court of Justice in respect of racist practices: To establish ... and to enforce, distinction, exclusions, restrictions and limitations exclusively based on grounds of race, color, descent or national or ethnic origin which constitute a denial of fundamental human rights is a flagrant violation of the purposes and principles of the Charter.

Articles 2(1), 3, and 26 of the ICCPR set forth five related principles: the principle of equal enjoyment of rights; the general principle of equality and the corollary principle of equality between men and women; the principle of equality before the law and equality before the courts; the principle of equal protection before the law; and the principle of non-discrimination. The covenant's preparatory works indicate that, notwithstanding differences in terminology, the principles of equality and non-discrimination in the document were intended to be the same principles as those contained in the UN Charter, the UDHR, and the ICESCR. The meaning of equality and non-discrimination in all of these instruments can be taken from the modern international law of human rights.

Equal enjoyment of enumerated rights

Article 2 of the covenant requires states parties to respect and ensure "the rights recognized in the present Covenant, without distinction of any kind, such as race, color, sex ..." Unlike Article 26, the article does not forbid distinction or discrimination generally, but only distinctions and discriminations in the enjoyment of the rights recognized in the covenant. However, since the covenant recognizes equal protection of law (Article 26), distinctions forbidden by the latter article also violate Article 2(1).

Article 2(1) requires that the enjoyment of rights be respected "without distinction of any kind, such as race, color or sex." The clear implication is that the grounds enumerated are not exclusive, and other

Equality 75

grounds for distinction are also barred. However, the grounds barred are others similar to race, color "or other status." Even some types of "status" may be a permissible ground to deny rights if it is relevant. This includes, for example, being under age, mentally incompetent, and for some specified purposes, alienage. The covenant does not forbid depriving or limiting rights for misconduct, for example on conviction for crime.

Non-discrimination

In addition to equality and equal protection, the covenant prohibits discrimination on particular grounds. Article 2 prohibits discrimination on forbidden grounds in respecting or ensuring the rights recognized by the covenant. Article 26 forbids discrimination on the same grounds in respect of equality before the law and the equal protection of the law. Discrimination on forbidden grounds is expressly prohibited also in the enjoyment of particular rights, such as the rights of children (Article 18). Article 2 forbids discrimination in the enjoyment of the rights of the covenant, but Article 26 forbids discrimination with respect to the equal protection of laws generally.

Discrimination versus distinction

During drafting, the question arose whether the word "discrimination" or "distinction" should be used. Ultimately, both words were used interchangeably, even within the same covenant. During consideration of Article 26 of the ICCPR in the Third Committee in 1961, some representatives stressed the differences between "discrimination" and "distinction."[3] The following year, when Article 2(1) of the ICESCR was being drafted, the Italian, Argentine, and Mexican delegations proposed an amendment to replace the word "distinction" with "discrimination" on the grounds that "some distinction might be justified— for example, preferential treatment for certain under-privileged groups—and that it was discrimination which should be condemned."[4] Some delegations, however, argued that the proposal was questionable on legal grounds.[5]

In the end, however, it was decided to insert the word "discrimination" in the ICESCR. When the Third Committee considered a similar provision of the ICCPR the following year, this same decision was not repeated. As a result, the ICESCR uses the term "discrimination," and the ICCPR uses the term "distinction." It is clear from both debates that the drafters intended to include the higher level of protection, whichever word was used, in both covenants. Representatives proposing each word argued that it would give the higher level of protection. It is clear in the preparatory works of both covenants, however, that both terms exclude only arbitrary or unjust distinction or discrimination.[6]

A memorandum submitted by the division of human rights of the UN Secretariat to the Sub-Commission on Prevention of Discrimination and Protection of Minorities stated: "Discrimination implies, essentially, unequal and unfavorable treatment, either by the bestowal of favors or the imposition of burdens. Any of a number of grounds may underlie such unequal treatment." Four of them are mentioned in the charter—race, sex, language, and religion. The prevention of discrimination is, therefore, the implementation of the principle of equality of treatment.[7] A later memorandum elaborated further: "The following delimitation of the meaning of the term discrimination may be suggested: discrimination includes any conduct based on a distinction made on grounds of natural or social categories, which have no relation either to individual capacities or merits, or to the concrete behavior of the individual person."[8]

The European Court of Human Rights, referring to the criteria for determining whether a given difference in treatment contravenes Article 14 of the European Convention, has stated that:

> [T]he principle of equality of treatment is violated if the distinction has no objective and reasonable justification. The existence of such a justification must be assessed in relation to the aim and effects of the measure under consideration, regard being had to the principles which normally prevail in democratic societies. A difference of treatment in the exercise of a right laid down in the Convention must not only pursue a legitimate aim: Article 14 is likewise violated when it is clearly established that there is no reasonable relationship of proportionality between the means employed and the aim sought to be realized.[9]

Affirmative action

When both covenants were being drafted, it was accepted that prohibiting discrimination or distinction does not preclude positive measures taken in favor of disadvantaged groups. When Article 26 of the ICCPR was being written, it was recognized that "the word, 'discrimination' ... was used ... in a negative sense only, to mean a distinction of an unfavorable kind."[10] Similarly, it was said that the word "discrimination" conveyed the idea of a distinction made without any objective basis.[11] The representatives of Chile, the Netherlands, and Uruguay pointed out that equality did not mean identity of treatment.

During discussions on the ICESCR in 1962, the Indian representative pointed out that implementing non-discrimination raised certain problems, such as in the case of certain groups in under-developed countries. Thus, it was suggested that the committee add an article reading: "Special measures for the advancement of any socially and educationally backward sections of society shall not be construed as distinctions under this article."[12] The committee endorsed the point made by the Indian representative,[13] and the position adopted by the Third Committee followed that also made by the World Court in a case regarding minority schools in Albania.[14]

General Comment 18/37 of the Human Rights Committee (non-discrimination)

In General Comment 18/37 of 9 November 1989, the Human Rights Committee provided useful guidance on the ICCPR provisions dealing with equality and non-discrimination. The committee noted that the covenant did not define the term "discrimination" or indicate what constituted discrimination. It noted, however, that Article 1 of the International Convention on the Elimination of All Forms of Racial Discrimination provided that the term "racial discrimination" means any distinction, exclusion, restriction, or preference based on race, color, descent, or national or ethnic origin that intends to nullify equal enjoyment or exercise of human rights and fundamental freedoms in the political, economic, social, cultural, or any other field of public life. Similarly, Article 1 of the Convention on the Elimination of All Forms of Discrimination against Women provides that "discrimination against women" means any distinction, exclusion, or restriction made on the basis of sex that impairs or nullifies women's enjoyment or exercise of human rights and fundamental freedoms.

While these conventions only address cases of discrimination on specific grounds, the Human Rights Committee believed that the term "discrimination," as used in the covenant, should be understood to imply any distinction, exclusion, restriction, or preference that is based on any ground, such as race, color, sex, language, religion, political or other opinion, national or social origin, property, birth or other status. Moreover, such distinction should also nullify or impair the recognition, enjoyment, or exercise by all persons—on equal footing—of all rights and freedoms. However, the term "enjoyment of rights and freedoms on an equal footing" does not mean identical treatment in every instance. The committee also pointed out that the principle of equality sometimes requires states parties to take affirmative action to diminish or eliminate conditions that cause or perpetuate discrimination.

In an important clarification, the Human Rights Committee stated that Article 26 of the covenant does not merely duplicate the guarantee already provided in Article 2 but provides an autonomous right. It prohibits discrimination in law or in any field regulated and protected by public authorities. Article 26 is, therefore, concerned with the obligations imposed on states parties regarding their legislation and the application of it. Thus, when legislation is adopted by a state party, it must comply with the requirement in Article 26 that its content should not be discriminatory. In other words, the application of the principle of non-discrimination in Article 26 is not limited to those rights enumerated in the covenant.

Finally, the Human Rights Committee observed that not every differentiation of treatment will constitute discrimination if the criteria for differentiation are reasonable and objective and if the aim is to achieve a purpose legitimate under the covenant.[15]

General Comment 4/13 of the Human Rights Committee (gender equality)

In General Comment 4/13, of 28 July 1991, the Human Rights Committee provided important guidance on the international law of human rights regarding gender equality, specifically under Articles 2(1), 3, and 26 of the ICCPR. Importantly, the committee began with the observation that these articles require measures of protection but also affirmative action to ensure the positive enjoyment of rights. This cannot be done simply by enacting laws. Hence, more information has generally been required to ascertain what measures, in addition to law, are required to give effect to the obligations under Article 3 and to ascertain what progress is being made or what factors or difficulties are being met in this regard. However, the positive obligation undertaken by states parties may have an inevitable impact on legislation or administrative measures designed to regulate matters other than those addressed in the covenant but which may adversely affect rights recognized in the covenant. As an example, the committee mentioned the degree to which immigration laws that distinguish between men and women may adversely affect women's rights to marry non-citizens or hold public office.

The Human Rights Committee advised that it might assist states parties if special attention were given to a review by specially appointed bodies or institutions of laws or measures that inherently draw a distinction between men and women if those laws or measures adversely affect covenant rights. The committee also considered that it might help the states parties implement this obligation if more use could be made of existing means of international cooperation to exchange experience and organize assistance to solve the practical problems connected with ensuring equal rights for men and women.[16]

The Beijing World Conference on Women's Rights (1995)

The fourth World Conference on Women's Rights, held in Beijing in September 1995, was a landmark in efforts to advance gender justice.[17] The conference recognized that the status of women had advanced in some important respects in the previous decade. Nonetheless, progress had been uneven, inequalities between women and men persisted, and obstacles remained. The conference also recognized that the increasing poverty affecting many people, particularly women and children, exacerbated the situation.

The conference reaffirmed the commitment to equal rights and the human dignity of women and men enshrined in the UN Charter, the UDHR, and other international human rights instruments, in particular the Convention on the Elimination of All Forms of Discrimination against Women and the Convention on the Rights of the Child, as well as the Declaration on the Elimination of Violence against Women and the Declaration on the Right to Development.

The conference emphasized that women's empowerment and their full participation in society, including in the decision-making process and access to power, were fundamental to achieve equality, development, and peace. It insisted that "women's rights are human rights." Furthermore, equal rights, opportunities and access to resources, equal sharing of familial responsibilities by men and women, and a harmonious partnership between them were critical to people's well-being and that of their families as well as to the consolidation of democracy.

The conference expressed its conviction that explicit recognition and reaffirmation of women's right to control all aspects of their health, in particular their own fertility, was basic to their empowerment.

The conference expressed its determination to ensure the full enjoyment of all human rights and fundamental freedoms by girls and women and to take effective action against violations of these. It further expressed its determination to take all necessary measures to eliminate discrimination against women and girls, and remove all obstacles to gender equality and the advancement and empowerment of women.

80 *Equality*

The conference expressed its determination to:

- prevent and eliminate all forms of violence against women and girls;
- ensure equal access to and equal treatment of women and men in education and health care, and enhance women's sexual and reproductive health as well as education;
- promote and protect all human rights of women and girls;
- intensify efforts to ensure equal enjoyment of all human rights and fundamental freedoms for all women and girls who face multiple barriers to their empowerment and advancement because of factors such as race, age, language, ethnicity, culture, religion, or disability, or because they are indigenous people;
- ensure respect for international law, including humanitarian law to protect women and girls, in particular; and
- develop the fullest potential of girls and women of all ages, ensure their full and equal participation in building a better world for all, and enhance their role in the development process.

Two years before the conference on 20 December 1993, the GA adopted the Declaration on the Elimination of Violence Against Women.[18] The GA reaffirmed that women were entitled to equal enjoyment and protection of all human rights and fundamental freedoms in the political, economic, social, cultural, civil, or any other field. These rights included the right to life; the right to equality; the right to liberty and security of person; the right to equal protection under the law; the right to be free from all forms of discrimination; the right to the highest standard attainable of physical and mental health; the right to just and favorable conditions of work; and the right not to be subjected to torture, or other cruel, inhuman or degrading treatment or punishment.

The GA called on states to condemn violence against women and to refrain from invoking any custom, tradition, or religious consideration to avoid their obligation to do so. Further, states should pursue policies to eliminate violence against women by all appropriate means and without delay. The GA defined violence against women as encompassing but not limited to:

- physical, sexual and psychological violence occurring in the family, including battering, sexual abuse of female children in the household, dowry-related violence, marital rape, female genital mutilation and other traditional practices harmful to women, non-spousal violence and violence related to exploitation; and

- physical, sexual and psychological violence occurring within the general community, including rape, sexual abuse, sexual harassment and intimidation at work, in education institutions and elsewhere, trafficking in women and enforced prostitution.

The Durban World Conference Against Racism, Racial Discrimination, Xenophobia and Related Intolerance (2001)

The Durban Declaration, adopted in 2001 by the World Conference Against Racism, Racial Discrimination, Xenophobia and Related Intolerance, described victims of racism, racial discrimination, xenophobia, and related intolerance as individuals or groups of individuals who are or have been negatively affected by, subjected to, or targets of those scourges. It recognized that people of African descent have been victims of racism, discrimination and enslavement, and of history's denial of their rights for centuries. It also recognized that they, as well as Asians and people of Asian descent, faced barriers as a result of social biases and discrimination.

Strongly condemning racism and discrimination against migrants and the stereotypes often applied to them, the declaration reaffirmed states' responsibility to protect their human rights and governments' responsibility to safeguard and protect them against illegal or violent acts perpetrated with racist or xenophobic motivation.

Noting that racism, discrimination, and xenophobia contributed to forced displacement and movement of people as refugees and asylum seekers, the declaration recognized that intolerance against refugees, asylum seekers, and internally displaced persons continued despite efforts to combat them. It underlined the urgency of addressing the root causes of displacement and of finding durable solutions, particularly voluntary return to countries of origin and resettlement in third countries.

The declaration recognized the existence of intolerance against religious communities, particularly limitations on their right to practice their beliefs freely, as well as the emergence of increased negative stereotyping, hostile acts, and violence against such communities because of their religious beliefs and their ethnic or so-called racial origins.

The declaration strongly reaffirmed that victims of human rights violations resulting from racism, discrimination, xenophobia and intolerance should be assured access to justice. Access to justice includes legal assistance where appropriate, and effective and appropriate protection and remedies, including the right to seek just and adequate reparation or satisfaction for any damage suffered.

The declaration condemned the persistence and resurgence of neo-Nazism, neo-fascism, and violent nationalist ideologies based on racial or national prejudice. It also condemned political platforms and organizations based on racism, xenophobia, or doctrines of racial superiority and related discrimination; and legislation and practices based on racism, discrimination, xenophobia and intolerance as incompatible with democracy and with transparent and accountable governance.

Conclusion

As demonstrated in this chapter, equality remains one of the principal pillars of the international human rights movement. The idea has been well spelled out in the UN Charter, the UDHR, and a succession of international treaties. The jurisprudence on equality is also quite rich. Nevertheless, the practical implementation of equality remains illusory in many parts of the world. Discrimination on the grounds of race and gender is widespread. The UN has set a determined course to promote and vindicate equality. This, however, would require progress in advancing human rights across the board and in implementing the other concepts discussed in this book, particularly development. Pope Francis has been particularly eloquent in making the case for equality and for access to development for the poor.

Notes

1 Communication no. 35/1978, *Shirin Aumeeruddy-Cyiffra et al. v. Mauritius*, views adopted 9 April 1981; Report of the Human Rights Committee, *GAOR*, 36th Session, Supplement no. 40 (A/36/40), 134–42.
2 Hersch Lauterpacht, *An International Bill of the Rights of Man* (New York: Columbia University Press, 1945), 115.
3 Italy, UN General Assembly Document A/C.3/SR.1099, para. 10 (1961).
4 Italy, UN General Assembly Document A/C.3/SR.1185, para. 14 (1962).
5 USSR, UN General Assembly Document A/C.3/SR.1203, para. 16 (1962).
6 See for example, the remarks of the Danish representative, UN Doc.A/C.3/SR.1184, para. 17 (1962). See similarly the representative of Pakistan, UN Doc. A/C.3/SR.1185, para. 52 (1962).
7 Definitions of the Expressions "Prevention of Discrimination" and "Protection of Minorities" (Memorandum by the Division of Human Rights), UN Doc. E/CN.4/Sub.2/8, 2 (1947).
8 UN Doc. E/CN.4/Sub.2/40, paras. 33–36 (1949).
9 ECHR, "Belgian Linguistic Case," *Yearbook of the European Convention on Human Rights* 11, no. 832 (1968): 34.
10 Philippines, UN Doc. A/C.3/SR.1102, para. 53 (1961).
11 UN General Assembly Document. A/C.3/SR.1101, para. 24 (1961).

Equality 83

12 UN Doc. A/C.3/SR.1259, para. 18 (1963). The Indian representative was supported by his colleagues from Australia and the United Arab Republic. UN Doc. A/C.3/SR.1258, paras. 45, 48 (1963).
13 UN Doc. A/C.3/SR.1258, paras 33–34 (1963).
14 There the court recognized: "It is perhaps not easy to define the distinction between the notions of equality in fact and equality in law; nevertheless, it may be said that the former notion excludes the idea of a merely formal equality; that is indeed what the Court laid down in the Advisory Opinion of September 10, 1923, concerning the case of the German settlers in Poland (Opinion No. 6), in which it was said that 'there must be equality in fact as well as ostensible legal equality in the sense of the absence of discrimination in the words of the law'. Equality in law precludes discrimination of any kind; whereas equality in fact may involve the necessity of different treatment in order to attain a result which establishes an equilibrium between different situations" (*PCIJ* [1923], ser. A/B, no. 64, at 19).
15 See Manfred Novak, *UN Convention on Civil and Political Rights: CCPR Commentary* (Kehl, Germany: N.P. Engel Publisher, 2005), 1109–11.
16 Novak, *UN Convention and Civil on Political Rights: CCPR Commentary*, 1091.
17 See generally, Rosemary Agonito, *History of Ideas on Woman* (New York: Putnam's Sons, 1977); Rebecca Cook, *Human Rights of Women: National and International Perspectives* (Philadelphia: University of Pennsylvania Press, 1994); and *The International Human Rights of Women: Instruments of Change* (Washington, DC: ABA Section of International Law and Practice, 1998).
18 General Assembly resolution 48/104.

6 Democracy

- **Self-determination**
- **Democracy in the contemporary world order**
- **The content of democracy**
- **Promoting the right to democracy**
- **Conclusion**

> We will spare no effort to promote democracy and strengthen the rule of law as well as respect for all internationally recognized human rights and fundamental freedoms, including the right to development.
> (Millennium Declaration, paragraph 24)

> Democracy is based on the freely expressed will of the people to determine their own political, economic, social and cultural systems and their full participation in all aspects of their lives.
> (Vienna Declaration, paragraph 8)

In Zambia, a parliamentary candidate was prevented from participating in the general election campaign and preparing his candidacy for his party. After trying to bring his case to his national courts, Peter Chiko Bwallia brought his case to the Human Rights Committee under the Optional Protocol to the ICCPR. The committee held that Article 25 of the covenant had been violated.[1]

This chapter looks at democracy as a human rights idea, examining the related idea of self-determination and proceeding to discuss the role of democracy in the contemporary world order. Thereafter, efforts to reinforce democracy are examined, including the CHR's efforts to underscore that democracy is a fundamental human right.

Self-determination

Self-determination has been a foundation principle of international order and law since US President Woodrow Wilson articulated his famous 14 points in 1917. The UN Charter and the international covenants on human rights enshrine the principle of self-determination. On the 25th anniversary of the UN, on 24 October 1970, the General Assembly adopted a declaration on the principles of international law grounded in the UN Charter that codified the principle of self-determination.[2] The declaration stated that all people have the right to determine freely their political status and pursue their economic social and cultural development based on the charter's principles of equal rights and self-determination. Moreover, the UN Charter requires that every state respect this right. The right of self-determination can be implemented by establishing a sovereign and independent state, free association or integration with an independent state, or entering any political status freely determined. Every state must refrain from any action aimed at disrupting—whether totally or partially—the national unity and territorial integrity of any other state or country. Further, the declaration continued, every state must promote—through joint and separate action—universal respect for the observance of human rights and fundamental freedoms.

Pursuing the principle of self-determination, the UN has worked assiduously for decolonization, and there are no longer any significant territories that are colonial or dependent. The principle of self-determination has had great success since the UN was established.

However, does implementation of the principle of self-determination cease when external self-determination has been achieved? Or should self-determination also be considered internally in the form of democracy? This has been hotly debated, with many governments insisting that after external self-determination has been achieved, outside states or international organizations should not interfere in internal affairs. This was seen in 2007 when the World Bank published its *Worldwide Governance Indicators* report rating the countries' performance in the area of governance. Many countries vehemently objected to the bank engaging in this activity. Argentina, for example, protested the bank's assessment that its quality of governance had declined between 1998 and 2006. China was also unhappy about its low rating on "voice and accountability."[3] A total of nine of the World Bank's 24 executive directors addressed a letter to the bank president expressing doubts about the institution's role in making such judgments.[4]

As a matter of principle and law, there can be no doubt that the principle of self-determination applies in the external and internal spheres. Antonio Cassese argued that self-determination had both internal and external dimensions in the international covenants on human rights. Article 1 intends to convey two ideas: first, that the choice of domestic political institutions and authority must be free of outside interference; and second, that that choice must not be conditioned, manipulated, or tampered with by domestic authorities.[5]

Cassese insisted that the test for gauging whether self-determination was recognized or denied "is whether or not there is a democratic decision-making process." It followed that self-determination was a continuing and permanent right.[6]

Democracy in the contemporary world order

The principle of democratic legitimacy is one of the foundation principles of international human rights law and the contemporary world order.[7] There are at least eight aspects that are particularly important: conflict prevention, development, justice, human rights, terrorism, world order, democratic legitimacy and international security.

In the afterword to a three-volume collection of the papers of former UN Secretary-General Boutros Boutros-Ghali, Bruce Russet referred to the significance of the secretary-general's *Agenda for Democracy*, issued at the end of 1995. Russet stated: "Internationally as well as nationally, institutions must be seen as legitimate, not just as immediately effective. In the long run, effectiveness depends on legitimacy. Democracy is an instrument for achieving both."[8]

Democracy is also an important factor in preventing conflicts. As David Hamburg has put it, "The building of democratic institutions would be one of the greatest conflict prevention measures that could be taken, especially if one thinks in terms of both political and economic democratic structures."[9]

In his *Agenda for Democracy*, Boutros-Ghali emphasized the role of democracy in conflict prevention:

> Lacking the legitimacy or real support offered by free elections, authoritarian Governments all too often take recourse to intimidation and violence in order to suppress internal dissent. They tend to reject institutions such as a free press and an independent judiciary which provide the transparency and accountability necessary to discourage such governmental manipulation of citizens. The resulting atmosphere of oppression and tension, felt in neighboring countries, can heighten the fear of war. It is for this reason that the Charter declares that one of the first purposes of

the United Nations is "to take effective collective measures for the prevention and removal of threats to the peace." Threatened by the resentment of their own people, non-democratic Governments may also be more likely to incite hostilities against other States in order to justify their suppression of internal dissent or forge a basis for national unity.[10]

It has been suggested that democratic legitimacy should be one of the leading policy planks of the HRC. The following principles should guide the council in advancing constitutional, democratic legitimacy:

- the existence of a constitution that has popular support and represents the populace's hopes and aspirations;
- the right of people to determine freely their own political, economic, and social systems;
- the importance of democratic legitimacy for peace, human rights, and development;
- democratic legitimacy and governance is a basic human right;
- constitutional democratic legitimacy can play a role in preventing conflicts;
- constitutional democratic governance can play a role in spurring development;
- constitutional democratic governance can play a role in preventing terrorism; and
- constitutional democratic governance can play a role in advancing justice and equity, both locally and internationally.

According to philosophers, including Mortimer Adler,[11] justice should be the supreme inspirational principle of all human societies. The pursuit of justice can best be conducted in an environment of democratic legitimacy. It was in recognition of this that Article 21 of the UDHR proclaimed that the will of the people shall be the basis of the authority of government. This should be expressed in periodic and genuine elections by universal and equal suffrage and shall be held by secret vote or by equivalent free voting procedures.

According to Article 25 of the ICCPR, everyone should have the right and the opportunity, without any of the distinctions mentioned in Article 2 or any unreasonable restrictions: 1) to take part in public affairs directly or through freely chosen representatives; 2) to vote and be elected at genuine periodic elections that are by universal and equal suffrage and shall be held by secret ballot, guaranteeing the free expression of the will of the electors; and 3) to have equal access to public service in his or her country.

Likewise, the European Convention on Human Rights and Fundamental Freedoms calls for an effective political democracy. In the Handyside case, the ECHR referred to the notions of pluralism, tolerance, and broadmindedness, which should be characteristics of a democratic society.[12] In the Klass case, the court considered that one of the fundamental principles of a democracy is the rule of law. Justice is best served by constitutional democracy under the rule of law.[13]

Not only is democratic legitimacy an important requirement for justice, but some claim that democracy is a basic human right. The World Conference on Human Rights declared that democracy, development, and respect for human rights are interdependent and mutually reinforcing. It emphasized that the "international community should support the strengthening and promoting of democracy, development and respect for human rights and fundamental freedoms of the entire world."

The late Louis Henkin has argued that:

> The human rights ideology and the law of human rights represented in the International Covenant [on Civil and Political Rights] include, I believe, a right to democracy in the sense of constitutional democracy and its elements—authentic popular sovereignty, respect for individual rights, the rule of law, due process of law and commitment to the principle of justice. I think that these principles of justice were what those who drafted the Covenant contemplated and what states that became parties to the Covenant committed themselves to abide by.[14]

In human rights treaties and case law, there are important expressions of the links between democracy and human rights. In some instances, limitations are accepted if they are perceived to be necessary in a democratic society. The Human Rights Committee has held that the principles of legality and the rule of law require that fundamental requirements of a fair trial must be respected during a state of emergency.[15] The European Commission of Human Rights has held that measures affecting fundamental rights must be subject to some form of adversarial proceedings before an independent and competent tribunal.[16]

Democratic legitimacy is key to preventing and suppressing terrorism. Moreover, human rights monitoring bodies have made an important distinction between democracies and dictatorships when deciding whether there is an emergency threatening the life of the nation. Regional and international supervisory human rights bodies have granted the governments of democracies, as opposed to those of unrepresentative governments, a wider margin of appreciation in determining whether a state of emergency exists, whether from an external or internal threat. However, national courts and regional or international supervisory bodies hold themselves competent to supervise the application of emergency measures. In scrutinizing the application of such measures, the principles of legality, proportionality, non-derogability of certain fundamental rights, and the principle of non-discrimination are kept in mind.

In *Ireland v. The United Kingdom* (1978), the ECHR declared:

> It falls in the first place to each Contracting State, with its responsibility for "the life of the nation," to determine whether that life is threatened by a public emergency... By reason of their direct and continuous contact with the pressing needs of the moment, the national authorities are in principle in a better position than the international judge, to decide ... on the presence of such an emergency.
>
> ... In this matter, article 15(1) leaves those authorities a wide margin of appreciation.[17]

The domestic margin of appreciation is subject to supervision and control by the ECHR, and case law indicates that a democratic government's opinion on whether a public emergency exists will not be questioned by the convention organs. However, in the Greek case, the European Commission of Human Rights disagreed with Greece's military government regarding the existence of a state of emergency.[18]

At the UN, attention to the issue of new and restored democracies began to be emphasized in 1988, with 13 countries participating in the first international conference on this topic in Manila. By the time the conference was held in Doha in 2006, over 100 countries were present, together with a large number of participants in the parliamentarians and civil society forums.

In a report to the GA, the secretary-general announced his intention to ask relevant UN entities to initiate a study on the comparative advantages, complementarity, and desirable distribution of labor of intergovernmental democracy movements, organizations, and institutes, and how the UN system has worked and could work further with them in a mutually supportive way.

There is significant recent practice of the recognition and application of the principle of democratic legitimacy. According to a study covering the period from 1993 through 2000, the UNSC referred to democracy in 53 resolutions. The council, according to the same study, praised democratic governance for reasons ranging from its role in fostering national reconciliation, to ensuring security in states recently emerging from civil war, to assisting in reconstructing governing infrastructures.

The council has refused to recognize those regimes as legitimate that overthrew elected leaders. It has also authorized the use of armed force to return elected leaders to office. In addition, the UNSC and the AU have stated that they will not accept the violent overthrow of a democratically elected government.

The content of democracy

On 16 September 1997, the Council of the Inter-Parliamentary Union (IPU) adopted the Universal Declaration on Democracy, which stated that strengthening the democratization process and representative institutions would greatly contribute to achieving peace and development in the world. The Universal Declaration contained principles of democracy, the elements of democratic government, and the international dimension of democracy. Its salient provisions are set out here.

On democracy, the declaration stated that it is a universally recognized ideal as well as a goal based on common values held by peoples throughout the world, irrespective of cultural, political, social, and economic differences. It is a basic right of citizenship to be exercised under conditions of freedom, equality, transparency, and responsibility, with due respect for the plurality of views and in the interest of the polity.

Democracy, the declaration continued, is both an ideal to be pursued and a mode of government to be applied according to modalities that reflect the diversity of experiences and cultural particularities without derogating from internationally recognized principles, norms, and standards. It is thus a constantly improving and always perfectible state or condition whose progress depends on a variety of political, social, economic, and cultural factors.

As an ideal, democracy aims to preserve and promote the dignity and fundamental rights of the individual, achieve social justice, foster a community's economic and social development, strengthen the cohesion of the society and enhance national tranquility, and create a climate that is favorable for international peace. As a form of government, democracy is the best means of achieving these objectives; it is also the only political system that has the capacity for self-correction.

Achieving democracy presupposes a genuine partnership between men and women in the conduct of the affairs of society in which they work in equality and complementarity, drawing mutual enrichment from their differences.

A state of democracy ensures that the processes by which power is acceded to, wielded, and alternates allow for free political competition and are the product of open, free, and non-discriminatory participation by the people, exercised in accordance with the rule of law.

Democracy is inseparable from international human rights. Those rights must, therefore, be applied effectively and their proper exercise must be matched with individual and collective responsibilities. Democracy was founded on the primacy of the law and the exercise of human rights. In a democratic state, no one is above the law, and all are equal before the law. Peace and economic, social, and cultural development were both conditions for and fruits of democracy. Thus, there was interdependence between peace, development, respect for and observance of the rule of law and human rights.

On the elements and exercise of democratic government, the declaration added that democracy was based on the existence of well-structured and well-functioning institutions, as well as on a body of standards and rules and on the will of society as a whole, fully conversant with its rights and responsibilities. Democratic institutions should mediate tensions and maintain equilibrium between the competing claims of diversity and uniformity, individuality and collectivity, to enhance social cohesion and solidarity.

Furthermore, democracy was founded on everyone's right to take part in public affairs; it therefore requires representative institutions at all levels and, in particular, a parliament in which all components of society are represented and which has the requisite powers and means to express the will of the people by legislating and overseeing government action.

The key element in the exercise of democracy is the holding of free and fair elections at regular intervals. These elections must be held on the basis of universal, equal, and secret suffrage so all voters can choose their representatives in conditions of equality, openness, and transparency. To that end, civil and political rights are essential, and, more particularly among them, the rights to vote and to be elected, the rights to freedom of expression and assembly, access to information, and the right to organize political parties and carry out political activities. Party organization, activities, finances, funding, and ethics must be properly regulated in an impartial manner to ensure the integrity of the democratic processes.

It is an essential function of the state to ensure the enjoyment of civil, cultural, economic, political, and social rights for all citizens. Democracy thus goes hand in hand with an effective, honest, and transparent government, freely chosen and accountable for its management of public affairs.

Public accountability, essential to democracy, applied to all who hold public authority, whether elected or non-elected, and to all bodies of public authority. Accountability entails a public right of access to information about government activities, the right to petition government and to seek redress through impartial administrative and judicial mechanisms.

Public life must be characterized by a sense of ethics and transparency, and appropriate norms and procedures must be established to uphold both. Individual participation in democratic processes and public life at all levels must be regulated fairly and impartially and must avoid any discrimination, as well as the risk of intimidation by state and non-state actors.

Judicial institutions and independent, impartial, and effective oversight mechanisms guarantee the rule of law. For these institutions and mechanisms to ensure respect for the rules, improve the fairness of the processes, and redress injustices, all people must have equal access to administrative and judicial remedies.

While the existence of an active civil society is essential in democracies, the capacity and willingness of individuals to participate in democratic processes and make governance choices cannot be taken for granted. It is, therefore, necessary to develop conditions conducive to the genuine exercise of participatory rights, while also eliminating obstacles that prevent, hinder, or inhibit this exercise. It is, therefore, indispensable to ensure the permanent enhancement of equality, transparency and education, and to remove obstacles such as ignorance, intolerance, apathy, the lack of genuine choices and alternatives, and the absence of measures designed to redress imbalances or discrimination.

A sustained state of democracy requires a democratic climate and culture constantly nurtured and reinforced by education and other vehicles of culture and information. Hence, a democratic society must be committed to education in the broadest sense of the term, and, more particularly, civic education and the shaping of a responsible citizenry.

Democratic processes are fostered by a favorable economic environment. Therefore, in its overall effort for development, society must be committed to satisfying the basic economic needs of the most disadvantaged, ensuring their full integration in the democratic process. The state of democracy presupposes freedom of opinion and expression. This right implies freedom to hold opinions without interference and to seek, receive, and impart information and ideas through any media and regardless of frontiers.

The institutions and processes of democracy must accommodate all people's participation in homogeneous and heterogeneous societies to safeguard diversity, pluralism, and the right to be different in a climate of tolerance. Democratic institutions and processes must also foster decentralized local and regional government and administration, which is a right and a necessity, and which makes it possible to broaden the base of public participation.[19] The Universal Declaration on Democracy is a helpful statement of the core content of this concept.

Promoting the right to democracy

In 1999, the Clinton Administration secured a major victory at the then CHR when it negotiated the passage of a resolution affirming democracy as a fundamental human right. Since then, OHCHR has organized international seminars that have adopted significant recommendations on strengthening democracy as a human right.

In its Resolution 1999/57, adopted by 51 votes (with no votes against and two abstentions), the CHR affirmed that democracy fostered the full realization of human rights and vice versa. The commission also affirmed that the rights of democratic governance include:

- rights to freedom of opinion and expression, thought, conscience and religion, and peaceful association and assembly;
- the right to seek, receive, and impart information and ideas through any media;
- the rule of law, including legal protection of citizens' rights, interests and personal security, fairness in the administration of justice and independence of the judiciary;
- the right of universal and equal suffrage, as well as free voting procedures and periodic and free elections;
- the right of political participation, including equal opportunity for all citizens to become candidates;
- transparent and accountable government institutions;
- the right of citizens to choose their governmental system through constitutional or other democratic means; and
- the right of equal access to public service in one's own country.

A UN seminar on the subject, held in 2005, noted that the triangle formed by the concepts of rule of law, human rights, and democracy is not an equilateral one; circumstances may often require that greater emphasis be placed on one element, without detaching it from the others. Thus, a state whose institutions have broken down may need to re-establish democratic institutions and the rule of law to ensure respect for human rights and fundamental freedoms. States in which authoritarian rule or a populist majority have denied people's rights may give priority to restoring human rights and fundamental freedoms and their system of protection, including the administration of justice.[20]

The seminar underlined that free, fair, and periodic multi-party elections are a key component of democracy, the rule of law, and the protection of human rights They also have autonomous value as a means of self-realization and recognition of human dignity. Periodic elections are essential to ensure accountability of representatives to exercise the legislative or executive powers vested in them. The conduct of elections should be entrusted to an independent mechanism that is free from interference that could undermine the fairness of elections.[21]

At the seminar, participants stated that General Comment no. 25 of the Human Rights Committee concerning Article 25 of the ICCPR should guide the implementation of the right to participate in public affairs, voting rights, and the right of equal access to public service. According to this general comment, the conduct of public affairs is a broad concept that relates to the exercise of political power, in particular the exercise of legislative, executive, and administrative powers. It covers all aspects of public administration, and the formulation and implementation of policy at the international, national, regional, and local levels. The allocation of powers and the means by which individual citizens exercise the right to participate in the conduct of public affairs should be established by the constitution and other laws.[22]

In 2000, the United Nations Development Programme (UNDP) established democratic governance as one of its main areas of focus within its development cooperation program. In 2002, UNDP published the *Human Development Report 2002: Deepening Democracy in a Fragmented World*, which provided an in-depth study of the linkages between human development and democracy, and incorporated a rights-based approach.[23] The UN Democracy Fund helps finance projects that build and strengthen democratic institutions, promote human rights, and ensure the participation of all groups in democratic processes.

The International Conference on New and Restored Democracies is an intergovernmental movement that seeks to advance democratization. It has organized several international conferences, such as that which took place in Qatar in 2006. A parallel conference of democracies has met to promote democratic governance. The International Institute for Democracy and Electoral Assistance (IDEA), based in Stockholm, promotes sustainable democracy worldwide. IDEA seeks to blend research and field experience and develop practical tools to improve democratic processes. The IPU, founded in 1889, is an international organization of parliaments that promotes inter-parliamentary dialogue and democracy.

Conclusion

The democracy idea is of great importance to the future of human progress and prosperity with justice. In large parts of the world, undemocratic governments ride roughshod over people who often have little say in the governance of their countries. Because of this, the growing emphasis on democratic governance and democracy as a human right is extremely important. Democratic governance can help countries draw on their resources efficiently and fairly. Democratic governance can help ensure that all parts of the population are given a stake in the future of their country. Democracy can contribute to lessening conflicts. Democracy can enrich regional and international cooperation. The idea of democracy deserves heightened emphasis in the future of the human rights movement.

Notes

1 Article 25 reads that: "every citizen shall have the right and the opportunity, without unreasonable restrictions, to take part in the conduct of public affairs, directly or through freely chosen representatives and to vote and to be elected at genuine periodic elections which shall be by universal and equal suffrage and shall be held by secret ballot, guaranteeing the free expression of the will of the electors."
2 *Declaration on Principles of International Law Concerning Friendly Relations and Cooperation among States in Accordance with the Charter of the United Nations*, General Assembly resolution 2625 (XXV).
3 Krishna Guha, "World Bank Ratings Spark Anger," *Financial Times*, 11 July 2007.
4 Krishna Guha and Richard McGregor, "World Bank Directors Test Zoellick," *Financial Times*, 18 July 2007.
5 Antonio Cassese, "The Self-Determination of Peoples," in *The International Bill of Rights: The Covenant on Civil and Political Rights*, ed. Louis Henkin (New York: Columbia University Press, 1981), 97.
6 Cassese, "The Self-Determination of Peoples," 98.
7 David Beetham, *Democracy and Human Rights* (Cambridge: Polity Press, 1999); Robert Dahl, *A Preface to Democratic Theory* (Chicago, Ill. and London: University of Chicago Press, 1956); Edward Newman and Roland Rich, *The UN Role in Promoting Democracy: Between Ideals and Reality* (Tokyo, New York, and Paris: United Nations University Press, 2004); and Inter-Parliamentary Union, *Democracy: Its Principles and Achievement* (Geneva, Switzerland: IPU, 1998).

8 Charles Hill, *The Papers of United Nations Secretary-General Boutros Boutros-Ghali*, 3 (New Haven, Conn.: Yale University Press, 2003), 2070.
9 See "Foreword," in Larry Diamond, *Promoting Democracy in the 1990s: Actors and Instruments, Issues and Imperatives* (New York: Carnegie Commission on Preventing Deadly Conflict, 1995), vii.
10 Hill, *The Papers of United Nations Secretary-General Boutros Boutros-Ghali*, 2018.
11 Mortimer Adler, *Six Great Ideas* (New York: Macmillan Publishing Co., 1981).
12 *Handyside v. The United Kingdom* (App. 5493/72), ECHR judgment of 7 December 1976.
13 *Klass and others v. Germany* (App. 5029/71), ECHR judgment of 6 September 1978.
14 *Commemorative Volume on the Occasion of the Twenty-fifth Anniversary of the Human Rights Committee*, ed. N. Ando (The Hague, the Netherlands: Martinus Nijhoff), 176. See also Tom Franck, "The Emerging Right to Democratic Governance," *American Journal of International Law* 86, no. 46 (1992): 541. Larry Diamond has also asserted the universal right to democratic governance in *Promoting Democracy in the 1990s* (New York: Carnegie Corporation of New York, December 1995).
15 UN OHCHR, *Digest of Jurisprudence of the United Nations and Regional Organizations on the Protection of Human Rights While Countering Terrorism* (New York and Geneva, Switzerland: UN, 2003), 40.
16 *Al Nashif v. Bulgaria* (App. 50963/99), ECHR judgment of 20 June 2002.
17 *Ireland v. The United Kingdom*, 18 January 1978, series A, no. 25 (1979–80) 2 *EHRR* 25, para. 207.
18 See Iain Cameron, *National Security and the European Convention on Human Rights* (The Hague, the Netherlands: Kluwer Law International, 2000).
19 IPU, *Democracy: Its Principles and Achievement* (Geneva, Switzerland: IPU, 1998), iv–vii.
20 E/CN.4/2005/58, para. 33.
21 E/CN.4/2005/58, para. 34.
22 E/CN.4/2005/58, para. 35.
23 UNDP, *Human Development Report 2002* (Oxford: Oxford University Press, 2002).

7 Development

- The UN Charter
- Differing interpretations and the proposal for an international convention on the right to development
- The International Covenant on Economic, Social and Cultural Rights
- The Declaration on the Right to Development
- The Millennium Declaration and MDGs
- Preventable poverty
- African Commission on Human and Peoples' Rights
- Conclusion

> The World Conference on Human Rights reaffirms the right to development, as established in the Declaration on the Right to Development as a universal and inalienable right and an integral part of fundamental human rights.
> (Vienna Declaration, paragraph 10)

In the contemporary world, hundreds of thousands of women are trafficked into slavery and prostitution, and children are sexually exploited. Many of these women and children are lured by the promise of better opportunities or earnings. Poverty has a great deal to do with the plight of the victims. How can this still take place in the twenty-first century? Could the declaration and implementation of a right to development help remove such conditions?

Many parts of the developing world that were subjected to colonialism entered into independence impoverished and ravaged. A prominent Third World historian, Walter Rodney, made a powerful presentation in his book *How Europe Underdeveloped Africa*.[1] On the island of Gore, off the coast of Senegal, a holding depot held captured slaves before they were shipped to the New World. Keba Mbaye, a Senegalese jurist, that country's chief justice, and also its representative on the UN Commission on Human Rights, was so moved by the plight of his ancestors and the impact of slavery on his continent that, in an address at the International Institute of Human Rights in Strasbourg in 1972, he articulated, for the first time, the notion of the right to development.[2] The right to development is the subject of one of the major contemporary human rights debates.

Some of the debates concern questions such as: Is development a human right, and what does it mean? Whose right is it? Is it applicable in the internal sphere within countries or only in the external relations among states, implying a duty of developed countries to assist developing countries? Is there a genuine consensus over the right, which, as seen above in the epigraph to this chapter, was endorsed by the World Conference on Human Rights in 1993? This chapter examines the journey of the idea of development as a human right, starting with the UN Charter, then proceeding to the ICESCR, the UN Declaration on the Right to Development (1986), the Millennium Development Goals (MDGs), and ongoing efforts to implement the right to development.

The UN Charter

The link between development and human rights has been prominent since the UN was established. Article 55 of the charter set out the interdependence and interrelatedness of peace, development, and human rights:

> With a view to the creation of conditions which are necessary for peaceful and friendly relations among nations based on respect for the principle of equal rights and self-determination of peoples, the United Nations shall promote:
>
> a   Higher standards of living, full employment, and conditions of economic and social progress and development;
> b   Solutions of international economic, social, health, and related problems, and international cultural and educational cooperation;
> c   Universal respect for, and observance of, human rights and fundamental freedoms for all without distinction as to race, sex, language, or religion.

The importance of development for human rights and the need to integrate human rights in the development process have been emphasized since the charter was drafted, and there have been extensive debates about rights-based approaches to development and the role of human rights in poverty reduction strategies. While related, these are distinct from the right to development, and further examination of the substance of this idea, as well the different interpretations given by developing and developed countries, is required.

Differing interpretations and the proposal for an international convention on the right to development

These divergent interpretations could be seen in debates at the HRC. In 2007, a working group on the right to development met to consider how to advance implementation of the right. In the working group,[3] African states underscored the centrality of the right to development in promoting and protecting human rights and its importance in relation to the HRC's mandate. According to the African states, only a comprehensive approach—including equitable international trade rules and a response to energy, raw materials, and debt burden issues—could reduce the growing gap between developing and developed countries. In the framework of fighting poverty, the African states called for international cooperation without conditionality and advocated an international convention on the right to development.[4] As will be shown later, this is a contested idea at the United Nations.

The countries belonging to the Non-Aligned Movement (NAM) emphasized the importance and centrality of the right to development in the HRC and complained that since the Declaration on the Right to Development had been adopted 20 years before, the international community had done very little to implement this right. In the current globalization context, the NAM underscored developing countries' lack of autonomy in formulating their own development policies. Rather, many development policies are seen to act against the interests of developing countries—the so-called decapitalization of developing countries: unfair trade rules and practices that restrict market access and allow export subsidies, failed commitments on official development assistance (ODA) and transfer of technology, and heavy debt burdens. Elaborating on the right to development, the NAM reaffirmed the duty of states to cooperate to create conditions conducive to realizing the right to development. It called for cooperation that was not subject to conditionality or treated as charity.[5]

For their part, the European Union and associated countries reaffirmed their "firm commitment to the realization of the right to development and underscored the primary responsibility of states for the promotion and protection of all human rights, including the right to development; responsibility to create internal conditions favorable to their development, and to cooperate at an international level in eliminating obstacles to development."[6]

As seen above, developing countries emphasized the international dimensions of the right to development while opposing discussion of the internal dimensions of this right. The developed countries, on the other hand, emphasized the internal dimensions, also viewing international cooperation as related. This difference in approach between developing and developed countries could be seen in the deliberations of the working group, whose report called for a comprehensive and coherent set of standards. Developing countries advocated drafting and adopting a convention on the right to development. The working group explained that these standards "could take various forms, including guidelines on the implementation of the right to development, and evolve into a basis for consideration of an international legal standard of a binding nature, through a collaborative process of engagement." This was diplomatic language for a convention.

The NAM made this clear in annex III to the report: "The Non-Aligned Movement interprets the phrase 'international legal standard of a binding nature' contained in paragraph 52 of the conclusions and recommendations to mean 'internationally legally binding convention'."[7] Canada objected, stating that it "does not believe it is appropriate for the Working Group or high-level task force to consider the development of a legally binding instrument."[8] The European Union and Australia made similar reservations.[9]

It remains to be seen whether developing countries, which are in the majority at the UN, will press for an international convention on the right to development, what would be included in such an instrument, who would support it, and how it would interpret the right to development. Before such a document is adopted, the ICESCR, the 1986 Declaration on the Right to Development, and the MDGs can be examined for insight into international views on the right to development.

The International Covenant on Economic, Social and Cultural Rights

An examination of the covenant illustrates development performing six roles. First, development comes closest to being recognized as a right in Article 11, which refers to the right to an adequate standard of living "and to the continuous improvement of living conditions." The covenant follows a deliberate scheme in which many articles define the right recognized and then proceed to indicate the steps to be taken, nationally and internationally, to promote rights such as the right to an adequate standard of living.

Second, development is sometimes cast as derivative of a recognized right. This is the case, for example, in Article 1, which addresses the right to self-determination and also states that by "virtue of that right," people fully pursue their economic, social, and cultural development.

Third, development is cast as a goal to be pursued when trying to realize the rights recognized in the covenant. One may see this, for example, in article 15 on the right to take part in cultural life. This article specifies that states parties should include the "development and the diffusion of science and culture." Another example is Article 13(2e), which includes "the development of a system of schools at all levels" among the steps to be taken to implement the right to education.

Fourth, in some instances development is cast Article 12 on the right to enjoy the highest attainable standard of physical and mental conditions requires states to take steps "for the healthy development of the child." Likewise, Article 13, after recognizing the right to education, adds that "education shall be directed to the full development of the human personality." (One might have thought that the "full development of the human personality" should have featured explicitly in the core definition of the right to development in the declaration adopted by the GA in 1986.)

Fifth, development is also included in the covenant as a means to realize the rights that the document recognizes. This is evident, for example, in Article 6, which recognizes the right to work and specifies that the steps necessary to achieve this right should include "policies and techniques to achieve steady economic, social and cultural development." One also sees this in Article 11(2a), which refers to the need for developing or reforming agrarian systems to achieve the most efficient development and utilization of natural resources.

Sixth, and finally, one sees the concept of development in determining the extent of a state's obligations to guarantee the covenant's economic rights to non-nationals.

The above-mentioned instances indicate that the covenant's drafters definitely had development issues at the forefront of their minds. However, they did not consider it necessary, at that stage, expressly to include the right to development. This has now been done in the Declaration on the Right to Development and at the World Conference on Human Rights.

The Declaration on the Right to Development

Article 9 of the Declaration on the Right to Development, which was adopted by the GA in 1986, states that all aspects of the right to development are indivisible and interdependent and each of them should be considered in the context of the whole.[10] Is an "aspect" the same as an "element of the definition" of a right? The declaration may help answer this question. The nearest that the declaration comes to defining the right to development is Article 1(1), which states that "the right to development is an inalienable human right by virtue of which every human person and all peoples are entitled to participate in, contribute to, and enjoy economic, social, cultural and political development, in which all human rights and fundamental freedoms can be fully realized." One could also possibly include Article 8 in this definition, which provided that:

1 States should undertake, at the national level, all necessary measures for the realization of the right to development and shall ensure, inter alia, equality of opportunity for all in their access to basic resources, education, health services, food, housing, employment and the fair distribution of income. Effective measures should be undertaken to ensure that women have an active role in the development process. Appropriate economic and social reforms should be made with a view to eradicating all social injustices.
2 States should encourage popular participation in all spheres as an important factor in development and in the full realization of all human rights.

The remaining articles make a number of statements that serve different purposes. There are collateral statements such as Article 6, which states that all human rights and fundamental freedoms are indivisible and interdependent. It identifies the subjects and beneficiaries of the right to development in Article 1(1), which refers to the right to development as one to which "every person and all peoples are entitled." Article 2(1) specifies that the human person is the central subject of development and should be the active participant and beneficiary of the right to development. Paragraph 3 of the same article adds that states have the right and duty to formulate appropriate national development policies. The possible subjects and beneficiaries are, therefore, the individual, the state, and all peoples.

The declaration also explains what the right to development implies. Article 1(2) states that the right to development implies the full realization of the right to self-determination (as will be seen below, development is cast as a derivative of the right to self-determination). It also indicates what the right to development requires, such as Article 3(2), which states that the right to development requires full respect for the principles of international law concerning friendly relations and cooperation among states. Article 4(2) adds that sustained action is required to promote more rapid development. Effective international cooperation is also essential.

The declaration also indicates responsibilities. Article 2(2) states that all human beings have a responsibility for development. Article 3(1) adds that states have the primary responsibility to create national and international conditions favorable to realize the right to development. It also indicates duties of the subjects and beneficiaries of the right to development. Some examples are presented here:

- Article 2(2): Individuals should promote and protect an appropriate political, social, and economic order for development;
- Article 2(3): States have the right and duty to formulate appropriate national development policies;
- Article 3(3): States have the duty to cooperate to ensure development and eliminate obstacles to development;
- Article 4: States have the duty to take steps, individually and collectively, to formulate international development policies to facilitate the full realization of the right to development. Sustained action is required to promote more rapid development of developing countries. Effective international cooperation is essential;
- Article 5: States shall take resolute steps to eliminate massive and flagrant violations of human rights;
- Article 6: All states should cooperate to promote, encourage, and strengthen universal respect for and observance of all human rights and fundamental freedoms; states should also take steps to eliminate obstacles to development resulting from failure to observe civil and political rights as well as economic, social, and cultural rights;
- Article 7: All states should promote the establishment, maintenance, and strengthening of international peace and security;
- Article 8: States should undertake, at the national level, all necessary measures to realize the right to development. States should encourage popular participation in all spheres as an important factor in development and the full realization of human rights; and
- Article 10: Steps should be taken to ensure the full exercise and progressive enhancement of the right to development.

Although all of the above are contained in the Declaration on the Right to Development, they cannot all form parts of the definition of the right to development. The elements that seem to be new—the normative statements that have been added to the existing human rights norms—are in Article 1(1), which rests on the notions of participation in, contribution to, and enjoyment of development. Thus, the declaration adds a new right to the list of human rights: "The right to development is an inalienable human right by virtue of which every human person and all peoples are entitled to participate in, contribute to, and enjoy economic, social, cultural and political development, in which all human rights and fundamental freedoms can be fully realized." This is the first time that such an explicit statement has been made in an authoritative international instrument.

The declaration insists that development has to be of such a nature that "all human rights and fundamental freedoms can be fully realized." This point is further emphasized in Articles 5 and 6. In other words, development is vitiated when there is gross violation of human rights and fundamental freedoms.

The declaration insists on the indivisibility and interdependence of all human rights. It urges full respect for principles of international law and calls on all states to promote the establishment, maintenance, and strengthening of international peace and security. These are essentially statements about interrelationships and interlinkages. The right to development cannot, therefore, be considered a synthesis right that some claim encompasses and subsumes other rights. Peace, disarmament, respect for human rights, and fundamental freedoms are required for development to take place. They are not, however, subsumed in an overarching "right to development."

Development is conceptually employed in the declaration in several ways: narrowly, in the legal sense of a right (Article 1(1)), broadly as a goal, relatively as a guide, and practically as a means. Its conception as a new right is an advance from the ICESCR, which does not contain a specific affirmation of the right to development. The covenant, though, contains some traces of the notion. The Declaration on the Right to Development and the covenant cover very similar ground in calling for national and international measures to realize economic, social, and cultural rights.

The Millennium Declaration and MDGs

In successive policy documents, the UN has sought to set development goals and pursue development strategies to tackle massive economic and social problems, particularly the extreme poverty that two thirds of the global population faces (see Table 7.1). The Millennium Declaration is the latest example of such a policy document.

In the Millennium Declaration, which was adopted on 8 September 2000, heads of states and governments reaffirmed their commitment to the UN Charter, expressing their determination to establish a just and lasting peace. Signatories to the document stated that the central challenge is to ensure that globalization is a positive force for the world's peoples. They considered certain fundamental values to be essential to international relations, such as freedom, equality, solidarity, tolerance, respect for nature, and shared responsibility.

In the document, governments declared their intention to spare no effort to free people from the scourge of war. They also resolved to strengthen the rule of law in international and national affairs and make the UN more effective in maintaining peace and security. The declaration stated that member states would spare no effort "to free our fellow men, women and children from the abject and dehumanizing conditions of extreme poverty." They resolved, in particular, to halve by 2015 the proportion of the global population who live on less than one dollar a day, suffer from hunger, and lack access to safe water. They also committed to ensure that all children would be able to complete a full course of primary schooling. Similar goals were set to reduce maternal mortality, tackle HIV/AIDS and malaria, and improve the lives of slum-dwellers.

The declaration included the intention to protect the vulnerable and protect and assist children and civilian populations that disproportionately suffer the consequences of natural disasters, genocide, armed conflicts, and other humanitarian emergencies. They promised to make the UN a more effective instrument to pursue development and fight against poverty, ignorance, disease, injustice, terror and crime, and degradation and destruction of "our common home."

Heads of states and governments also undertook specific commitments regarding human rights, democracy, and good governance. They resolved to strengthen their capacity to implement principles of democracy and respect for human rights, including minority rights. They further resolved to eliminate all forms of violence against women; take measures to protect the human rights of migrants, migrant workers, and their families; eliminate acts of racism and xenophobia; and promote greater tolerance in all societies.

Further, in the declaration, governments pledged to strengthen cooperation between the UN and national parliaments, and give greater opportunities to the private sector, NGOs, and civil society to contribute to realizing UN goals and programs. They requested that the GA review the progress

Development

Table 7.1 World development and poverty indicators

Facts
MDG 1: Eradicating extreme poverty The proportion of people in developing countries living on less than US$1.25 a day decreased from 43.1 percent in 1990 to 20.6 percent in 2010. Some 40 percent of developing countries have already achieved the first MDG. Going forward, while growth projections seem positive, especially in East Asia and the Pacific and South Asia, growth in the poorest region, sub-Saharan Africa, will face challenges as they seem unlikely to meet the goal of halving poverty rates by 2030.
MDG 2: Achieve universal primary (elementary) education This goal, the oldest of all the MDGs, reached around 90 percent for developing countries as a whole in 2009 but has since stalled. No region has made any gains since. Full enrollment remains elusive in parts of South Asia and sub-Saharan Africa.
MDG 3: Promote gender equality and empowerment The elementary school enrollment rate of girls, which was at 86 percent that of boys in 1990, increased to 97 percent in 2011. Girls' enrollment also rose for secondary school: from 77 percent of boys' in 1990 to 96 percent in 2011. However, in low-income countries girls lag far behind and only eight of 36 countries reached or exceeded equal education for girls in primary and secondary education. Wealthy households fare better than poorer ones. Women work long hours and are paid less overall for their labor. More women take part in public life at the highest echelons. Better data are needed on women's role in the economy.
MDG 4: Reduce child mortality Whereas in 1990, 13 million children died before age five, by 1999 fewer than 10 million did. In 2012, 7 million did so. Over this period under-five mortality rate in developing countries fell 46 percent, from an average of 99 percent per 1,000 live births in 1990 to 53 in 2012. Of all regions, South Asia and sub-Saharan Africa face continued high rates of under-five mortality. Most children die from causes that are easy to prevent or cure with existing forms of intervention, such as pneumonia (17 percent), diarrhea (9 percent) and malaria (7 percent). Vaccination campaigns in low- and lower-middle-income economies have so far not improved the plight of many children.
MDG 5: Improve maternal health There has been an estimated 47 percent decline in maternal deaths from 1990 to 2010. In the latter year 287,000 were recorded. The vast majority were in developing countries and in 2010 half were in sub-Saharan Africa and a quarter in South Asia, though the latter has made significant progress in this area. While overall progress is a positive sign, the rate of progress has not matched projections by the MDGs.

Facts

MDG 6: Combat HIV/AIDS, Malaria, and other diseases

Poverty, armed conflict, and natural disasters contribute to the spread of disease. Malaria, tuberculosis, and AIDS exact a great toll on health and productivity. In 2012, 35 million people lived with HIV/AIDS and 2.3 million more acquired the disease. Sub-Saharan Africa remained the epicenter of the epidemic, though the proportion of adults living with AIDS began to fall. At the end of 2012, 9.7 million in developing countries were receiving antiretroviral drugs. In 2012, 8.6 million people were newly diagnosed with tuberculosis, though incidence, prevalence, and death rates were falling. There were some 200 million cases of malaria in 2012, causing 600,000 deaths. Malaria "is a disease of poverty."

MDG 7: Ensure environmental sustainability

This goal, the "most far reaching" is one that will "affect each person now and in the future." The World Bank notes that failure to reach agreement on limiting greenhouse gas emissions into the atmosphere will leave billions of people vulnerable to climate change, "with the effects expected to hit hardest in developing countries." The world released 33.6 billion metric tons of carbon dioxide in 2010, up 5 percent over 2009 and a considerable rise of 51 percent since 1990—the baseline for Kyoto Protocol requirements. Global emissions in 2013 were estimated at an unprecedented 36 billion tons. In 1990, 1.3 billion people worldwide lacked access to drinking water from a convenient, protected source. By 2012 this figure improved to 752 million people, representing a 41 percent reduction. While the proportion of people in developing countries with access to an improved water source rose from 70 percent in 1990 to 87 percent in 2012, almost 27 percent of countries are "seriously off track toward meeting the water target." While sanitation conditions have improved, 2.5 billion people still lack access to improved sanitation. The divide between rural and urban areas is striking, as 43 percent of the population in rural areas has access to improved sanitation compared to 73 percent in urban areas.

MDG 8: Developing a global partnership for development

Developing a global partnership for development faced a setback following the financial crisis of 2008. Commitments to ODA have fallen. Since 2010, ODA has fallen 6 percent. Debt relief continues to progress. Some 39 countries were eligible for the Heavily Indebted Poor Countries Debt Relief Initiative and the Multilateral Debt Relief Initiative. The ratio of debt service to exports in low- and middle-income economies fell to 9.8 percent in 2012, far below the 21.1 percent level at the start of the decade. The situation for telecommunications infrastructure also improved. By 2012, there were 6.3 billion mobile phone subscriptions and 2.5 billion people using the Internet worldwide. Since 2000, Internet users per 100 people in developing countries has grown 28 percent a year, but low-income countries of South Asia and sub-Saharan Africa lag behind.

Source: World Bank, *World Development Report 2014*, data.worldbank.org/sites/default/files/wdi-2014-ch1.pdf.

made in implementing the declaration's provisions and asked the secretary-general "to issue periodic reports" to the GA as a basis for further action.[11]

The MDGs were derived from the declaration. During the 1990s, a number of global conferences had taken place, defining the main objectives of the development agenda, now collectively known as the MDGs, which are eight goals to be achieved by 2015. Goal 8 called for a global partnership for development with the following targets:

- addressing the special needs of the least developed countries, landlocked countries and small island developing states;
- developing further an open, rule-based, predictable, non-discriminatory trading and financial system;
- dealing comprehensively with developing countries' debt;
- in cooperation with developing countries, developing and implementing strategies for decent and productive work for youth;
- in cooperation with pharmaceutical companies, providing access to affordable essential drugs in developing countries; and
- in cooperation with the private sector, making available the benefits of new technologies, especially information and communications to developing countries.

The MDGs are based more on partnership and cooperation than on the right to development, but they have been invoked by developing countries in support of the right to development, particularly alleviating extreme poverty.

In 2015 the GA was due to adopt a set of sustainable development goals to carry on the effort begun by the MDGs. The Human Rights Council's Working Group on the Right to Development is advocating that the right to development feature prominently in the new development goals. The group was also working on criteria to elaborate on the content of the right to development with the eventual aim of the adoption of a set of binding norms in a convention on the topic. It remains to be seen whether a consensus can be achieved on the drafting and adoption of such an instrument.

Preventable poverty[12]

The first goal of the MDGs is eradicating extreme poverty and hunger. In 2014, the Food and Agriculture Organization reported that chronic hunger had declined in developing countries, but that global hunger continued, with an estimated 805 million people in the developing world affected by chronic undernourishment.[13]

The Committee on Economic, Social and Cultural Rights, a body established by ECOSOC and operating under the ICESCR, adopted a statement on poverty in 2001, which noted that poverty could arise when people lack access to resources because of who they are, what they believe, or where they live. Thus, discrimination may cause poverty, just as poverty may cause discrimination.[14] According to the UN Charter and the ICESCR, governments should use their resources to meet the needs of their people, there should be no discrimination in the allocation of resources, and governments should cooperate to realize the rights enumerated in the charter, the UDHR, and the international covenant. Nowadays, there is understandable emphasis on implementing the right to development, on how globalization impacts on governments' ability to fulfill their human rights obligations, and on the adverse effects of an inequitable international economic order. These are all deserving issues, but they do not gainsay a government's obligation to meet the basic needs of its people, especially those in extreme poverty.

The concept of preventable poverty requires that situations of extreme poverty should be monitored, and national strategies should be proposed to tackle them. Regional and international assistance should be targeted to such situations as a matter of priority. There are national, regional, and international bodies that can help identify such situations and call for action to redress them. The Committee on Economic, Social and Cultural Rights could take the lead on this. The HRC's Special Rapporteur on Extreme Poverty could do likewise. UNDP, the World Bank, and regional development banks or institutions could also play a part. It surely must be fair to expect priority attention to be devoted to alleviating extreme poverty as issues of prevention, protection, and justice. Regional prevention mechanisms could also play their part.

African Commission on Human and Peoples' Rights

On the right to development, the African Commission recently handed down a path-breaking decision on the right to development of the Endorois community in Kenya, which contains valuable guidance on principles and policies required to guarantee the development of indigenous communities.[15] The commission had earlier, in 2001, delivered a decision of great importance on the situation of the people of Ogoniland in Nigeria, which addressed the right of that people to livelihood and protection.[16]

The commission found that the Endorois community had suffered a violation of its right to development at the hands of the Kenyan government: moved off their land without proper consultations, denied compensation, and not given matching land to pursue their livelihood. The commission took the view that the right to development is both constitutive and instrumental—both a means and an end. A violation of either the procedural or substantive element violates the right to development. The commission endorsed the submissions of the complainants in the case that giving effect to the right to development requires fulfilling five main criteria: policies must be equitable, non-discriminatory, participatory, accountable and transparent, with equity and choice as important overarching themes. A government bears the burden for creating conditions favorable to a people's development. It is obliged to ensure that the indigenous community is not left out of the development process or its benefits.

The commission underlined the importance of free choice of development for indigenous peoples, endorsing the view that they must not be coerced, pressured, or intimidated in their choice of development. It stressed the importance of participation and empowerment, and drew attention to the fact that in the right to development, the UN declaration includes active, free, and meaningful participation in development. The results of development should be empowerment of the indigenous community. It is not sufficient for the authorities merely to give food aid; the capabilities and choices of the indigenous people must improve in order for the right to development to be realized.

The commission found that Kenya had not obtained the prior, informed consent of all the Endorois before designating their land a game reserve and commencing their eviction. A government must consult with respect to indigenous peoples, especially when dealing with sensitive issues such as land. The community representatives must not be in an unequal bargaining position. It is incumbent on the government to conduct the consultation process in such a manner that allows their representatives to be fully informed of the issues at stake and participate in developing parts crucial to the life of the community. The Kenyan government did not impress upon the Endorois any understanding that they would be denied all rights of return to their land, including unfettered access to their grazing land and the medicinal salt licks for their cattle. The commission took the view that as regards any development or investment projects that would have a major impact within the Endorois territory the state had a duty not only to consult with the community, but also to obtain their free, prior, and informed consent, according to their customs and traditions. To the contrary, the Endorois representatives at discussions with the government had been illiterate, impairing their ability to understand the documents produced by the latter. The government did not ensure that the Endorois were accurately informed of the nature and consequences of the process, a minimum requirement that had been set out by the Inter-American Commission of Human Rights in the 2002 Dann case.[17] Free, prior, and informed consent is essential for the protection of indigenous peoples in relation to major development projects.

Endorsing earlier decisions of the Inter-American Court of Human Rights, the commission held that benefit sharing is vital both in relation to the right to development and the right to property. The former is violated when any development decreases the well-being of the community. The commission cited with approval a recommendation of the Committee on the Elimination of Racial Discrimination that not only the prior informed consent of communities must be sought when major exploitation activities are planned in indigenous territories but also that the equitable sharing of benefits to be derived from such exploitation be ensured.

In the Ogoni case, which involved the desecration of their lands in the extraction of oil, the African Commission had found several violations and appealed to the government of Nigeria to protect fully the environment, health, and livelihood of the people in Ogoniland. The government, it held, should take measures to ensure that appropriate environmental and social impact assessment are undertaken in case of future oil development activities.

It also pointed out that closely allied with the right to development is the issue of participation. It cited with approval a decision of the Inter-American Court of Human Rights in the Saramaka case, concerning Suriname, which, in ensuring the effective participation of the Saramaka people in development or investment plans within their territory, the state has a duty to consult the community actively according to their customs and traditions.[18] This duty requires the state both to accept and disseminate information, and entails constant communication between the parties.

Conclusion

This chapter has shown the emphasis given to the pursuit of development and the implementation of economic, social, and cultural rights—alongside civil and political rights—since the UN was established. Development and human rights are intrinsically related, and they require each other for their full realization. The GA and the World Conference on Human Rights have declared the existence of a right to development, and development is widely accepted as a human right, even if differing interpretations are given for it. Even so, the emergence of the right to development has not been free of controversy, and many contend that it is not a human right. This raises profound questions about the meaning of a human right. If one takes the legalistic view that a human right must be legally enforceable, then development might not be considered a human right everywhere. However, if one agrees with Amartya Sen that rights form part of social ethics, are situated within the process of public reasoning, and may inspire legislation, then surely the concept of the right to development is sound. The international community, assembled at the World Conference on Human Rights, considered development so important that it was consensually agreed as a human right. This is a strong argument that development is a human right. The task ahead is implementation, beginning with the implementation of the right to development at the national level.[19]

Notes

1. Walter Rodney, *How Europe Underdeveloped Africa*, revised 2nd edn (Washington, DC: Howard University Press, 1982).
2. Keba M'Baye, "Le droit au dévelopement, comme un droit de l'homme" (The Right to Development as a Human Right), Inaugural lecture at the International Institute for Human Rights, Strasbourg, France, 1972. See also Keba M'Baye, "Emergence of the 'Right to Development' as a Human Right in the Context of a New International Economic Order," address to a meeting of experts on human rights, human needs, and the establishment of a new international economic order, 16 July 1979, SS-78/CONF.630/8.
3. Working Group on the Right to Development, A/HRC/4/47, 14 March 2007.
4. Working Group on the Right to Development, para. 18.
5. Working Group on the Right to Development, para. 19.
6. Working Group on the Right to Development, para. 20.
7. Working Group on the Right to Development, para. 60.
8. Working Group on the Right to Development, paras 61–62.
9. Working Group on the Right to Development, paras 63–64.
10. See generally, Subrata R. Chowdhury, Erik M.G. Denters and Paul J. de Waart, eds, *The Right to Development in International Law* (Dordrecht, the Netherlands: Martinus Nijhoff Publishers, 1992); and Paul J. de Waart, Paul Peters, and Erik Denters, eds, *International Law and Development* (Dordrecht, the Netherlands: Martinus Nijhoff, 1988).
11. *Millennium Declaration*, para. 31.
12. See Thomas Wieder, "Prévenir la pauvreté plutôt que la guerir" (Preventing rather than curing poverty), *Le Monde*, 18 May 2007.
13. FAO, *The State of Food Insecurity in the World 2014* (Rome: FAO, 2014).
14. ECOSOC, E/C.12/2001/10 (10 May 2001), para. 11.
15. African Commission on Human and Peoples' Rights, "Centre for Minority Rights Development (Kenya) and Minority Rights Group International on

Behalf of Endorois Welfare Council v. Kenya," doc. no. 276/03, 2003, www.achpr.org/communications/decision/276.03.
16 African Commission on Human and Peoples' Rights, "The Social and Economic Rights Action Center and the Center for Economic and Social Rights v. Nigeria," doc. no. 155/96, 2001, www1.umn.edu/humanrts/africa/comcases/155-96.html.
17 *Mary and Carrie Dann v. United States*, case 11.140, report no. 75/02, Inter-American Court of Human Rights, doc. 5 rev. 1, 2002, 860, www1.umn.edu/humanrts/cases/75-02a.html.
18 *The Saramaka People v. Suriname*, Inter-American Court of Human Rights, judgment of 28 November 2007 (Preliminary Objections, Merits, Reparations and Costs).
19 Bertrand G. Ramcharan, *The Right to Development in Comparative Law: The Pressing Need for National Implementation*, University of Cape Town Faculty of Law, Institute of Development & Labour Law, Monograph 1/2010.

8 International cooperation and dialogue

- The principle of cooperation
- Human rights cooperation under the UN Charter
- The World Conference on Human Rights
- Cooperation in the Human Rights Council
- International cooperation under human rights treaties and jurisprudence
- Cooperation with human rights mechanisms and procedures
- Cooperation in the detection, arrest, extradition, and punishment of persons guilty of war crimes and crimes against humanity
- Enhancing international cooperation in the field of human rights
- The practice of human rights dialogues
- Bilateral human rights dialogues
- Dialogue with non-state actors
- Dialogue with business
- The African Peer Review Mechanism
- Dialogue with the human rights treaty bodies
- Dialogue with the UN human rights special procedures
- Dialogue with the UN high commissioner for human rights
- The UN High Commissioner for Refugees (UNHCR)
- The OSCE high commissioner on national minorities
- The promotion of democracy and the rule of law
- Conclusion

> We recognize that, in addition to our separate responsibilities to our individual societies, we have a collective responsibility to uphold the principles of human dignity, equality and equity at the global level. As leaders we have a duty therefore to all the world's people, especially the most vulnerable and, in particular, the children of the world, to whom the future belongs.
>
> (UN Millennium Declaration, paragraph 2)

International cooperation and dialogue 115

In the UN's evolving approaches and programs for dealing with human rights, growing emphasis is being put on cooperation and dialogue. One could already see this in the UN Charter, at the International Conference on Human Rights in Tehran in 1968, the World Conference on Human Rights held in 1993, and the resolution establishing the HRC.

The people of Darfur, Sri Lanka, and Syria have suffered from conflict and gross violations of human rights for many years. Thousands have been killed, displaced, tortured, and raped in Syria, and there is no end in sight. Insisting that these were an internal conflicts, the governments of these countries continued to maintain that the outside world should not get involved. When the situations came before the HRC, governments resisted condemnatory language against those responsible for atrocities, insisting on the softest possible language in the HRC decisions. This highlights the question of whether justice can be served when dialogue takes precedence over principle. This chapter highlights some of the salient issues involved in processes of cooperation and dialogue.

The principle of cooperation

As the UN Charter envisioned, international cooperation plays a central role in the international system. All countries were expected to cooperate to achieve the charter's principles and the UN's economic, social, and human rights goals. Further, all countries were expected to pool their efforts to realize human rights in accordance with Articles 1(3), 55, and 56.

In the human rights field, the idea of international cooperation has the following dimensions. First, states must live up to their obligations under the charter and international human rights instruments. Second, governments must cooperate with international human rights bodies. Third, governments must cooperate with special procedures and mechanisms established by the UN. Fourth, where national action cannot protect and promote human rights norms, states should cooperate toward this end. Fifth, states and the international community should cooperate to protect human rights.

At a recent seminar on international cooperation organized by OHCHR, the following elements were distilled in the seminar report:

- international human rights norms must be the foundation and benchmarks for international cooperation across the board;
- there must be more invocation and application of conscience in the practice of international cooperation, especially when dealing with international crimes and gross violations of human rights;

- international cooperation must be brought to bear on the prevention, alleviation, and remedying of gross violations of human rights, civil, economic, political, and social;
- bilateral, regional, and international cooperation should be aimed at addressing the adverse impact of consecutive and compounded global crises, such as financial and economic crises, food crises, climate change, and natural disasters, on the full enjoyment of human rights; and
- there is room for the enhancement of international cooperation on issues such as human rights education; the UPR [Universal Periodic Review] process; follow-up to recommendations of human rights organs; interactions among national human rights institutions; the right to development; international migration; the protection of children against being sold, prostitution and pornography; violence against women; South-South cooperation; and mainstreaming of the theme of international cooperation.[1]

Human rights cooperation under the UN Charter

According to the charter's first article, the purposes of the UN are, among others, to achieve international cooperation in solving international problems of an economic, social, cultural, or humanitarian character, promote and encourage respect for human rights and fundamental freedoms, and be a center for harmonizing nations' actions to attain these common ends. Article 55 of the charter gives the UN a mandate to promote universal respect for and observance of human rights and fundamental freedoms for all. In Article 56, all members pledged to take joint and separate action with the organization to achieve the purposes set forth in Article 55.

In Resolution 2625 (XXV) of 24 October 1970, the GA adopted the Declaration on Principles of International Law Concerning Friendly Relations and Cooperation Among States in accordance with the UN Charter, which is considered a codification of the charter's legal principles. In that declaration, the GA proclaimed that:

> States have the duty to cooperate with one another, irrespective of the differences in their political, economic and social systems, in the various spheres of international relations in order to maintain international peace and security and to promote international stability and progress, the general welfare of nations and international cooperation free from discrimination based on such differences. To

this end: states shall cooperate with other states in the maintenance of international peace and security; states shall cooperate in the promotion of universal respect for, and observance of, human rights and fundamental freedoms for all, and in the elimination of all forms of racial discrimination and all forms of religious intolerance; states shall conduct their international relations in the economic, social, cultural, technical and trade fields in accordance with the principles of sovereign equality and nonintervention; states members of the United Nations have the duty to take joint and separate action in cooperation with the United Nations in accordance with the relevant provisions of the Charter.

Furthermore, states should cooperate in the economic, social, and cultural fields as well as in science and technology, and promote international cultural and educational progress. States should also cooperate to promote economic growth, especially in developing countries.[2]

In their commentary on the charter, Leland Goodrich, Edvard Hambro, and Anne Simons noted that the UN was not intended to have the powers of a government. Rather, it should promote cooperation between states in finding solutions to common problems and achieve maximum support from members for the organization's work.[3]

On the legal thrust of Article 56, Goodrich, Hambro, and Simons pointed out that the phrase "in cooperation with the Organization" does not mean that UN recommendations are binding. However, it does mean "that members are obligated to refrain from obstructionist tactics and to cooperate in good faith to achieve the goals specified in Article 55."[4]

The commentary on the charter edited by Bruno Simma noted that, as far as the protection of human rights was concerned, Article 1(3) had been invoked to improve the effective enjoyment of human rights and fundamental freedoms, and with respect to particular human rights issues and situations generally within the UN system.[5]

The same commentary concluded that Article 56 specifies member states' obligations set forth in Articles 2(2) and 55. This specification dealt with the three elements of Article 56: joint action, separate action, and cooperation with the organization. It also addressed the obligations assumed under Article 55. In his commentary on Article 56, Rüdiger Wolfrum agreed with Goodrich, Hambro, and Simons that Article 56 requires "that member states cooperate with the UN in a constructive way; obstructive policies are thus excluded."[6]

The World Conference on Human Rights

The World Conference on Human Rights, held in Vienna in June 1993, provided an unchallenged consensus of the international community on human rights issues, including on human rights cooperation and dialogue. The preamble to the Vienna Declaration and Program of Action reaffirmed the commitment in Article 56 to take joint and separate action, placing emphasis on developing effective international cooperation. The conference reaffirmed states' commitment to fulfill their obligations to promote universal respect for and observance and protection of all human rights and fundamental freedoms. Further, the conference declared that "the universal nature of these rights and freedoms is beyond question." In this framework, "enhancement of international cooperation in the field of human rights is essential for the full achievement of the purposes of the United Nations."[7]

The Vienna conference declared that promoting and protecting human rights and fundamental freedoms must be a priority objective of the UN and a centerpiece of international cooperation. In this regard, "the promotion and protection of all human rights is a legitimate concern of the international community."[8]

The conference emphasized that all human rights were universal, indivisible, interdependent, and interrelated.[9] Democracy, development, and respect of human rights and fundamental freedoms were interdependent and mutually reinforcing.[10] The conference reaffirmed the right to development as established in the Declaration on the Right to Development as a universal and inalienable right and an integral part of fundamental human rights. As stated in the declaration, the human person is the central subject of development. While development facilitated the enjoyment of all human rights, "the lack of development may not be invoked to justify the abridgement of internationally recognized human rights."[11]

The conference recognized the important role of NGOs in promoting human rights and emphasized the importance of continued dialogue and cooperation between governments and NGOs.

The Vienna Program of Action contained a separate section on "cooperation, development, and strengthening of human rights," which recommended that priority be given to national and international action to promote democracy, development, and human rights.[12] It strongly supported establishing a comprehensive program within the UN to help states build and strengthen adequate national structures to observe human rights and maintain the rule of law.[13] It appealed to governments, competent agencies, and institutions to increase considerably the resources devoted to building well-functioning legal systems that can protect human rights, and to national institutions working in this area.[14]

The conference considered human rights education, training, and public information essential to promote and achieve stable and harmonious relations among communities and to foster mutual understanding, tolerance, and peace. It called on all states and institutions to include human rights and humanitarian law in the curricula of all learning institutions.[15]

The conference further expressed its dismay at massive violations of human rights, especially in the form of genocide, ethnic cleansing, and systematic rape of women in war situations. It strongly condemned such abhorrent practices and called for perpetrators of such crimes to be punished.[16] It also expressed dismay and condemnation that gross and systematic violations and situations that obstructed the full enjoyment of human rights continued to occur.[17] It reaffirmed the importance of ensuring the universality, objectivity, and non-selectivity of human rights issues.[18]

The conference called on states to abrogate legislation leading to impunity for those responsible for grave violations of human rights, such as torture, and to prosecute such violations, thereby providing a firm basis for the rule of law.[19] It reaffirmed that efforts to eradicate torture should, first and foremost, be concentrated on prevention.[20]

The conference declared that widespread extreme poverty inhibited the full and effective enjoyment of human rights; its immediate alleviation and eventual elimination must remain a high priority for the international community.[21] It affirmed that extreme poverty and social exclusion constituted a violation of human dignity and called for urgent steps to achieve better knowledge of extreme poverty and its causes to promote the human rights of the poorest.[22]

The conference affirmed that respect for human rights and fundamental freedoms is a fundamental rule of international human rights law. The speedy and comprehensive elimination of racism and racial discrimination, xenophobia, and related intolerance was a priority for the international community.[23] The conference urged the full and equal enjoyment by women of all human rights, adding that this should be a priority for governments and the UN.[24]

The conference underlined the importance of preserving and strengthening the system of special procedures, rapporteurs, representatives, experts, and working groups of the CHR and its sub-commission to enable them to carry out their mandates. All states were asked to cooperate fully with these procedures and mechanisms.[25]

Cooperation in the Human Rights Council

GA resolution 60/251 establishing the HRC recognized that the promotion and protection of human rights should be based on the "principles of cooperation and genuine dialogue" aimed at strengthening member states' capacity to comply with their human rights obligations. Operative paragraph 4 of the resolution stated that the work of the HRC shall be guided by the principles of "universality ... constructive international dialogue, and cooperation, with a view to enhancing the promotion and protection of all human rights." Operative paragraph 5(8) also declared that the council shall work "in close cooperation in the field of human rights" with governments, regional organizations, national human rights institutions, and civil society. Operative paragraph 9 decided that council members should uphold the highest standards in promoting and protecting human rights, fully cooperate with the council, and be subject to the UPR mechanism during their term of membership. As shown here, international cooperation thus features prominently in the scheme of the HRC. This chapter endeavors to elucidate the content of the idea of international cooperation.

International cooperation under human rights treaties and jurisprudence

The duty to cooperate has been spelled out in the jurisprudence of bodies such as the Human Rights Committee, which has repeatedly pointed out that states must investigate allegations made against them and inform the committee of their findings.

A state's failure to furnish its observations leads the committee to give due weight to the allegations, and a state's failure to respond to a petition submitted to the committee could lead to an adverse finding against the state. In *Dante Piandiong et al. v. The Philippines* (Communication no. 869/1999), the Human Rights Committee concluded that by ratifying the Optional Protocol on the procedure for individual communications, a state undertakes to cooperate with the committee to permit and enable it to consider a communication. Moreover, it ruled that a state party commits a grave breach of its obligations under the optional protocol if it prevents or frustrates consideration of the committee's communication. Specifically, a state breaches its obligations under the protocol if, having been notified of the communication, it proceeds to execute the alleged victim.[26]

Cooperation with human rights mechanisms and procedures

Over a number of sessions, the former CHR and the current HRC have adopted resolutions on cooperation with representatives of UN human rights bodies that urged governments to refrain from all acts of intimidation or reprisal against individuals who cooperate with representatives of UN human rights bodies, or who have provided testimony to them, individuals who have availed themselves of UN procedures to protect human rights and fundamental freedoms, and those who have provided legal assistance to people for this purpose, individuals who submit or have submitted communications under procedures established by human rights instruments, and, finally, relatives of victims of human rights violations.[27]

Cooperation in the detection, arrest, extradition, and punishment of persons guilty of war crimes and crimes against humanity

On 3 December 1973, the GA adopted the Principles of International Cooperation in the Detection, Arrest and Punishment of Persons Guilty of War Crimes and Crimes against Humanity. This included a set of principles of international cooperation in the detection, arrest, extradition, and punishment of persons guilty of war crimes and crimes against humanity. The document stated:

> States shall cooperate with each other on a bilateral and multilateral basis with a view to halting and preventing war crimes and crimes against humanity, and shall take domestic and international measures necessary for that purpose;
> States shall cooperate with each other in the collection of information and evidence which would help to bring to trial persons against whom there is evidence that they have committed war crimes and crimes against humanity;
> In cooperating with a view to the detection, arrest and extradition of persons against whom there is evidence that they have committed war crimes and crimes against humanity and, if found guilty, their punishment, states shall act in conformity with the provisions of the Charter of the United Nations and of the Declaration on Principles of International Law concerning Friendly Relations and Cooperation among States in accordance with the Charter of the United Nations.[28]

Enhancing international cooperation in the field of human rights

The former CHR adopted a series of resolutions to enhance international cooperation in human rights, which emphasized that international cooperation was essential to achieve the purposes of the UN, including the effective protection and promotion of all human rights. According to the commission, it was one of the purposes of the UN and the responsibility of all member states to promote, protect, and encourage respect for human rights and fundamental freedoms through international cooperation. It considered that "international cooperation in this field, in conformity with the purposes and principles set out in the Charter of the United Nations and in international law, should make an effective and practical contribution to the urgent task of preventing violations of Human Rights and of fundamental freedoms for all."[29] The commission recognized that states have a collective responsibility to uphold the principles of human dignity, equality, and equity at the global level. The commission also invited states and relevant UN human rights mechanisms to pay attention to the importance of mutual cooperation, understanding, and dialogue to ensure the promotion and protection of human rights.

The practice of human rights dialogues

The concept of a human rights dialogue has a long history. At the birth of international humanitarian law, nongovernmental efforts were marshaled to persuade governments to accept and observe these emerging norms. Inter-state representations constituted an emerging humanitarian dialogue. Subsequently, the International Committee of the Red Cross (ICRC) has consistently sought to work cooperatively with governments to the fullest extent possible. The principles of ICRC dialogue and contacts emphasize discreet confidence building.

The International Labour Organization (ILO) has also developed a tradition of dialogue. Its direct contact procedures provide opportunities to pursue dialogue and cooperation. Since its adoption of the declaration on fundamental labor standards, the ILO has accentuated its practice of dialogue.

Following the entry onto the scene of the human rights treaty bodies, their consideration of reports and visits to countries (in the case of bodies such as the Committee Against Torture) have established a rich tradition of human rights dialogue. General Comment no. 31 of the Human Rights Committee is significant in this regard.

International cooperation and dialogue 123

Human rights dialogues have been practiced by the European Commission on Human Rights (now the European Court of Human Rights), the Inter-American Commission and Court, and the African Commission. Each has a solid body of practice. The peer review panel of the New Partnership for Africa's Development (NEPAD) is blazing a new trail in developing human rights dialogue. The Organization for Security and Co-operation in Europe (OSCE) high commissioner on national minorities, the UN high commissioner for human rights, and the Council of Europe commissioner on human rights also have significant practice. Under the procedure established by ECOSOC resolution 1503, there had been a long-standing practice of dialogue in the confidential proceedings of the CHR and through direct contacts with countries. There has also been a significant practice of bilateral human rights dialogues between countries, and between multilateral or regional organizations and individual countries. Finally, there have been examples of thematic dialogues in human rights bodies on human rights issues of international concern.

At the UN, more recently, there has been a distinct policy emphasis on human rights dialogues. GA resolution 48/141, which established the post of UN high commissioner for human rights, mandated that the high commissioner engage in a dialogue with all governments to secure respect for all human rights. GA resolution 60/251 establishing the HRC recognized that promoting and protecting human rights should be based on cooperation and genuine dialogue aimed at strengthening member states' capacity to comply with their human rights obligations.[30] Furthermore, the GA decided that the council's methods of work shall be transparent, fair, and impartial and enable genuine dialogue, be result oriented, allow subsequent follow-up discussions to recommendations and their implementation, and allow for substantive interaction with special procedures and mechanisms.

Based on the above, it can be concluded that a human rights dialogue involves substantive cooperation in good faith by all participants and participation of governments and civil society, is based on international human rights law or international humanitarian law, aims to promote and protect human rights, works to strengthen national protection capacity in each country, includes an understanding of the circumstances and history of each country, should be result oriented, and has appropriate follow-up.

Keeping this in mind, the remaining sections of this chapter highlight the dialogue practice of some selected human rights/humanitarian institutions and practitioners.

Bilateral human rights dialogues

A study of human rights dialogues commissioned by the Swiss Federal Department of Foreign Affairs and published by the German Institute of Human Rights provided a useful summary of bilateral human rights dialogues.[31] The study contains a number of suggestions for human rights dialogues. One suggestion is that planning a human rights dialogue should take up existing international material, in particular the concluding observations by UN treaty bodies and the recommendations of special procedures. Furthermore, partners should avoid privileging political over social rights and vice versa. A human rights dialogue should always respect that human rights are indivisible and that effective human rights protection poses major challenges for all countries.

Dialogue with non-state actors

The issue of human rights and non-state actors certainly attracts differences of views.[32] As a general proposition, it may be readily agreed that everyone who can promote and protect human rights should be encouraged to do so. International actors pursuing human rights dialogues with particular countries can and sometimes do maintain dialogue with non-state actors. The purpose of such dialogue could be to understand better the capacity-building needs of a country in human rights where national, regional, or international action might be most beneficial to regions or groups, and how human rights education could be enhanced. International or regional partners would need to pursue such dialogue with the understanding and support of the government concerned. This would be within the spirit of partnership in a common cause.

If the country is experiencing human rights problems, international or regional dialogue partners may need to consult non-state actors to ascertain and assess the problems to help the government solve the problems. This would be a more delicate process and would need to be accompanied by confidence-building measures to assure all sides that the dialogue partner is intending to be helpful in a time of need.

If there is an armed conflict within the country, the international or regional dialogue partner should be particularly discerning. Governments facing insurrection are naturally sensitive about foreign contacts with insurrectionists. Where insurrectionists are committing acts contrary to international human rights or humanitarian law, international and regional actors must not be shy of calling on them to cease such acts. If international or regional dialogue partners consider that being in contact with such insurrectionists could help reduce outrages on the population, they should explain this to the government and endeavor to use their good offices to protect human rights.

Dialogue with business

As with non-state actors, the subject of business and human rights also gives rise to differing viewpoints. The Compact with Business, which was launched by former Secretary-General Annan, sought to sensitize business on how it might help promote and protect human rights and of the importance of not contributing to violations of human rights. The initiative of the former Sub-Commission on the Promotion and Protection of Human Rights had similar objectives and even took this one step further by advocating a code of conduct for business organizations when it came to protecting human rights. More recently, the special representative of the secretary-general on business and human rights has sought to find middle ground on these issues.

Business organizations may contribute to the spread of human rights education in primary and secondary schools and in higher institutions of learning. Business organizations may contribute to human rights capacity building within countries. Business organizations may contribute to alleviating the plight of vulnerable groups such as minorities, indigenous populations, migrants, and the victims of trafficking. Business organizations may use their good offices with governments to help prevent, mitigate, or stop human rights violations, and to promote justice and redress. International business organizations could make an important contribution to strengthening the universality of human rights on the basis of the UDHR.

The implementation of the "Ruggie Principles" is leading to significant international cooperation on the role of business in contributing to the promotion and the protection of human rights.[33]

The African Peer Review Mechanism

The African Peer Review Mechanism (APRM) has existed for a decade. In March 2003, the heads of state of NEPAD and its Government Implementation Committee, meeting in Abuja, Nigeria, adopted a memorandum of understanding (MOU) on the APRM. The MOU, which operates as a treaty, came into effect immediately with the agreement of six countries to participate in the process.

The APRM process is based on a self-assessment questionnaire developed by the APRM's secretariat and is divided into four sections: democracy and political governance; economic governance and management; corporate governance; and socioeconomic development. The APRM base document, which was adopted at the AU summit in Durban in 2002, provided four types of review: 1) base review, which is carried out within 18 months of a country becoming a member of the APRM; 2) periodic review, which is carried out every two to four years; 3) requested review, under which any country can request an additional review for its own reasons; and 4) crisis review, which occurs when early signs of impending political or economic crisis would trigger a review.

Each participating country is required to have a national coordinating structure to conduct broad-based and inclusive consultation of key stakeholders in the public and private sectors. When the panel conducts a review, it appoints an APR country review team that is constituted for the period of the review visit.

The review process has a preliminary phase during which a support mission seeks to ensure a common understanding of the philosophy, rules, and processes of the APRM and to help countries that need support with the national processes. Under stage one, the country in question must answer a detailed questionnaire for the purposes of self-assessment. The APRM secretariat makes a background study of the country's governance and development. This is shared with the country concerned and other partner institutions. After the self-assessment is complete, the country must issue a draft program of action. After the questionnaire and the program of action have been submitted to the APR secretariat, it draws up an issues paper on matters that require further assessment.

In stage two, the review team visits the country and carries out the widest possible range of consultations with the government, officials, political parties, parliamentarians, and representatives of civil society organizations. In the third stage, a draft report is compiled, which is based on the findings of the review team from its visit, the background research of the APR secretariat, and the issues paper prepared by the secretariat. The draft report is then discussed with the government concerned. In stage four, the review team's report and the final program of action compiled by the government are sent to the APR secretariat and the APR panel. The report is then submitted to the APR forum of participating heads of state and government which recommends necessary action. Peer pressure may be applied at this stage if necessary.

In stage five, the report is tabled in key regional and sub-regional structures such as the Pan-African Parliament, the African Commission on Human and Peoples' Rights, the Peace and Security Council, and the Economic, Social and Cultural Council of the AU. The report becomes publicly available at this point.

After the review has been completed, the subject country is expected to implement its program of action, and foreign donors are expected to support the implementation of the plan of action. After a review is concluded, a periodic review should be undertaken every two to four years.[34]

Dialogue with the human rights treaty bodies

The bodies established under UN or regional human rights treaties engage in different forms of dialogue with governments and others. In the first place, when they are considering reports or petitions, the treaty bodies solicit information from states parties, engage in periodic discussions with them, make representations to them, and indicate concluding observations that suggest follow-up efforts. The aim here is to foster compliance with the treaty concerned. Where a state is late in submitting reports, comments, or information, representatives of treaty bodies may engage in discreet contacts with governments to encourage cooperation.

In the second place, the principal UN human rights treaty bodies now regularly exchange views with representatives of states parties to the particular treaty. This may take place in Geneva or New York, where the state representatives are present. These exchanges intend to allow the state representatives to express views and share their experiences on the treaty's implementation arrangements. The conversations also allow the treaty bodies to share their insights with the state representatives.

In the third place, the series of general comments adopted by human rights treaty bodies represents a form of dialogue with the states collectively. Based on their experience in considering reports by states, the treaty bodies provide insights on how governments could work to give effect to the treaty.

General Comment no. 31 of the Human Rights Committee, discussed above, is a particularly good example of this.

Dialogue with the UN human rights special procedures

The term UN human rights special procedures refers to the various rapporteurs, experts, representatives, working groups, and similar mechanisms established by the CHR, now the HRC. Some of these special procedures have structural or thematic mandates. Examples of this are the special procedures on international solidarity and human rights, structural adjustment, and debts as they impact on human rights, environmental dangers, and the right to development. On such topics, those that hold the mandates of special procedures gather and analyze information, consult with all concerned to obtain their insights and pertinent information, and distil recommendations. They are, in effect, engaged in a process of global dialogue on these structural issues.

Asimilar process takes place regarding thematic procedures on economic, social, civil, or political rights. The special procedures on the rights to food, education, health, and adequate standard of living, including housing, endeavor to gather information and insights on their mandates and also to distil recommendations. A global dialogue is also underway here.

The special procedures against torture, extra-judicial executions, arbitrary detention, enforced and involuntary disappearances, violence against women, trafficking in human beings, and on the human rights of minorities, indigenous people, terrorism and human rights, and similar subjects seek to gather information on their topics globally, to be in touch with all who could provide information or shed light on their topic, distil recommendations, and understand the situation where problems are encountered in particular countries. They regularly visit countries to pursue their mandates.

There are some country-specific special procedures. Some of these benefit from the cooperation of the country concerned and endeavor to create dialogue with the government to help restore or strengthen human rights in the country. There have been instances where such dialogue has been particularly beneficial and appreciated by the government concerned. Almost invariably, they are particularly appreciated by the people of the country. Country dialogue, if carried out in a spirit of confidence building and cooperation and with the objective of protecting human rights, can be of great service.

Finally, special procedure mandate holders have an annual dialogue with the HRC and, in some instances, with the Third Committee of the GA. Typically, the special procedure mandate holder introduces his or her report and engages in a dialogue with representatives of the countries directly concerned in the report and with representatives of UN member states. The aim here is to deepen the process of cooperation to protect human rights. In the past, special procedures had been squeezed for time in the CHR. The HRC has allocated more time for dialogues with special procedure mandate holders, and this has been much appreciated by the human rights community.

As the dialogue deepens between the HRC and the special procedures, there is a hope for increased emphasis on preventive human rights strategies—specifically, heading off potential violations before they occur. The HRC has an explicit mandate for dialogue and prevention, and it would be natural to pursue a synthesis between the two: a dialogue for prevention, and a dialogue for promotion and protection.

Dialogue with the UN high commissioner for human rights

Since the position was established, the UN high commissioner for human rights has pursued different forms of dialogue. First, the high commissioner has annual dialogue sessions with the GA and the HRC. This is an occasion for member states to listen to the experience and insights of the high commissioner, communicate their views, and help develop cooperative approaches to advance the promotion and protection of human rights.

In the second place, the high commissioner maintains an ongoing dialogue with partner departments and organizations of the UN system, regional organizations, NGOs, and civil society. In the third place, high commissioners have pursued contacts with representatives of national human rights institutions and have sought to foster stronger national systems to promote and protect human rights.

Fourth, successive high commissioners have established a pattern of visiting countries for dialogue to support the strengthening of national human rights systems. They have also sought to emphasize human rights capacity building generally.

In her 2006 report to the GA, then UN High Commissioner Louise Arbour emphasized country engagement, which aimed to address protection gaps through a consultative process involving governments, civil society, and other relevant international and national counterparts. OHCHR, she emphasized, was not an arbiter or judge. Rather, Arbour saw its work as an ongoing dialogue, bringing duty bearers and rights holders together toward more effective promotion and protection of human rights. To this end, country-level monitoring of human rights developments and collection of information are indispensable for an objective analysis of the human rights situation. This, in turn, is fundamental in order to devise the most adequate forms of technical cooperation.[35]

The high commissioner considered national human rights institutions a key element of the OHCHR country-engagement strategy. Further, according to Arbour, OHCHR's expanded presence in the field, both at country and regional levels, would allow it to achieve the greatest impact.[36] Cooperation with the UN resident coordinator system and UN country teams was also becoming more structured and systematic.

Arbour's successors have continued this policy of giving priority to the role of human rights field offices and at the time of writing, in late 2014, there were more than 50 such offices in different parts of the world.

The UN High Commissioner for Refugees (UNHCR)

In the past, UNHCR has also deployed dialogue and good offices to help head off problems. Prince Sadruddin Aga Khan, a former high commissioner, identified three criteria for action by the high commissioner's office. First, the needs to be met and the necessary action to be undertaken should be of a strictly humanitarian and nonpolitical character. Second, there should be a request to the high commissioner from the government directly concerned. Third, the persons for whom the assistance program is to be implemented must qualify as refugees or be in a situation analogous to that of refugees.[37]

In its more recent history, UNHCR has used international conferences and plans of action to respond to refugee and displacement crises, help contain them, and also stem situations that could lead to refugee outflows. UNHCR has used conferences and/or plans of action for refugees in Southeast Asia, Central America, and Central Africa. A UNHCR plan of action successfully addressed the situation following the break-up of the Soviet Union and the fears of refugee movements in the countries of the Commonwealth of Independent States.[38]

The OSCE high commissioner on national minorities

In 1990, the Conference on Security and Co-operation in Europe (CSCE, later OSCE) established the position of high commissioner on national minorities to provide early warning and, where appropriate, early action regarding tensions involving national minority issues that have not yet developed beyond an early warning stage but could develop into a conflict within the CSCE area, affecting peace, stability, or relations between participating states. Within this mandate, the high commissioner is required to work in confidence and to act independently of all parties directly involved in the tensions.

If, on the basis of exchanges of communications and contacts with relevant parties, the high commissioner concludes that there is a risk of potential conflict, he/she may issue an early warning, which will be communicated promptly by the chairman-in-office to the Committee of Senior Officials. The high commissioner may recommend that he/she be authorized to enter into further contact and closer consultations with the parties concerned with a view to possible solutions, according to a mandate decided by the committee.

The promotion of democracy and the rule of law

Article 21 of the UDHR proclaimed that the will of the people shall be the basis of government authority. This will shall be expressed in periodic and genuine elections conducted by universal and equal suffrage and held by secret vote or by equivalent free voting procedures.

According to Article 25 of the ICCPR, everyone shall have the right and the opportunity: 1) to take part in the conduct of public affairs, directly or through freely chosen representatives; 2) to vote and to be elected at genuine periodic elections that are held according to universal and equal suffrage and by secret ballot, guaranteeing the free expression of the will of the electors; and 3) to have equal access to public service in his or her country.

The UN has had extensive experience in monitoring popular consultations and elections in colonies and trust territories. The aim of the UN's involvement was to ensure that the people could exercise their choice freely. UN supervision varied according to the circumstances of the case and the mandate established by the GA, the Trusteeship Council, or other UN organs. A distinction was also drawn between supervising popular consultations and observing them. Supervision was wider in scope and covered the organizational aspects as well as the observation stage.

Prior to the 1990s, the UN had observed elections in a few independent countries.[39] However, from the 1990s, the UN saw a determined push for more involvement in promoting democracy and free elections. There is a Division for Electoral Assistance within the UN Department of Political Affairs, which provides advice and technical assistance at government request. It has helped organize some elections and has observed many others. All three facets of the division's activities— advice and assistance, organization, and observation to help countries conduct free elections and, in some instances, avoid conflict that could occur over the conduct or results of elections—involve dialogue and cooperation.

Since 1989, the UN has received numerous requests for electoral assistance from member states. Since the Electoral Assistance Unit/Division was established in 1992, the UN has provided various forms of electoral assistance to dozens of member states.

Conclusion

From the foregoing discussion, it can be concluded that cooperation as a human rights concept involves practical action in good faith to promote and protect human rights. The above discussion presented seven categories in which international law and practice requires meaningful and substantive cooperative action. Dialogue as a human rights concept is also intended to advance the promotion and protection of human rights in good faith. Both cooperation and dialogue are meant to enhance human rights or their protection. Human rights cooperation and dialogue can serve optimally if they are marshaled in aid of the protection of human rights.

Notes

1 UN General Assembly, "Report of the Seminar on Enhancement of International Cooperation in the Field of Human Rights," UN doc. A/HRC/23/20, 23 April 2013, para. 58, daccess-dds-ny.un.org/doc/UNDOC/GEN/G13/133/61/PDF/G1313361.pdf?OpenElement.
2 General Assembly resolution 2625 (XXV), 24 October 1970.
3 Leland Goodrich, Edvard Hambro, and Anne Simons, *Charter of the United Nations: Commentary and Documents* (New York and London: Columbia University Press, 1969), 35.
4 Goodrich et al., *Charter of the United Nations*, 381.
5 Bruno Simma, ed., *The Charter of the United Nations: A Commentary* (Oxford: Oxford University Press, 1985), 55–56.
6 In Simma, *The Charter of the United Nations*, 794.
7 *Vienna Declaration*, para. 1.
8 *Vienna Declaration*, para. 4.
9 *Vienna Declaration*, para. 5.
10 *Vienna Declaration*, para. 8.
11 *Vienna Declaration*, para. 10.
12 *Vienna Declaration*, para. 66.
13 *Vienna Declaration*, para. 69.
14 *Vienna Declaration*, para. 74.
15 *Vienna Declaration*, paras 78 and 79.
16 *Vienna Declaration*, para. 28.
17 *Vienna Declaration*, para. 30.
18 *Vienna Declaration*, para. 32.
19 *Vienna Declaration*, para. 60.
20 *Vienna Declaration*, para. 61.
21 *Vienna Declaration*, para. 14.
22 *Vienna Declaration*, para. 25.
23 *Vienna Declaration*, para. 15.
24 *Vienna Program of Action*, para. 36.
25 *Vienna Program of Action*, para. 95.

26 Raija Hanski and Martin Scheinin, eds, *Leading Cases of the Human Rights Committee* (Turku/Abo, Finland: Institute for Human Rights, Abo Akademi University, 2003), 12–13.
27 See for example, Commission resolution 2003/9, *Cooperation with Representatives of United Nations Human Rights Bodies*.
28 General Assembly resolution 3074 (XXVIII), 3 December 1973.
29 See Commission resolution 2003/60, *Enhancement of International Cooperation in the Field of Human Rights*.
30 Preamble, para. 10.
31 Anna Wurth and Frauke L. Seidensticker, *Indices, Benchmarks, and Indicators: Planning and Evaluating Human Rights Dialogues* (Berlin, Germany: German Institute of Human Rights, 2005).
32 See generally Andrew Clapham, *Human Rights Obligations of Non-State Actors*, Vol. XV/1 (Oxford: Oxford University Press, 2006).
33 United Nations, "Guiding Principles on Business and Human Rights," UN doc. HR/PUB/11/04, 2011.
34 See *African Peer Review Mechanism: Organization and Processes*, NEPAD/HGSIC-3-2003/APRM/Guideline/O&P, 9 March 2003.
35 A/61/36, para. 3.
36 A/61/36, paras 3–4.
37 Prince Sadruddin Aga Khan, "Legal Problems Relating to Refugees and Displaced Persons," *Recueil des Cours de l'Académie de Droit International* 149 (1976): 287–352.
38 Interview with Francois Fouinat, former chef de cabinet to High Commissioner Sadako Ogata, Geneva, 6 December 2006.
39 Korea, Haiti, Costa Rica, and Cambodia.

9 Protection

- Human rights protection at the national level
- The continuing need for international protection
- Antecedents of international protection
- The nature of protection: scholarly views
- The responsibility to protect
- Preventive, curative, and remedial or compensatory protection
- International protection
- The United Nations
- UNHCR
- The United Nations Human Rights Council
- UN field operations and human rights: The Brahimi Report
- Universal criminal jurisdiction
- Conclusion

> The World Conference on Human Rights ... expresses its dismay and condemnation that gross and systematic violations of human rights and situations that constitute serious obstacles to the full enjoyment of all human rights continue to occur in different parts of the world.
> (Vienna Declaration, paragraph 30)

Lack of protection is the Achilles heel of the human rights movement. In its 2007 *World Report*, Human Rights Watch lamented:

> Each government these days seems to have a ready excuse for ignoring human rights. High-minded pronouncements occasionally ring from capitals or from ambassadors to the United Nations, but without the sustained follow-through needed for change. Commitments are crabbed by caveats, engagements by escape clauses ... [T]he excuses for inaction overwhelm the imperative of decisive action.[1]

This is a sobering assessment that remains valid. Yet the idea of the protection of human rights is a foundation of the contemporary human rights movement and the international law of human rights.[2] Protection has preventive, curative, and remedial or compensatory aspects. National authorities are, first and foremost, responsible for protection of human rights. Where this is lacking, protection may be exercised regionally pursuant to regional human rights conventions or internationally pursuant to the UN Charter or international human rights conventions where applicable. This chapter examines the idea of protection of human rights in its different aspects and contexts.

Human rights protection at the national level

As discussed in Chapter 2, every country should be able to show that it has an adequate and effective national protection system in place, with constitutional, legislative, judicial, educational, institutional, and preventive components. National protection systems are, strategically, among the most important for future human rights strategies and a key concept for preventive human rights strategies. Based on the work of international human rights treaty bodies, special procedures, and the empirical work of UN institutions such as UNDP and OHCHR, more efforts should be deployed to strengthen national protection systems in the future. Before these systems are strengthened, however, the need for international protection remains staggering.

The continuing need for international protection

While it is an accepted rule of international law that each government is primarily responsible for protecting the human rights of persons within its jurisdiction, the need for international protection is an empirically observable fact that continues to be evident today. The sheer number and scale of situations involving shocking human rights violations proves that international protection of human rights is a continuing necessity. The following reasons for international protection may be noted.

There may, first of all, simply be a breakdown of government, resulting in excesses being committed against persons within the government's jurisdiction. For such persons, international protection may be the only line of defense. The spate of extra-judicial killings in the world is an example. Second, national laws or judicial policies may actually be inconsistent with internationally recognized human rights standards, and the only way to alter such laws may be through an international forum. Third, the domestic judicial system may simply fail, for example, when a person is unable to obtain any remedy for a violation of his or her human rights. Fourth, in highly charged situations, such as in international or internal conflicts or in emergency situations, an international presence may be indispensable to avoid or minimize excesses or inhumane actions. Fifth, in a world undergoing unprecedented political, economic, social, and cultural transformations, the pressures on governments are manifold, which can easily lead to harsh treatment of some parts of the population. The refugee and displacement crises in many parts of the world come to mind. Sixth, the potential for barbarism continues to break out frequently, wanton disregard for the elementary principles of humanity is rampant. Incidents of piracy against refugees are vivid examples. Seventh, there are some particularly vulnerable groups whose protection, experience has shown, can only be assured by urgent international action. This is the case for victims of institutionalized racism and racial discrimination, victims of slavery and slavery-like practices such as trafficking, minorities, and indigenous populations.

In the Nottebohm case (second phase), the ICJ, referring to the institution of diplomatic protection, commented that to "exercise protection, is to place oneself on the plane of international law. It is international law which determines whether a state is entitled to exercise protection."[3] On an earlier occasion, in the Reparation case, the court had expressly recognized the UN's capacity to engage in international protection.[4]

A third strand of the court's jurisprudence is provided in the Barcelona Traction case, which drew attention to obligations "towards the international community as a whole," which were derived in contemporary international law from the principles and rules concerning the basic rights of the human person, including protection from slavery and racial discrimination. "Some of the corresponding rights of *protection*," the court affirmed, "have entered into the body of general international law."[5]

These three cases indicate that the concept of international protection is an established part of international customary law.

Antecedents of international protection

The notion of protection (initially domestic protection) may be traced back to times when organized human societies were emerging, and notions of law and justice were evolving. As previously discussed, in *Freedom in the Ancient World*, H.J. Muller showed how law codes—written or unwritten—provided protection for the individual. Muller also traced the "efforts of kings to protect ordinary men against the abuses of power and privilege."[6] Bello has found notions akin to protection in African customary humanitarian law and has reported that, while not generally the case, during armed conflicts in certain parts of Africa, some tribes "took pride in according respect and human rights to women, children and old persons."[7] In Asia, Charles Alexandrowicz found that high standards of protection of foreigners have existed historically, irrespective of religion or civilization.[8]

In Europe in the sixteenth century, the institution of "protecting powers" developed, as European powers obtained, through capitulation treaties, the "right to exercise exclusive, extra-territorial jurisdiction over their nationals in the Ottoman Empire, and later on in the other independent countries of the Middle and Far East." The institution of protecting powers, which could also be found in diplomatic and consular practice, subsequently evolved to become the "cornerstone of the system of implementation of the Geneva Conventions" of 1949 on the laws of armed conflicts.[9]

The use of treaties to protect human rights, which was known even in the practice of the ancient Greeks, began to assume prominence in the seventeenth century. The Treaty of Westphalia (1648) sought to ensure equality of rights for Roman Catholics and Protestants in Germany. During the seventeenth century, in peace treaties, some governments undertook to respect the rights of Roman Catholic subjects of Protestant princes. In 1774, vis-à-vis Russia, Turkey aimed to protect the Christian religion and its churches within its territory. The Congress of Vienna of 1815 provided for the free exercise of religion and equality, irrespective of religion, in various cantons of Switzerland as well as for the equality of Christian denominations in Germany. The congress also contained provisions aiming to improve the civil status of Jews.[10]

The doctrine and practice of humanitarian intervention may also be included among the antecedents of the practice of international protection. In previous centuries, when a state was so abusive to its own population that it shocked the conscience of humanity, other states have claimed the right to threaten or use force to assist the oppressed persons. Setting aside the issue of the validity of such interventions in contemporary international law, the practice does offer guidance on one set of circumstances that warrants international protection: when atrocities reach such a scale as to shock the conscience of humanity.

The concept of international protection may, furthermore, be traced in the movements to abolish slavery, establish international humanitarian law concerning the conduct of hostilities and the protection of human rights during periods of armed conflict, and develop international social and labor legislation.

The institution of diplomatic protection, one of the hallowed institutions of international law, has also contributed to the development of the concept of international protection of human rights. Diplomatic protection proceeds from a state's right to protect its nationals abroad. As the Permanent Court of International Justice stated in the Mavrommatis Palestine Concessions case, "it is an elementary principle of international law that a state is entitled to protect its subjects, when injured by acts contrary to international law committed by another state, from whom they have been unable to obtain satisfaction through the ordinary channels."[11] In traditional international law, the responsibility of states for damage done in their territory to the person or property of foreigners was a part of the international standard of justice and the principle of the equality of nationals and aliens. As the General Claims Commission held in the Neer case, the propriety of governmental acts should be put to the test of international standards.

In an important submission, Francisco V. Garcia-Amador, former rapporteur of the International Law Commission, argued that what was formerly the object of these two principles—the protection of the person and of his property—is now intended to be accomplished by the international recognition of the essential rights of human beings.[12]

In some peace treaties, special minorities treaties, and declarations made after World War I, some states of Central and Eastern Europe and Iraq accepted obligations toward their racial, linguistic, and religious minorities, according to which all of their nationals were equal before the law and enjoyed equal civil and political rights. The relevant treaties stated that their provisions constituted obligations of international concern rather than domestic matters, and all were placed under the guarantee of the League of Nations.

At the drafting of the UN Charter in San Francisco, the question arose whether the charter should define the role of the UN in terms of promotion or protection. The drafters opted for language calling for the achievement of international cooperation in promoting and encouraging respect for human rights and fundamental freedoms. Notwithstanding the use of the term promotion, the practice of the UN has confirmed the organization's competence to protect human rights. In 1972, one commentator wrote:

> In the actual practice of the various organs of the United Nations over the past 25 years the obstacles to taking action based on the human rights provisions of the Charter have proved to be far less

formidable than the cleavage of theoretical opinions of scholars and of abstract statements by governments would lead one to assume. In the practice of the United Nations and its Members neither the vagueness and generality of the human rights clauses of the Charter nor the domestic jurisdiction clause have prevented the United Nations from considering, investigating, and judging concrete human rights situations, provided there was a majority strong enough and wishing strongly enough to attempt to influence the particular development.[13]

The nature of protection: scholarly views

According to one expert, the institutions responsible for implementing human rights are usually entrusted with one of two tasks—promoting or protecting human rights. The promotion of human rights implies action directed toward the future, while the protection of human rights is intended to ensure the observance of human rights under existing law. Protection relies mainly on court processes, whereas promotion makes use of every available legislative technique, including studies, research, reports, and the drafting of texts.[14]

The same source listed political supervision among the techniques used by institutions to protect human rights. Specifically, this means supervision by the political organs of international organizations, such as the UN General Assembly, and supervision by means of reports, petitions, or complaints.

Atle Grahl-Madsen, who specialized in international refugee law, defined protection as denoting measures of some kind or other taken by a subject of international law to safeguard or promote the integrity, rights, or interest of an individual. Protection may take many shapes. One might distinguish between internal protection (the protection of the law) and external protection (diplomatic or consular protection). Moreover, protection may be active or passive.[15]

A third scholar writing in the field of international humanitarian law employed the concepts of constraints and protection:

> "Constraints" is the most appropriate concept if the supervision of the application of the norms rests with the parties themselves (self-control). "Protection" would be an adequate description if some agency other than the parties could, on their own initiative, take steps to halt violations of the norms. "Rights" is the adequate notion if the persons in whose interests the norms were given could avail themselves of a formal procedure to secure that the norms were

respected. These persons, who would be the actual or potential victims of the armed conflict, would therefore have to have access to some kind of an impartial tribunal or other institution not subjected to the command of one of the parties to the conflict.[16]

An expert on the ICRC, discussing that organization's protection functions, placed them into two categories: direct protection and indirect protection. He submitted that the ICRC's three basic roles had both a direct and an indirect dimension: 1) ad hoc diplomacy; 2) development of law; and 3) application of the law.[17] There is much merit in this frame of direct and indirect protection, which offers a conceptual approach that corresponds closely to international protection as practiced in the UN.

The responsibility to protect

The International Commission on Intervention and State Sovereignty launched the concept of the responsibility to protect.[18] In the commission's view, the responsibility to protect embraced three specific responsibilities:

- the responsibility to prevent—namely, to address both the root causes and direct causes of internal conflict and other man-made crises putting populations at risk;
- the responsibility to react—namely, to respond to situations of compelling human need with appropriate measures, which may include coercive measures like sanctions and international prosecution, and in extreme cases military intervention; and
- the responsibility to rebuild—namely, to provide, particularly after a military intervention, full assistance with recovery, reconstruction and reconciliation, addressing the causes of the harm the intervention was designed to halt or avert.

The commission was firm in its view that prevention was the single most important dimension of the responsibility to protect. Prevention options should always be exhausted before intervention was contemplated, and more commitment and resources must be devoted to it. The exercise of the responsibility to prevent and react should always involve less intrusive and coercive measures before more coercive and intrusive ones are applied.

The UN Summit of World Leaders in 2005 endorsed the responsibility to protect. Leaders further declared their readiness to refer situations of genocide, ethnic cleansing, crimes against humanity and war crimes to the UNSC.

Preventive, curative, and remedial or compensatory protection

International protection may be grouped into three categories: anticipatory or preventive, mitigatory or curative, and remedial or compensatory. Preventive protection means that the national authorities, regional organizations, or the UN should try to anticipate and head off potential situations of human rights violations before they occur. This is a new thrust in the efforts of the human rights movement, and prevention is still in its infancy.[19] Prevention should be an essential part of any national protection system.

Among the preventive measures taken by international bodies, mention may be made of urgent appeals addressed on behalf of victims or of interim measures undertaken on their behalf. On some occasions, the UNSC and the HRC have met to consider a situation and possibly intercede. Special procedures of the HRC address urgent appeals to governments in cases of concern. The UN high commissioner for human rights may do likewise or may make public statements expressing concern. The secretary-general may intercede if this is considered helpful. The European Court and the Inter-American Commission on Human Rights have an established practice of interceding urgently if they conclude that an individual is in serious danger of irreparable harm. The good offices of international officials, such as the director-general of the ILO, may also be called on.[20]

Aside from these limited measures, such as appeals, interim measures, or the use of humanitarian good offices, the area of anticipation and prevention represents one of the major gaps in the international protection of human rights. In 1980, Theo C. van Boven, then director of the UN Division of Human Rights stated:

> We are frequently faced in the United Nations with serious and urgent problems of violations of human rights which arise in different parts of the world, but, apart from statements of the Secretary-General issued in a humanitarian spirit, or the exercise of his good offices in certain cases, the organization is mostly unable to take action in a situation where every day counts heavily notwithstanding the hope and expectations of the international community for such action. In the ILO, for example, the Director-General has been granted the competence, in urgent cases, to approach the government concerned to receive a mission from the organization

urgently to look into allegations of violations of trade unions rights within the country in question ... We, in the United Nations, similarly receive many complaints and disturbing reports about grave human rights problems in this as well as in other countries ... but there is no similar possibility for action open to us. In my view, this is a major deficiency in the arrangements.[21]

The situation has not changed markedly since then.

Curative protection involves efforts to mitigate and stop gross violations of human rights. The UNSC, the HRC, special procedures of the HRC, the UN high commissioner for human rights, and the secretary-general endeavor to engage in mitigatory and curative protection.

Various procedures exist within different international organizations, which aim to stop or to mitigate excesses or cure or redress situations giving rise to such excesses. Among these are the UN procedures for dealing with complaints of human rights violations, ILO's complaints procedures, UNESCO's complaints procedures, intergovernmental complaints procedures (such as those under the European Convention on Human Rights, the American Convention on Human Rights or the International Covenant on Civil and Political Rights), investigation and fact finding under various procedures in the UN, ILO, the Council of Europe, and the Organization of American States (OAS), visits or the establishment of international presences, the activities of the ICRC, the UN high commissioner for human rights, and UNHCR, the activities of NGOs, the exercise of good offices, and public denunciations of violations of human rights.

Some of the procedures within the different international organizations are intended to provide protection through remedies or compensation. Of particular significance in this regard are the petition systems under the European and American conventions on human rights, and under the Optional Protocol to the ICCPR, and some other treaties. Judicial measures of protection such as those provided by the European Court and the Inter-American Court of Human Rights are also relevant in this regard. Also related are the efforts made within the UN to provide reconstruction assistance to countries that have experienced extensive violations of human rights, as well as to individuals who have been subjected to such violations.[22]

Remedial and compensatory protection involves processes of establishing the truth about what took place in a situation of gross violations of human rights, bringing perpetrators to justice where possible, and providing redress to victims of violations or to their families. Truth and reconciliation commissions seek to ascertain and record what took place. National or hybrid courts or the ICC, or ad hoc tribunals—such as the international criminal tribunals for the Former Yugoslavia, Rwanda, Sierra Leone, and Cambodia—may deal with justice issues.

It should be pointed out that although preventive/anticipatory, curative/mitigatory, and remedial/compensatory procedures have been discussed, many procedures perform functions belonging to more than one of these categories.

International protection

The international protection of human rights is called into the picture when there has been a failure of national protection (see Table 9.1). It may be exercised even if regional bodies are aware of the situation. If a situation of gross violations of human rights threatens or breaches international peace and security, the primary (although not the exclusive) protection actor should be the UNSC. The Security Council usually engages in political protection—namely, it acts as it sees appropriate according to the political circumstances. The UNSC may engage in a higher standard of protection if it considers this appropriate, and it may even decide to refer situations to the ICC, as it did in the case of Darfur. Further, it may choose, acting under the mandatory chapter of the charter, to establish an international criminal tribunal to try those accused of criminal violations of human rights.[23]

Among the contemporary agencies of international protection are: the UN (including the UNSC, the HRC, the Human Rights Committee, the Committee on Economic, Social and Cultural Rights, the Committee on the Elimination of Racial Discrimination, the Committee on the Elimination of Discrimination against Women, the Committee on the Rights of the Child, the UNHCR, the UN high commissioner for human rights, and the Office for the Coordination of Humanitarian Affairs), the ILO, UNESCO, the ICRC, the Council of Europe, the ECHR, the OAS (the Inter-American Commission and the Court of Human Rights), the AU, the League of Arab States, and NGOs such as Amnesty International, Human Rights Watch, the International Commission of Jurists, the International Association of Democratic Lawyers, and the International League for Human Rights.

The degree of protection actually provided by these bodies is not commensurate with the needs on the ground. Table 9.2 depicts the performance of these bodies on a scale of zero to five. The only body that comes out respectably is the ECHR.

Table 9.1 The protection roles of international human rights institutions

Institution	Roles
The Security Council	*Can* act to prevent gross violations of human rights that may threaten international peace and security
	Can act urgently to mitigate and arrest gross violations of human rights that actually threaten or breach international peace and security
	Can deal with situations of criminal violations of human rights by referring them to the International Criminal Court
The General Assembly	*Can* respond to situations of gross violations of human rights that are of international concern
ECOSOC	*Can* act to prevent situations of gross violations of economic, social and cultural rights
	Can respond to situations of gross violations of economic, social and cultural rights
The International Criminal Court	Tries charges of international crimes brought before it by the prosecutor of the ICC
The Human Rights Council	Promotes international cooperation for the universal protection of human rights
	Can act to prevent situations of gross violations of human rights
	Can respond urgently to situations of gross violations of human rights
The Human Rights Committee	Considers reports from states parties
	Considers individual petitions from states parties that have accepted this competence
The Committee on Economic, Social and Cultural Rights	Considers reports from states parties
	Considers individual petitions from states parties that have accepted this competence
The Committee on the Elimination of Racial Discrimination	Considers reports from states parties
	Considers petitions under Article 14
The Committee on the Elimination of Discrimination against Women	Considers reports from states parties
	Considers individual petitions from states parties that have accepted this competence

Institution	Roles
	Conducts investigations if states parties accept this competence
The Committee Against Torture (CAT)	Considers reports from states parties
Sub-Committee on the Prevention of Torture	Visits places of detention in order to prevent torture
The Committee on the Rights of the Child	Considers reports from states parties
	May make visits to states parties that have accepted this competence
	Considers individual petitions from states parties that have accepted this competence
The Committee on the Rights of all Migrant Workers and Members of their Families	Considers reports from states parties
	Convention envisages a petitions procedure that is not yet in force
The European Court of Human Rights	Considers petitions from individuals in states parties to the European Convention
The Committee on Enforced Disappearances	Considers reports from states parties
	Considers individual petitions from states parties that have accepted this competence
	May conduct confidential investigations of allegations of grave or systematic violations
The Committee on the Rights of Persons with Disabilities	Considers reports from states parties
	Considers individual petitions from within states parties that have accepted its competence
The Inter-American Commission on Human Rights	Makes periodic visits to states parties
	Considers some individual petitions from within states parties
The Inter-American Court of Human Rights	Considers cases referred to it by the Inter-American Commission or by states parties
The African Commission on Human and Peoples' Rights	Considers reports from states parties
The African Court on Human and Peoples' Rights	Considers cases referred to it

146 Protection

Table 9.2 The performance of the international protection system

	Performance
UN Security Council	**
UN General Assembly	**
ECOSOC	–
The Human Rights Council	***
The special procedures of the HRC	***
UN human rights treaty bodies	***
European Court of Human Rights	****
Inter-American Court of Human Rights	***
African Commission on Human and Peoples' Rights	**
African Court of Human Rights	–
Arab Commission on Human Rights	–
ASEAN Intergovernmental Commission on Human Rights	–
National human rights institutions worldwide	**

Notes: Five-star rating: 0 = no protection; 5 = highest protection.

Shades of protection: direct and indirect

The international protection of human rights in the contemporary world can be described as direct or indirect. Direct international protection means the intercession of an international entity either at the behest of a victim, by persons on their behalf, or by the international protecting agency to halt a violation of human rights. Examples of direct international protection are the activities of the UNHCR, the UN high commissioner for human rights, the ICRC, and the various petitions or complaints procedures such as that provided under the Optional Protocol to the ICCPR.

However, much of the protection activities undertaken in the international community may be classified as indirect protection. Among these are the creation of an international environment that is conducive to the realization of human rights; the elaboration of norms and standards; education, teaching, training, research, and the dissemination of information;[24] and the provision of advisory services and technical assistance in human rights.

The next section examines how various organizations and procedures have approached the application of direct protection.

The League of Nations: the concept of "guarantee"

Some treaties concluded after World War I entrusted the task of guaranteeing rights for minority groups to the League of Nations. The Tittoni Report, which was accepted by the Council of the League of Nations in 1920, addressed the meaning of the term guarantee:

> [I]t may be advisable at the outset to define clearly the exact meaning of the term "guarantee" of the League of Nations. It seems clear that this stipulation means, above all, that the provisions for the protection of minorities are inviolable, that is to say, they cannot be modified in the sense of violating in any way rights actually recognized, and without the approval of the majority of the Council of the League of Nations.[25]

The *International Protection of Minorities Under the League of Nations*, a report written by the UN in 1947, noted that in exercising the supervision that it assumed under the minorities treaties, the League Council had used the methods of persuasion or pressure of a purely moral or political nature to the exclusion of compulsory measures. This was due mainly to the fact that an accused state had a seat on the council if it were charged with having infringed its obligations and could use its veto to block any adverse discussion. In response to the question "Could the Council give orders or injunctions to a state which was violating the obligations assumed in respect of the treatment of minorities and lay down how it should behave?" the report answered: "It might be thought so, from reading the very general provisions on the subject ... The council could consider, discuss or publicly criticize the conduct of any State and note failures to comply with the obligations assumed."[26]

The International Labour Organization

In the UN system, the ILO has come closest to developing a quasi-judicial protection system. In brief, the ILO approach to protection encompasses prescription of standards on matters within its competence; supervisory procedures to oversee the application of those standards; quasi-judicial complaints procedures to deal with allegations of human rights violations; and measures of fact finding, mediation, conciliation, direct contacts, and good offices.

ILO organs have repeatedly insisted on the strictest compliance with the terms of international labor conventions by states, irrespective of their political, economic or social systems, or of their level of economic development. International labor organs have also insisted that the protection provided for by international labor conventions is international protection. This principle was admirably brought out by an ILO commission of inquiry in 1956. Responding to Greece's contention that it had proclaimed a state of emergency in accordance with its national law and that the government was the sole judge of the need to proclaim a state of emergency, the commission stated:

> The Commission understands perfectly the argument that conformity with the constitution would make the Government in the eyes of Greek Law the sole judge of the need to proclaim a state of emergency. But it has not that effect in international law. The Commission takes the view that it is an accepted principle of international law that a State cannot rely on the terms of its national law, or otherwise invoke the concept of national sovereignty, to justify non-performance of an international obligation. Any doubt concerning the extent of such obligations must be determined by exclusive reference to the relevant principles of international law, whether made express by the parties to a treaty or derived from another source of international law, in particular, international custom and general principles of law.

The commission added:

> All the main legal systems accept in some form the principle that pleas of justification on grounds such as self-defense are subject to legal review. If a plea of emergency is to be treated in international law as a legal concept there similarly has to be appraisal by an impartial authority at the international level. It is for this reason that international tribunals and supervisory organs, when seized of such a plea, have invariably made an independent determination of whether the circumstances justified the claim, and have not allowed the State concerned to be the sole judge of the issue.[27]

The International Committee of the Red Cross

During the 1970s, the ICRC undertook a comprehensive review of its role and activities. One of the background papers prepared for that review described Red Cross protection as embracing three categories of activities to protect individuals in conflicts: helping to develop international humanitarian law; helping to apply that law; and engaging in ad hoc diplomacy on the basis of humanitarian motivation.[28]

An ICRC committee that discussed the results of this in-depth review noted that the final report "does not define the meaning of 'protection' but it obviously refers to the protection of victims of armed conflicts or internal disorders who are in the hands of adverse authority or of an authority which does not afford them appropriate guarantees." A footnote to this passage added:

> Like the Report, the Geneva Conventions, and the Red Cross Statutes contain no definition of "protection," undoubtedly because it is a concept that is easily understood. Yet if a definition were required one might say that in the Red Cross *action "to protect" implies preserving victims of conflicts who are in the hands of an adverse authority from the dangers, sufferings and abuses of power to which they may be exposed, defending them and giving them support*. In a broader context, one might say that "protection" also includes developing, publicizing and ensuring application and respect for international humanitarian law.[29]

More recently, the ICRC published "Strengthening Protection in War," which summarized the reflections of four workshops of humanitarian scholars and humanitarian organizations. According to workshop participants, the concept of protection encompasses:

> ... all activities aimed at ensuring full respect for the rights of the individual in accordance with the letter and the spirit of the relevant bodies of law, i.e. human rights law, international humanitarian law and refugee law. Human rights and humanitarian organizations must conduct these activities in an impartial manner (not on the basis of race, national or ethnic origin, language or gender).[30]

The participants considered a protection activity to be any activity that prevents or puts a stop to a specific pattern of abuse and/or alleviates its immediate effects; restores people's dignity and ensures adequate living conditions through reparation, restitution, and rehabilitation; and fosters an environment conducive to respect for the rights of individuals in accordance with the relevant bodies of law. They recognized that "no single organization is able to meet the sheer diversity of protection needs as this requires a wide array of skills and means. It is therefore natural that various organizations operate in the same arena and often cater to the same beneficiaries, regardless of the situation."[31]

150 *Protection*

In 2003, another ICRC report, "International Humanitarian Law and the Challenges of Contemporary Armed Conflicts," stated:

> First, the ICRC believes ... that the four Geneva Conventions and their Additional Protocols, as well as the range of other international IHL [international humanitarian law] treaties and the norms of customary law provide a bedrock of principles and rules that must continue to guide the conduct of hostilities and the treatment of persons who have fallen into the hands of a party to an armed conflict. Second ... some of the dilemmas that the international community grappled with decades ago were, in general, satisfactorily resolved by means of IHL development. Today, the primary challenge in these areas is to either ensure clarification or further elaboration of the rules. Thirdly, international opinion—both governmental and expert, as well as public opinion—remains largely divided on how to deal with new forms of violence, primarily acts of transnational terrorism.[32]

Protecting powers under the Geneva Conventions

Georges Abi-Saab has classified the functions of protecting powers under the Geneva Conventions into the following categories:

1 Liaison functions between the detaining or occupying power, the protected persons and the power of origin. These include not only the communication of information requests or clarifications, but also exercising its good offices in cases of disagreement on the interpretation or application of the conventions or for the conclusion of special agreements.
2 Relief and assistance activities in favor of protected persons.
3 Scrutiny of the implementation of the convention by the detaining or occupying power. This function consists of supervising the treatment of the protected persons by the detaining power to make sure that it conforms with their rights under the conventions. More specifically, this implies having access to protected persons (the right to visit occupied territories, prisoners of war and internment camps, etc.) and the power to probe and investigate their conditions and the treatment they receive; it implies also having access to the occupying or detaining authorities in order to make presentations, to lodge complaints for violations of the conventions and to demand their rectification; and in general the right of assisting protected persons to obtain from the detaining power the

treatment which is guaranteed for them by the conventions. This is "protection" *sensu stricto*, although the term is used *sensu lato* to cover all of these functions.[33]

The United Nations

At the San Francisco Conference in 1945, draft proposals on human rights were considered by two committees. Committee I/1 adopted the sponsoring powers' proposal to promote and encourage respect for human rights, with only minor drafting changes. In its discussion, however, several important issues were raised. Some delegations commented on the meaning of the terms promotion and protection, and it was suggested that to promote human rights be replaced by stronger expressions, such as to assure or to protect human rights. However, subcommittee I/1/A held that "assuring or protecting such fundamental rights is primarily the concern of each state. If, however, such rights and freedoms were grievously outraged so as to create conditions which threaten peace or to obstruct the application of provisions of the Charter, then they cease to be the sole concern of each State."[34]

Committee II/3 incorporated an Australian proposal into Article 55 of the charter, which stated that the organization should not only promote respect for human rights but also the observance of human rights. When this provision was later discussed, it was explained that the committee intended "to reinforce 'respect,' which has the connotation of passive acceptance, by 'observance' which is intended to imply active implementation." It was added that "'observance' implies an obligation to change the laws of one's own country to implement this article, whereas 'respect' merely means respecting the laws of other countries in this regard."[35]

International organizations are growing institutions, and their competences and functions evolve through practice over time.[36] In 1980, the GA noted the "growing awareness of the international community of the need to ensure effective promotion and protection of human rights,"[37] and affirmed "that the efforts of the United Nations and its member states to promote and to protect civil and political rights, as well as economic, social and cultural rights, should continue."[38]

There can be little doubt that the UN is competent to act for the protection of human rights, particularly in situations where there is a consistent pattern of gross violations of human rights and fundamental freedoms. UN efforts to halt such violations are clear proof of this.

On 4 March 1966, in resolution 1102 (XL), ECOSOC invited the CHR to consider the question of the violation of human rights and fundamental freedoms as a matter of importance and urgency, and to submit to the council its recommendations on measures to halt such violations. In response to this resolution, the CHR adopted resolution 2 (XXII) of 25 March 1966, which informed ECOSOC that it would be necessary for the commission to consider fully the means by which it may be more "fully informed" of violations of human rights with a view to devising recommendations for measures to halt them. In resolution 1164 (LXI) the next year, the council welcomed the commission's decision to consider its tasks and functions and its role in relation to human rights violations, and concurred with the commission's view that it would be necessary for the commission to consider the means by which it might be kept more fully informed of violations of human rights, with a view to devising recommendations for measures to stop to these violations.

On ECOSOC's recommendation, made in the same year, the GA adopted resolution 2144 (XXI) of 26 October 1966, which invited ECOSOC and the CHR to give urgent consideration to ways and means of "improving the capacity of the United Nations" to put a stop to human rights violations.

Stemming from council resolutions 1102 and 1164 and GA resolution 2144, the CHR interpreted its competence as including "the power to recommend and adopt general and specific measures to deal with violations of human rights."[39] In the preamble to its resolution 1235 (XLII) and in paragraph 1, ECOSOC noted CHR resolution 8 (XXIII) and also:

> welcomed the decision of the Commission on Human Rights to give annual consideration to the item entitled "Question of the violation of human rights and fundamental freedoms, including policies of racial discrimination and segregation and of apartheid in all countries, with particular reference to colonial and other dependent countries and territories ..."

Paragraph 2 of the council's resolution authorized the commission to examine information relevant to gross violations of human rights and make a thorough study of situations that reveal a consistent pattern of violations of human rights.

From 1966 until its last session in 2005, the commission publicly considered the question of violations of human rights each year. During the annual debates, allegations of violations of human rights have been made against various countries. Situations of gross violations of human rights were also considered in the GA, the UNSC,

ECOSOC, and other organs. Moreover, many situations have been considered confidentially within the procedure established by council resolution 1503 (XLVIII). Indeed, in 1979, the GA, "conscious of the responsibility of the United Nations ... in dealing with situations of mass and flagrant violations of human rights," reaffirmed "that mass and flagrant violations of human rights are of special concern to the United Nations," and urged "the appropriate United Nations bodies, within their mandates, particularly the Commission on Human Rights, to take timely and effective action in existing and future cases of mass and flagrant violations of human rights." The assembly stressed "the important role that the Secretary-General can play in situations of mass and flagrant violations of human rights."[40]

The UN high commissioner for human rights has a mandate from the GA to promote and protect human rights. High commissioners have issued public statements about situations of concern to them, established investigations into some such situations, and have sought to exercise their good offices to protect human rights where, in their judgment, this might be useful.[41]

The secretary-general sometimes also acts to protect human rights. The secretary-general may speak out on occasion, establish investigations, or use good offices where considered appropriate.[42]

UNHCR[43]

Article 8 of the Statute of the Office of the United Nations High Commissioner for Refugees[44] defines that office's protection functions as follows:

> The High Commissioner shall provide for the protection of refugees falling under the competence of his Office by: (a) Promoting the conclusion and ratification of international conventions for the protection of refugees, supervising their application and proposing amendments thereto; (b) Promoting through special agreements with Governments the execution of any measures calculated to improve the situation of refugees and to reduce the number requiring protection; (c) Assisting governmental and private efforts to promote voluntary repatriation or assimilation within new national communities; (d) Promoting the admission of refugees, not excluding those in the most destitute categories, to the territories of States; (e) Endeavouring to obtain permission for refugees to transfer their assets and especially those necessary for their resettlement; (f) Obtaining from Governments information

concerning the number and conditions of refugees in their territories and the laws and regulations concerning them; (g) Keeping in close touch with the Governments and inter-governmental organizations concerned; (h) Establishing contact in such manner as he may think best with private organizations dealing with refugee questions; (i) Facilitating the co-ordination of the efforts of private organizations concerned with the welfare of refugees.

Article 9 adds that the "High Commissioner shall engage in such additional activities, including repatriation and resettlement, as the General Assembly may determine, within the limits of the resources placed at his disposal."

The Conclusions on the International Protection of Refugees, adopted by the executive committee of the UNHCR program, reaffirmed "the fundamental importance of the Statute of the Office of the United Nations High Commissioner for Refugees as a basis for the international protection function of the High Commissioner."[45] The "fundamental importance of international protection" has been reiterated[46] and the Executive Committee has also "reaffirmed the need to intensify its role in the field of protection."[47]

The UNHCR Handbook for Emergencies defines the aim of international protection as being to ensure that treatment of refugees is in accordance with internationally accepted basic standards, especially the principle of *non-refoulement*, according to which refugees may not be forcibly returned to a country where they have reason to fear persecution. Moreover, before this aim can be realized, asylum seekers must be admitted to the state where they are seeking refuge, without any discrimination as to race, religion, nationality, political opinion or physical incapacity. Therefore:

> When an influx of persons who may be of concern to UNHCR occurs, the overriding priority is to ensure that at least temporary asylum is granted to them. An on-the-spot presence and quick action are generally crucial to the attainment of United Nations HCR's objectives particularly where there is danger of refoulement or abuses of human rights such as arbitrary detention or mistreatment.

UNHCR does not, as a principle, favor granting temporary asylum or refuge, preferring rather to emphasize the need to grant durable asylum. However, this may not be immediately possible, and representatives and field officers may decide that, in the circumstances, only temporary asylum should be requested, without prejudice to subsequent efforts to obtain asylum.[48]

In 2002, the UNHCR published an *Agenda for Protection*, which had six goals: strengthening implementation of the 1951 Convention and 1967 Protocol; protecting refugees within broader migration movements; sharing burdens and responsibilities more equitably and building capacities to receive and protect refugees; addressing security-related concerns more effectively; redoubling the search for durable solutions; and meeting the protection needs of refugee women and children.[49]

The United Nations Human Rights Council

In its resolution establishing the HRC, the GA affirmed the need for all states to continue international efforts to enhance dialogue and broaden understanding among civilizations, cultures, and religions. It recognized that the promotion and protection of human rights should be based on the principles of cooperation and dialogue, and aimed at strengthening the member states' capacity to comply with their human rights obligations.

The core mandate given to the HRC was to promote universal respect for the protection of all human rights and fundamental freedoms for all without distinction of any kind. The council should address situations of violations of human rights, including gross and systematic violations, and make recommendations. Further, according to the GA, the work of the council should be guided by the principles of universality, impartiality, objectivity and non-selectivity, constructive international dialogue and cooperation with a view to enhanced promotion and protection of human rights.

The council is further mandated to promote human rights education and learning, as well as advisory services, technical assistance and capacity building to be provided in consultation and with the consent of the member states concerned; to serve as a forum for dialogue on thematic issues; to make recommendations to the GA for the further development of international law in the field of human rights; to promote the full implementation of human rights obligations undertaken by states and the follow-up of the goals and commitments related to the promotion and protection of human rights emanating from UN conferences and summits; to contribute, through dialogue and cooperation, to the prevention of human rights violations and respond promptly to human rights emergencies; to work in close cooperation in the field of human rights with governments, regional organizations, national human rights institutions, and civil society; to make recommendations with regard to the promotion and protection of human rights; and to undertake a universal periodic review of the fulfillment by each state of its human rights obligations and commitments.

So far, the HRC has emphasized cooperation and dialogue and has been selective in taking action on situations of gross violations of human rights. NGOs have expressed great concern about this selectivity (see Table 9.2).

Protection of civilians in armed conflict: UN Aide Memoire

The UN Aide Memoire on the Protection of Civilians in Armed Conflict[50] set out an agenda for protecting civilians, placing emphasis on prioritizing and supporting the immediate protection needs of displaced persons and civilians in host communities through measures to enhance security for displaced persons, measures to enhance security for civilians who remain in their communities, and for host communities living in or around areas where refugees or internally displaced persons take shelter.

The Aide Memoire called for facilitation of safe and unimpeded access to vulnerable populations as the fundamental prerequisite for humanitarian assistance and protection through appropriate security arrangements, engagement in sustained dialogue with all parties to the armed conflict, facilitation of the delivery of humanitarian assistance, compliance with obligations under relevant international humanitarian, human rights and refugee law, and counter-terrorism measures in full compliance with all obligations under international law, in particular international human rights, refugee and humanitarian law.

It urged strengthening the capacity of local police and judicial systems to protect civilians and enforce law and order through deployment of qualified and well-trained international civilian police, technical assistance for local police, judiciary and penitentiaries, reconstruction and rehabilitation of institutional infrastructure, and mechanisms for monitoring and reporting alleged violations of humanitarian, human rights, and criminal law.

It stressed the importance of addressing the specific needs of women for assistance and protection through measures to protect them from gender-based discrimination and violence, rape, and other forms of sexual violence; implementation of measures to report and prevent sexual abuse and exploitation of civilians by humanitarian workers and peacekeepers; mainstreaming of gender perspective, including the integration of gender advisors in peace operations. It also emphasized the need to address the specific needs of children by preventing or stemming the recruitment of child soldiers; initiatives to secure access to war-affected children; negotiated release of children abducted in situations of armed conflict; effective measures to disarm, demobilize, reintegrate and rehabilitate children recruited or used in hostilities; specific provisions for the protection of children (including, where appropriate, the integration of child protection advisors in peace operations); implementation of measures for reporting on and prevention of sexual abuse and exploitation of civilians by humanitarian workers and peacekeepers; family reunification of separated children; and monitoring and reporting on the situation of children.

Finally, the Aide Memoire called for putting an end to impunity for those responsible for serious violations of international humanitarian, human rights, and criminal law through establishing and using effective arrangements to investigate and prosecute serious violations of humanitarian and criminal law; exclusion of genocide, crimes against humanity and war crimes from amnesty provisions; and referral of situations to international courts and tribunals.

Protection of children in armed conflicts

A report of the secretary-general submitted to the GA in 2004 provided a comprehensive assessment of the UN system response to children affected by armed conflict.[51] The report grouped recommendations for improving and sustaining efforts on children and armed conflict (CAAC) into four categories, which constitute the medium-term strategic priorities for the UN system to improve its response to children affected by armed conflict: 1) continued vigorous advocacy for children affected by armed conflict; 2) an effective and credible monitoring and reporting system on child rights violations; 3) enhanced mainstreaming of CAAC issues across the UN system; and 4) improved coordination of CAAC issues across the UN system.[52]

On advocacy, the report concluded that there was continuing need for a special representative of the secretary-general (SRSG)-CAAC as an independent advocate reporting directly to the secretary-general, and recommended the introduction of appropriate mechanisms to measure progress against benchmarks established each year. The mandated functions of the SRSG-CAAC should focus on the following: integrating children's rights and concerns into the UN peace and security, humanitarian and development agendas throughout all phases of conflict prevention, peace-building, peace-making, and peacekeeping activities; unblocking political impasses to secure commitments from political actors on child protection on the national and regional levels and ensuring adequate follow-up to these commitments; and ensuring

158 *Protection*

the inclusion of children and armed conflict concerns in all relevant reports submitted to the UNSC by the secretary-general. It called for reporting child rights violations to relevant bodies, such as the secretary-general, the UNSC, governments, and regional mechanisms, and advocating the inclusion of appropriate measures in resolutions, such as sanctions, for actors violating CAAC norms and standards. It called for a collaborative process to produce the secretary-general's annual report to the UNSC on CAAC. The report should focus on progress in applying CAAC norms and standards, including reporting on child rights violations in situations of conflict; suggestions for measures to ensure compliance with norms and standards; and high-level analysis of CAAC trends with recommendations on improvements to the UN system response, particularly with suggestions on how UN peace and security mechanisms could respond better to CAAC and progress on developing a monitoring and reporting system for child rights violations.

The document recommended producing an annual report to the GA and the CHR, using inputs from key UN actors. The report should include a high-level analytical assessment of CAAC in all conflict situations (i.e. not just countries on the UNSC's agenda); progress in the UN system's advocacy, mainstreaming and coordination efforts on CAAC issues; and prioritizing next steps for the UN system in improving its response to CAAC.

The document recommended providing proactive advocacy support to the secretary-general, heads of agencies, special representatives, resident coordinators/humanitarian coordinators (RCs/HCs), and other high-level UN officials, primarily through inter-agency committees such as the Executive Committee on Humanitarian Affairs (ECHA), the Executive Committee on Peace and Security (ECPS), the Senior Management Group, and annual meetings of RCs and HCs; co-chairing a coordination mechanism at the UN on children affected by armed conflict; and maintaining a high-profile public awareness of CAAC issues as required to achieve political advocacy objectives, including cooperation with the Department of Public Information.[53]

The report further urged that the advocacy role of the ERC and the High Commissioner for Human Rights should also be systematically resorted to in support of CAAC concerns and issues.[54]

The report urged that a robust monitoring and reporting system for child rights violations in conflict situations should be developed in three distinct stages: developing an accepted, standardized and practical methodology to identify, document, and verify child rights violations; setting up and coordinating networks of actors to document child rights concerns, and establishing responsibilities and procedures for disseminating and leveraging the information.[55]

Protection of women

In resolution 1325 (2000), the UNSC called on all parties to armed conflict to respect international law applicable to the rights and protection of women and girls, especially as civilians, in particular the obligations applicable under the Geneva Conventions of 1949 and the Additional Protocols of 1977, the Refugee Convention of 1951 and the Protocol of 1967, the Convention on Elimination of All Forms of Discrimination against Women of 1979 and the Optional Protocol of 1999, and the UN Convention on the Rights of the Child of 1989 and the two Optional Protocols of 25 May 2000, and to bear in mind the relevant provisions of the Rome Statute of the ICC (paragraph 9). The council further called on all parties to armed conflict to take special measures to protect women and girls from gender-based violence, particularly rape and other forms of sexual abuse, and all other forms of violence in situations of armed conflict (paragraph 10).

Protection of internally displaced persons

The Guiding Principles on Internal Displacement provide that national authorities have the primary duty and responsibility to provide protection and humanitarian assistance to internally displaced persons within their jurisdiction. Certain internally displaced persons, such as children, especially unaccompanied minors, expectant mothers, mothers with young children, female heads of household, persons with disabilities, and elderly persons, are entitled to protection and assistance required by their condition and to treatment that takes account of their special needs.

All authorities and international actors should respect and ensure respect for their obligations under international law, including human rights and humanitarian law, to prevent and avoid conditions that might lead to displacement of persons. In addition to general principles, the principles contain guidance on protection from displacement (prevention), protection during displacement, humanitarian assistance, and principles relating to return, resettlement, and reintegration.

UN field operations and human rights: The Brahimi Report[56]

The Brahimi Report's wide-ranging recommendations advocated:

160   *Protection*

- the essential importance of the UN system adhering to and promoting international human rights instruments and standards and international humanitarian law in all aspects of its peace and security activities;
- improving respect for human rights through the monitoring, education, and investigation of past and existing abuses;
- providing technical assistance for democratic development;
- promoting conflict resolution and reconciliation techniques;
- addressing variables that affect peace implementation such as issues of ethnicity or religion or gross violations of human rights;
- addressing past violations of human rights; and
- working for respect of minority rights: "Long-term preventive strategies ... must ... work to promote human rights, to protect minority rights and to institute political arrangements in which all groups are represented."

Further, the report called for:

- the building of a culture of respect for human rights;
- observing international standards for democratic policing and human rights;
- integrating human rights specialists in peace-building missions;
- upholding the rule of law and respect for human rights through teamwork on the part of judicial, penal, human rights and policing experts;
- recognition of the critical role of the human rights components of a peace operation for effective peace building;
- training military, police and other civilian personnel on human rights issues and on the relevant provisions of international humanitarian law;
- a doctrinal shift in the use of civilian police, other rule of law elements and human rights experts in complex peace operations to reflect an increased focus on strengthening rule of law institutions and improving respect for human rights in a post-conflict environment;
- human rights monitoring;
- meeting threshold conditions in the implementation of ceasefire or peace agreements, such as consistency with international human rights standards; and
- rebuilding civil society and promoting respect for human rights in places where grievance is widespread, keeping in mind international conventions and declarations relating to human rights.

Universal criminal jurisdiction

The Princeton Principles on Universal Jurisdiction (2001) offered a recapitulation of international law that is relevant to the issue of impunity. Impunity has been identified as a key issue if successful prevention of violations of international human rights and humanitarian law is to be achieved. According to the principles:

> Universal jurisdiction may be exercised by a competent and ordinary judicial body of any state in order to try a person accused of committing serious crimes under international law, provided the person is present before such judicial body.[57]

Serious crimes under international law include: (1) piracy; (2) slavery; (3) war crimes; (4) crimes against peace; (5) crimes against humanity; (6) genocide; and (7) torture.[58]

Conclusion

The protection idea is crucial to the survival of the human rights movement. The idea that one should come to the aid of those whose rights are at risk or are being violated is at the heart of the human rights movement. Protection is a noble idea—but not an easy one to implement. Protection challenges the good faith and the efficiency of governments and of the international community. The massive violations of human rights that continue to take place in numerous parts of the world tell us that protection is largely illusory for millions of people worldwide. The international community must renew its resolve to strengthen human rights protection. This requires the development of strong national protection arrangements inside each country and efficient protection arrangements regionally and internationally. The GA's endorsement of the responsibility to protect must be given concrete application, particularly by the UNSC and the HRC. The challenges of protection remain daunting in the contemporary world.

Notes

1 Human Rights Watch, *World Report* (New York: HRW, 2007), 2.
2 See generally, Katarina Tomasevski, *Responding to Human Rights Violations 1946–1999* (The Hague, the Netherlands: Martinus Nijhoff Publishers, 2000).
3 *ICJ Reports*, 1955, 4.
4 *ICJ Reports*, 1949, 174.

162 *Protection*

5 *Barcelona Traction Light and Power Co. Ltd*, judgment of the ICJ, 5 February 1970, *ICJ Reports* (1970): 1 (emphasis added).
6 Herbert J. Muller, *Freedom in the Ancient World* (London: Secker and Warburg, 1962), 58–59. See also James Shotwell, *The Long Way to Freedom* (New York: Columbia University Press, 1960).
7 Emmanuel Bello, *African Customary Humanitarian Law* (Geneva, Switzerland: Oyez Publishing/The Red Cross, 1980), 29.
8 Charles H. Alexandrowicz, "The Afro-Asian World and the Law of Nations (Historical Aspects)," *Recueil des Cours de l'Académie de Droit International* 123, no. 1 (1968): 117–214.
9 For a concise and useful history of the institution of protecting power, see Georges Abi-Saab, "The Implementation of Humanitarian Law," in *The New Humanitarian Law of Armed Conflict*, ed. Antonio Cassese (The Hague, the Netherlands: Martinus Nijhoff, 1979), 310–48, at 311–18.
10 See Egon Schwelb, "Human Rights," in *Encyclopaedia Britannica*, vol. 8 (1974), 1183–89.
11 Mavrommatis Palestine Concessions case, *PCIJ*, series A, no. 2 (1924): 12.
12 Francisco V. Garcia-Amador, "Report on State Responsibility," *Yearbook of the International Law Commission II* (1956): 173–231.
13 Egon Schwelb, "The International Court of Justice and the Human Rights Clauses of the Charter," *American Journal of International Law* 66 (1972): 337–51.
14 Karel Vasak, "Distinguishing Criteria of Institutions," in *The International Dimensions of Human Rights*, ed. Karel Vasak (Paris: UNESCO, 1983), 215–16.
15 Atle Grahl-Madsen, *The Status of Refugees in International Law* (Leiden, the Netherlands: A.W. Sijthoff, 1966), 381.
16 Asbjørn Eide, "The New Humanitarian Law in Non-International Armed Conflict," in *The New Humanitarian Law of Armed Conflict*, ed. Antonio Cassese (The Hague, the Netherlands: Martinus Nijhoff, 1979), 277–309.
17 David P. Forsythe, *Humanitarian Politics: The International Committee of the Red Cross* (Baltimore, Md.: Johns Hopkins University Press, 1977), 28–32.
18 International Commission on Intervention and State Sovereignty (Ottawa, Canada), *The Responsibility to Protect*, December 2001. See also *The Responsibility to Protect: Research, Bibliography, Background*, December 2001.
19 See Linos-Alexandre Sicilianos, ed., *The Prevention of Human Rights Violations* (The Hague, the Netherlands: Martinus Nijhoff, 2001).
20 See Bertrand G. Ramcharan, *Humanitarian Good Offices in International Law* (The Hague, the Netherlands: Martinus Nijhoff, 1983).
21 Theodoor C. van Boven, *People Matter* (Amsterdam, the Netherlands: Meulenhoff, 1982), 73.
22 A United Nations Fund for Victims of Torture has existed since 1991.
23 See Jared Genser and Bruno Stagno Ugarte, eds, *The United Nations Security Council in the Age of Human Rights* (Cambridge: Cambridge University Press, 2014).
24 On this, see the Report of the ILA Sub-Committee on the International Protection of Human Rights by the Mobilisation of Public Opinion, submitted to the ILA Conference in 1976.
25 League of Nations document C.8M.5.1931.

26 E/CN.4/Sub.2/6, 8–9. See generally, "International Protection of Minority Rights: The League of Nations System and Post-World War II Arrangements," in Louis B. Sohn and Thomas Buergenthal, *International Protection of Human Rights* (Indianapolis and New York: Bobbs-Merrill Company, 1973), 213–336. See also Francesco Capotorti, *Study on the Rights of Persons Belonging to Ethnic, Religious and Linguistic Minorities* (New York: United Nations, 1979); and E/CN.4/Sub.2384/Rev.1.
27 Report of the Commission Appointed under Article 26 of the Constitution of the ILO to Examine the Complaints Concerning the Observance by Greece of the Freedom of Association and Protection of the Right to Organise Convention, 1948 (no. 87), and of the Right to Organise and Collective Bargaining Convention, 1949 (no. 98), made by a number of delegates to the 52nd session of the International Labour Conference. ILO, *Official Bulletin*, Special Supplement, LIV, no. 2 (1971): 25–26, paras 102–12.
28 David Forsythe, *Present Role of the Red Cross in Protection*, Background Paper no. 1 of the Joint Committee for the Reappraisal of the Role of the Red Cross (1975), 9.
29 *The ICRC, the League and the Tansley Report* (Geneva, Switzerland: ICRC, 1977), 18 and note 1 (emphasis added).
30 ICRC, *Strengthening Protection in War* (Geneva, Switzerland: ICRC, 2001), 20–21.
31 ICRC, *Strengthening Protection in War*, 28.
32 ICRC, "International Humanitarian Law and the Challenges of Contemporary Armed Conflicts," 28th International Conference of the Red Cross and Red Crescent in December 2003, 5–6.
33 Georges Abi-Saab, "The Implementation of Humanitarian Law," in Antonio Cassese, ed., *The New Humanitarian Law of Armed Conflict* (The Hague, the Netherlands: Martinus Nijhoff, 1979), 317–18.
34 Sohn and Buergenthal, *International Protection of Human Rights*, 510–11.
35 Sohn and Buergenthal, *International Protection of Human Rights*, 510–11.
36 "Throughout its history, the development of international law has been influenced by the requirements of international life." International Court of Justice, "Reparations for Injuries Suffered in the Service of the United Nations, 11 April 1949," *ICJ Reports* (1949): 174.
37 General Assembly resolution 35/176.
38 General Assembly resolution 35/174, para. 4. See similarly GA resolution 41/131, paras 12–14.
39 CHR resolution XXIII, para. 1.
40 General Assembly resolution 34/175.
41 See Bertrand G. Ramcharan, *A UN High Commissioner in Defence of Human Rights* (The Hague, the Netherlands: Martinus Nijhoff, 2005).
42 See Bertrand G. Ramcharan, *Humanitarian Good Offices: The Good Offices of the UN Secretary-General in the Field of Human Rights* (Dordrecht, the Netherlands: Martinus Nijhoff, 1983).
43 See Niklaus Steiner, Mark Gibney, and Gil Loescher, *Problems of Protection: The UNHCR, Refugees, and Human Rights* (New York and London: Routledge, 2003); and also Gil Loescher, *The UNHCR and World Politics: A Perilous Path* (Oxford: Oxford University Press, 2001).
44 General Assembly resolution 428 (V) of 14 December 1950, Annex.

164 *Protection*

45 See Conclusions on the International Protection of Refugees, UNHCR, 1980, no. 4 (XXVIII).
46 Conclusions on the International Protection of Refugees, Conclusion no. 2 (XXVII).
47 Conclusions on the International Protection of Refugees, Conclusion no. 2 (XXVII).
48 UNHCR, *Handbook for Emergencies* (1982), 10.
49 UNHCR, *Agenda for Protection* (2002), 29.
50 UNSC, "Statement by the President of the Security Council," 15 December 2003, S/PRST/2003/27.
51 UN General Assembly, "Comprehensive Assessment of the United Nations System Response to Children Affected by Armed Conflict," Report of the Secretary-General, 3 September 2004, A/59/331.
52 A/59/331, para. 46.
53 A/59/331, para. 49.
54 A/59/331, para. 51.
55 A/59/331, para. 52.
56 *Report of the Panel on United Nations Peace Operations*, A/55/305-S/2000/809 (UN General Assembly and Security Council document), 21 August 2000. See generally, William Durch, Victoria Holt, Caroline Earle, and Moira Shanahan, *The Brahimi Report and the Future of UN Peace Operations* (Washington, DC: The Henry L. Stimson Center, 2003).
57 *The Princeton Principles on Universal Jurisdiction* (Princeton, N.J.: LAPA, 2001), principle 1(2).
58 *The Princeton Principles on Universal Jurisdiction*, principle 2(1).

10 Justice, remedy, and reparation

- **Justice**
- **Remedy and reparation**
- **Conclusion**

> The World Conference on Human Rights expresses grave concern about continuing human rights violations in all parts of the world in disregard of standards as contained in international human rights instruments and international humanitarian law and about the lack of sufficient and effective remedies for the victims.
> (Vienna Declaration, paragraph 29)

For decades, Chile was a jewel of democracy in Latin America. Then, in 1973, General Augusto Pinochet overthrew the democratically elected government of President Salvador Allende and proceeded to imprison, kill, torture, and "disappear" people by the thousands.[1] While he ruled, General Pinochet had powerful backers.[2] Even after he left office, the law could not reach him.

Then a Spanish prosecutor, imbued with contemporary human rights ideas, sought to extradite him to Spain for prosecution in connection with the deaths of Spanish nationals. After Pinochet went to the United Kingdom for medical treatment, the Spaniards sought his extradition to Spain. The case reached the highest court in England, the House of Lords, which made important pronouncements on contemporary human rights ideas. However, General Pinochet was allowed to return to Chile on a technicality. Chilean prosecutors then sought to bring Pinochet to trial, but he evaded this on grounds of ill health and ended his years fighting off prosecution in his own country. The principle of justice had caught up with him—just as it did with Slobodan Milosevic and Charles Taylor.

The idea of justice is similarly at the heart of two major international campaigns currently underway: the campaign of the descendants of African slaves to be compensated for the crimes perpetrated against their ancestors, and the campaign of indigenous peoples for justice against genocides that were perpetrated against their ancestors.[3]

One would think it a simple and compelling idea—that those who have suffered gross violations of human rights are entitled to justice in their own countries if available, or in the international community if not.[4] However, often people do not receive justice, remedy, or reparation. The World Conference on Human Rights bemoaned this fact, as could be seen in the epigraph that opens this chapter. The human rights movement is swimming against strong currents of barbarism and bad governance, yet it tries to lay the foundations for justice, remedy, and reparation. This final chapter discusses three ideas that have been at the heart of the international human rights movement since the UN was established, but which have only been given limited practical expression worldwide thus far. The first two ideas, closely related to justice and remedy, are that victims of human rights violations are entitled to a remedy and to redress, and that victims of gross violations of human rights are entitled to have those responsible brought to justice. It is only recently, since the international criminal tribunals and the ICC were established, that these ideas have been given some practical, albeit limited, application.

The third idea—compensation or reparation for violations of human rights or for gross violations—is implicit in earlier ideas of justice and remedy. It is only recently that it has been explicitly elaborated in the international community with the GA's adoption of a set of guidelines on this topic in 2006.

The Second American Restatement of the Foreign Relations Law of the United States, as was discussed in an earlier chapter, is considered an authoritative summary of contemporary international law on human rights because of the high quality and objectivity of the experts who drafted it. It provides a succinct statement of the law on remedies in the following terms:

- a state party to an international human rights agreement has the remedies generally available for violation of an international agreement, as well as any special remedies provided by the agreement, or against any other state party violating the agreement;
- any state may pursue international remedies against any other state for violating the customary international law of human rights; and

- an individual victim of a violation of a human rights agreement may pursue any remedy provided by that agreement or by other applicable international agreements.[5]

Since this document was issued in 1987, the law has evolved and crystallized further, and it is now possible to offer the following additional propositions:

- a victim of a human rights violation is entitled to redress and, where called for, reparation in accordance with the international law of human rights and human rights treaties;
- the forms of redress vary depending on the facts of the case and as considered just in the eyes of the impartial decision maker;
- the reparation or compensation varies depending on the facts of the case and as considered just in the eyes of the impartial decision maker;
- those responsible for international crimes, such as genocide, ethnic cleansing, war crimes, crimes against humanity, and torture, are subject to international jurisdiction. If not tried objectively and seriously in a national court of their home country, the responsible individuals may be brought to justice before the courts of any other country or before the ICC, where its jurisdiction is applicable;
- in situations where gross violations of human rights have occurred, the victims and their families are entitled to a serious investigation to ascertain and record what occurred, identify those responsible, and indicate paths of reconciliation or justice; and
- the people of each country must decide freely which path they wish to follow to achieve reconciliation or justice.

The following pages examine justice, remedy, and reparation more closely.

Justice

Discussing justice, liberty, and equality, the philosopher Mortimer Adler argued for the sovereignty of justice:

> [W]e must note the sovereignty of justice. It regulates our thinking about liberty and equality. Without its guidance, certain errors are unavoidable and certain problems insoluble. [J]ustice is the supreme value, a greater good than either liberty or equality, and

one that must be appealed to for the rectification of errors with regard to liberty and equality.[6]

He continued:

> Only justice is an unlimited good ... One can want too much liberty and too much equality—more than is good for us to have in relation to our fellowmen, and more than we have any right to. Not so with justice. No society can be too just; no individual can act more justly than is good for him or his fellowmen.[7]

Those who have suffered gross violations of human rights are entitled to justice. In the international human rights movement, there is growing emphasis that victims of gross violations and/or their families have the right to a process that establishes the facts of what took place and draws lessons to prevent similar occurrences in the future. This is sometimes given the label of transitional justice.

According to the organization Transitional Justice, the major approaches to transitional justice include:

- domestic, hybrid, and international prosecutions of perpetrators of human rights abuse;
- determining the full extent and nature of past abuses through truth-telling initiatives, including national and international commissions;
- providing reparations to victims of human rights violations, including compensatory, restitutionary, rehabilitation, and symbolic reparations;
- institutional reform, including the vetting[8] of abusive, corrupt, or incompetent officials from the police and security services, the military, and other public institutions, including the judiciary;
- promoting reconciliation within divided communities, including working with victims on traditional justice mechanisms and forging social reconstruction;
- constructing memorials and museums to preserve the memory of the past; and
- taking into account gendered patterns of abuse to enhance justice for female victims.[9]

The prosecution and trial of those accused of genocide, ethnic cleansing, crimes against humanity, war crimes, and torture are considered essential to prevent such acts in the future. International law prohibits amnesties for such international crimes, and tribunals such as those established to deal with crimes in Cambodia, Rwanda, Sierra Leone, and the former Yugoslavia are adding important new practice and jurisprudence in the fight against criminal violations of human rights.

Since the ICC was established, the court's prosecutor has initiated prosecutions against persons accused of international crimes in Darfur, Sudan, the Democratic Republic of the Congo, northern Uganda, and Kenya. The former presidents of Liberia and the former Yugoslavia have appeared before ad hoc international criminal courts. The serving president of Kenya has appeared before the ICC. These groundbreaking precedents illustrate that those responsible for human rights violations, even at the highest levels, may be brought to justice. The ICC is a key human rights institution that deserves worldwide support.

Remedy and reparation

The remedy and reparation ideas affirm that victims of human rights violations are entitled to be compensated for their pain and suffering if the circumstances make this possible. In 2005, after years of study by independent experts and governmental comments, the CHR adopted a set of basic principles and guidelines on the right to remedy and reparation for victims of violations of international human rights law and international humanitarian law.[10] The document was subsequently endorsed by ECOSOC and adopted by the GA.[11] The principles may be far from being applied in practice, but they are vital to attaining justice in the future.

The CHR recommended that states take the basic principles and guidelines into account, promote respect of them, and bring them to the attention of executive bodies of governments, in particular law enforcement officials and military and security forces, legislative bodies, the judiciary, victims and their representatives, human rights defenders and lawyers, the media, and the public in general.

The commission recalled that the Rome Statute of the ICC required the establishment of "principles relating to reparation to, or in respect of, victims, including restitution, compensation and rehabilitation." It also called for the establishment of a trust fund for the victims (and their families) of crimes within the court's jurisdiction and mandated the court "to protect the safety, physical and psychological well-being, dignity and privacy of victims," and to permit the participation of victims at all "stages of the proceedings determined to be appropriate by the Court."

The commission affirmed that the principles and guidelines were directed at gross violations of international human rights law and serious violations of international humanitarian law which, by their very grave nature, constituted an affront to human dignity. It recalled that international law contained the obligation to prosecute perpetrators of certain international crimes according to international obligations of states and the requirements of national law or as provided for in the applicable statutes of international judicial organs. It further stated that the duty to prosecute reinforces the international legal obligations to be carried out in accordance with national legal requirements and procedures, and supports the concept of complementarity.

The commission declared its conviction that in adopting a victim-oriented perspective, the international community affirmed its human solidarity with victims of violations of international law, including international human rights law and international humanitarian law.

The basic principles and guidelines, as eventually adopted by the GA, contained 13 chapters with core provisions of international human rights law. Because of the clarity and firmness of the document, it is summarized below. The document is a magisterial summary of the contemporary international law on human rights, and the ideas of justice, remedy and reparation.

The basic principles and guidelines recall that the obligation to respect, ensure respect for, and implement international human rights law and international humanitarian law emanates from treaties to which a state is a party, customary international law, or the domestic law of states. The principles further urge that states should, as required under international law, ensure that their domestic law is consistent with their international legal obligations by:

- incorporating norms of international human rights law and international humanitarian law into their domestic law or otherwise implement them in their domestic legal system;
- adopting appropriate and effective legislative and administrative procedures and other appropriate measures that provide fair, effective, and prompt access to justice;
- making available adequate, effective, prompt, and appropriate remedies, including reparation, as defined below; and
- ensuring that their domestic law provides at least the same level of protection for victims as required by international obligations.

The principles further specify that the obligation to respect, ensure respect for, and implement international human rights law and international humanitarian law includes the duty to:

- take appropriate legislative and administrative and other appropriate measures to prevent violations;
- investigate violations effectively, promptly, thoroughly, and impartially and, where appropriate, take action against those allegedly responsible in accordance with domestic and international law;
- provide equal and effective access to justice for those who claim to be victims of a human rights or humanitarian law violation, irrespective of who may ultimately be the bearer of responsibility for the violation; and
- provide effective remedies to victims, including reparation, as described below.

The principles underline that states must investigate violations of international human rights law and international humanitarian law. Further, if there is sufficient evidence, they must also submit the person allegedly responsible for the violations to prosecution and, if found guilty, punish her or him. Moreover, in these cases, states should, in accordance with international law, cooperate with one another and assist international judicial organs in these violations.

To that end, where so provided in an applicable treaty or under other international law obligations, states should incorporate or otherwise implement appropriate provisions for universal jurisdiction within their domestic law. Moreover, where it is so provided for in an applicable treaty or other international legal obligations, states should facilitate extradition or surrender offenders to other states and to appropriate international judicial bodies. They should also provide judicial assistance and other forms of cooperation in the pursuit of international justice, including assistance to and protection of victims and witnesses. This should be done according to international human rights legal standards and subject to international legal requirements, such as those relating to the prohibition of torture and other forms of cruel, inhuman, or degrading treatment or punishment.

The principles specify that where provided for in an applicable treaty or other international legal obligations, statutes of limitations shall not apply to gross violations of international human rights law and international humanitarian law that constitute crimes under international law. Domestic statutes of limitations for other types of violations that do not constitute crimes under international law, including time limitations applicable to civil claims and other procedures, should not be unduly restrictive.

According to the principles, victims are people who individually or collectively suffered harm, including physical or mental injury, emotional suffering, economic loss, or substantial impairment of their fundamental rights, through acts or omissions that constitute gross violations of international human rights law or international humanitarian law. Where appropriate, and in accordance with domestic law, the term "victim" also includes the immediate family or dependants of the direct victim and persons who have suffered harm when intervening to assist victims in distress or prevent victimization. A person shall be considered a victim regardless of whether the perpetrator of the violation is identified, apprehended, prosecuted or convicted, and regardless of the familial relationship between the perpetrator and the victim.

The principles have further provisions on treatment of victims. They state that victims should be treated with humanity and respect for their dignity and human rights, and appropriate measures should be taken to ensure their safety, physical and psychological well-being, and privacy, as well as that of their families. The state should ensure that its domestic laws provide that a victim who has suffered violence or trauma should benefit from special consideration and care to avoid re-traumatization during legal and administrative procedures.

As remedies for gross violations of rights, the principles include the victim's right to equal and effective access to justice; adequate, effective, and prompt reparation for harm suffered; and access to relevant information concerning violations and reparation mechanisms.

According to the principles, victims of gross violations should have equal access to an effective judicial remedy as provided for under international law. Other remedies include access to administrative and other bodies, as well as mechanisms, modalities, and proceedings conducted in accordance with domestic law. Obligations arising under international law to secure the right to access justice and fair and impartial proceedings shall be reflected in domestic laws.

To that end, states should:

- disseminate information about all available remedies for gross and serious violations of international human rights law and international humanitarian law;
- take measures to minimize the inconvenience to victims and their representatives, protect against unlawful interference with their privacy, and ensure their safety from intimidation and retaliation, as well as that of their families and witnesses, before, during, and after judicial, administrative, or other proceedings that affect the interests of victims;
- provide proper assistance to victims seeking access to justice; and

- make available all appropriate legal, diplomatic, and consular means to ensure that victims can exercise their rights to remedy for gross and serious violations of international human rights law or international humanitarian law.

In addition to individual access to justice, states should endeavor to develop procedures to allow groups of victims to present claims for reparation and receive reparation. An adequate, effective, and prompt remedy for gross violations of international human rights law or serious violations of international humanitarian law should include all available and appropriate international processes in which a person may have legal standing and should be without prejudice to any other domestic remedies.

The principles stipulate that adequate, effective, and prompt reparation is intended to promote justice by redressing gross and serious violations of international human rights law or international humanitarian law. Reparation should be proportional to the gravity of violations and the harm suffered. In accordance with its domestic laws and international legal obligations, a state shall provide reparation to victims for acts or omissions that can be attributed to the state and constitute gross and serious violations of international human rights law or humanitarian law. In cases where a person, a legal person, or other entity is liable for reparation to a victim, such party should provide reparation to the victim or compensate the state if the state has already provided reparation to the victim.

States should endeavor to establish national programs for reparation and other assistance to victims if the party liable for the harm suffered is unable or unwilling to meet their obligations. States should also enforce domestic judgments for reparation against individuals or entities liable for the harm suffered and endeavor to enforce valid foreign legal judgments for reparation in accordance with domestic law and international legal obligations. To that end, states should provide effective mechanisms to enforce reparation judgments under their domestic laws.

In accordance with domestic and international law and taking account of individual circumstances, victims of gross and serious violations of international human rights law and international humanitarian law should, as appropriate and proportional to the gravity of the violation and the circumstances of each case, be provided with full and effective reparation as laid out in principles 19–23, which include restitution, compensation, rehabilitation, satisfaction, and guarantees of non-repetition.

Restitution should, whenever possible, restore the victim to the original situation before the violation occurred. Restitution includes, as appropriate: restoration of liberty, enjoyment of human rights, identity, family life and citizenship, return to one's place of residence, restoration of employment, and return of property.

Compensation should be provided for any economically assessable damage resulting from gross and serious violations of international human rights law and international humanitarian law, such as physical or mental harm; lost opportunities, including employment, education, and social benefits; material damages and loss of earnings, including loss of earning potential; moral damage; costs required for legal or expert assistance, medicine and medical services, and psychological and social services.

Rehabilitation should include medical and psychological care as well as legal and social services. Satisfaction should also include any or all of the following:

- effective measures aimed at the cessation of continuing violations;
- verification of the facts and full and public disclosure of the truth to the extent that such disclosure does not cause further harm or threaten the safety and interests of the victim, the victim's relatives, witnesses, or persons who have intervened to assist the victim or prevent the occurrence of further violations;
- the search for the whereabouts of the disappeared, the identities of abducted children, and the bodies of those killed, and assistance in the recovery, identification and reburial of the bodies in accordance with the expressed or presumed wish of the victims or the cultural practices of the families and communities;
- an official declaration or a judicial decision restoring the dignity, reputation, and the rights of the victim and of persons closely connected with the victim;
- public apology, including acknowledgment of the facts and acceptance of responsibility;
- judicial and administrative sanctions against persons liable for the violations;
- commemorations and tributes to the victims; and
- inclusion of an accurate account of the violations that occurred in international human rights law and international humanitarian law training, and in educational material at all levels.

Guarantees of non-repetition should include any or all of the following measures, which will also contribute to prevention:

- ensuring effective civilian control of military and security forces;
- ensuring that all civilian and military proceedings abide by international standards of due process, fairness, and impartiality;
- strengthening the independence of the judiciary;
- protecting persons in the legal, medical, and health care professions, the media and other related professions, and human rights defenders;
- providing human rights and international humanitarian law education to all sectors of society and training for law enforcement officials as well as military and security forces;
- promoting the observance of codes of conduct and ethical norms, in particular international standards, by public servants, including law enforcement, correctional, media, medical, psychological, social service, and military personnel, as well as by economic enterprises;
- promoting mechanisms for preventing and monitoring social conflicts and their resolution; and
- reviewing and reforming laws contributing to or allowing gross violations of international human rights law and serious violations of international humanitarian law.

The guidelines further call on states to develop means of informing the general public and, in particular, victims of gross violations of international human rights law and serious violations of international humanitarian law, of the rights and remedies addressed by the principles and of all available legal, medical, psychological, social, administrative, and all other services to which victims may have a right of access. Moreover, victims and their representatives should be entitled to seek and obtain information on the causes leading to their victimization and on the causes and conditions pertaining to the gross and serious violations of international human rights law and international humanitarian law, and to learn the truth about these violations.

The guidelines underline that the application and interpretation of its provisions must be consistent with international human rights law and international humanitarian law, and be without discrimination.

Conclusion

The ideas of justice, remedy, and reparation will be crucial to the success of the human rights movement in the twenty-first century. Governmental leaders who trample on the rights of their own people must know that they run the risk of being brought to justice—if applicable, before the ICC. People who have undergone gross violations of human rights are entitled to a process of reckoning and reconciliation to help heal their wounds and prevent atrocities in the future. Victims of gross violations of human rights are entitled to redress and appropriate reparation. Redress and reparation should be provided nationally. If the circumstances warrant, redress and reparation may also be required internationally. The ideas of justice, redress, and reparation buttress the entire human rights movement.

Notes

1 See Mark Ensalaco, *Chile under Pinochet: Recovering the Truth* (Philadelphia: University of Pennsylvania Press, 2000).
2 Christopher Hitchens, *The Trial of Henry Kissinger* (London and New York: Verso, 2001). See also Naomi Roht-Arriaza, *The Pinochet Effect: Transnational Justice in the Age of Human Rights* (Philadelphia: University of Pennsylvania Press, 2005).
3 See generally, Elazar Barkan, *The Guilt of Nations: Restitution and Negotiating Historical Injustices* (New York and London: W.W. Norton & Company, 2000). See also B. Hall, "Blair to Announce Regret over Slavery but no Apology," *Financial Times*, 27 November 2007.
4 See generally, Francesco Giglio, *The Foundations of Restitution for Wrongs* (Oxford: Hart Publishers, 2007); Menno T. Kamminga, "Interstate Accountability for Violations of Human Rights" (doctoral thesis, University of Leiden, 1990); and Katarina Tomasevski, *Responding to Human Rights Violations 1946–1999* (The Hague, the Netherlands: Martinus Nijhoff Publishers, 2000).
5 American Law Institute, *Restatement of the Law: The Foreign Relations Law of the United States*, 2 (St Paul, Minn.: American Law Institute, 1987), Article 703.
6 Mortimer Adler, *Six Great Ideas*, Touchstone edn (New York: Simon and Schuster, 1997), 135–36.
7 Adler, *Six Great Ideas*, 137.
8 Vetting refers to the process of excluding from public employment those known to have committed human rights abuses or been involved in corrupt practices.
9 See www.ictj.org/en/tj/, 16 May 2005.
10 Commission resolution 2000/35, adopted by 40 votes to none, with 13 abstentions.
11 General Assembly resolution 60/147.

11 Conclusion

At the end of this presentation of contemporary human rights ideas, we may ask: What will the role of these ideas be and how can we build on them in the twenty-first century? These questions are urgent because, when it comes to both dignity and freedom, humanity finds itself in a perilous condition at this stage in history. Earlier in this book, we touched on the fact that nearly a billion people in the world live in dire poverty, while the overwhelming majority experience deprivations and want.

The mapping of the human genome; experimentation in biotechnology; experiments such as cloning; the intrusiveness of modern telecommunications technology; global warming; gender and racial discrimination; the growing incidence of HIV/AIDS; mass migration across borders in search of economic opportunities; international criminality and human trafficking; violence and ill treatment of women; the exploitation of children; inequitable conditions for minorities and indigenous populations; continuing vast numbers of refugees and internally displaced persons; and the dangers of global terrorism—all present us with a vast array of predicaments and challenges that will test the human rights approach and the human rights ideas that have been discussed in this book.[1] How should these human rights ideas influence policies and strategies for improving the human condition in the future?

The opening chapter of this volume presented a sense of the rolling history of the human rights idea, with different societies learning from one another, cross-fertilizing, and contributing to the enrichment of rights. This brought us to the stage where the World Conference on Human Rights of 1993, representing countries throughout the globe, re-endorsed the international human rights norms contained in the UDHR and other instruments promulgated by the UN. The world conference was preceded by preparatory meetings in different parts of the world, and by great debates and discussions about human rights. The conference represented a consensus of humanity around contemporary human rights ideas.

We must always go forward, enriching and deepening the human rights project. Whatever the historic paths of different societies may have been, humanity came together at the end of the twentieth century and gave its blessings to the Vienna Declaration and Program of Action, some of whose provisions we have drawn on in different chapters. It is important to maintain a perspective of the world rallying together in unison behind shared values rather than harping on our different journeys to the twenty-first century.

The rolling perspective of the historical development of human rights also tells us that, in the future, we must further enrich and enlarge the stock of international norms on human rights. New problems and challenges will require human rights responses. As human beings interact more through migratory movements, and as global terrorism presents wrenching issues about the balance between human rights and security, it will be important to remember always the basic notion of the dignity of every human being and the principle of humanity in our treatment of everyone.

The idea of international obligation is vital to the cause at hand because it conveys a simple but powerful thought, namely, that under international law, the duty of governments to respect human rights is not a matter of discretion but a matter of legal obligation. Governments have freely consented to these obligations. They cannot claim differences of culture or religion or social systems as pretexts for noncompliance. International law is clear: governments must live up to the laws they have freely accepted. There are detailed legal instruments regulating the conduct of governments, and they must be held to compliance.

All governments have legal obligations under the UN Charter, international law, and treaties to respect, protect, and ensure the observance of human rights. The obligations under the UN Charter are firm and may have the status of *jus cogens*, for the charter is considered the core document of international constitutional law. There can be no doubt about governments' normative obligations. They are spelled out in the charter, the UDHR, the International Convention on the Rights of the Child (which has near-universal ratification), and in other human rights treaties. In practical terms, this means that we have long passed the stage where there can be debates about the meaning of human rights. Human rights have been firmly defined under international law, and states have distinct legal obligations to respect international and regional human rights norms.

Conclusion 179

The idea of international obligation, translated into action in the twenty-first century, requires all governments to live up to their international human rights commitments in good faith. At a time when human rights are adversely affected by poverty, conflicts, inequality, terrorism, state violence, and poor governance, this is admittedly no easy task. However, as a matter of principle and of policy, there can be no alternative to insisting that governments should be inspired by and should live up to their commitments to implement international human rights norms.

The processes under international and regional human rights treaties have an important role to play in helping guide governments along the path of compliance with their human rights obligations. The UN Human Rights Council has established a Universal Periodic Review process that requests all governments to appear before the council and report on progress and problems being encountered. Carried out meaningfully and in good faith, this process can help in the global implementation of human rights. The special procedures of the HRC—its thematic and country fact-finding and study experts—have a valuable role to play in helping governments live up to their international obligations. At the end of the day, improvement in the quality of governance is a matter of the highest priority.

The idea of the universality of human rights carries the powerful, simple message that every human being is entitled to respect for and protection of certain basic rights that are included in the UDHR. These include the right to be respected as a person before the law, the right not to be enslaved, the right not to be tortured, and the right to be free from arbitrary arrest or imprisonment. Here, again, universality may be more formal than real in many parts of the world, but this does not diminish the power of the idea, which has a magnetic pull. This idea is intended to beckon all societies toward the practical implementation of universal rights. Even though despots may violate human rights, they still pay lip service to the validity of the human rights idea. This is important for the future of humanity.

The idea of universality is a dynamic one and, in the circumstances of our times, should help remind us that all human beings are entitled to respect for their dignity and should be treated in accordance with the principle of humanity when it comes to civil, political, economic, social, and cultural rights. The idea of universality is a positive one for the poor and suffering masses of humankind, rather than an imposition of foreign values on different peoples. It surely must be accurate to say that no matter where an individual is born, he or she should be treated with respect and with dignity and should not have to undergo enslavement, torture, or discrimination—to mention only a few of the problems widespread today. All people have an interest in supporting and upholding the idea of universality. This is why a great deal of the academic questions about universality misunderstand the positive, pro-people thrust of the idea. Can anyone say that a human being should not be free of enslavement, torture, and discrimination? That women should be subjected to violence, honor killings, and trafficking? That children should be sexually exploited?

The idea of equality must drive us to strive for equal life chances and equitable treatment of peoples within and across societies and to combat the pernicious discrimination against people. In each society, the search for genuine equality must be an ongoing process within the constitutional and legal structure, the courts, educational institutions, and national human rights institutions. A society scrutinizes itself in the quest for more fairness and justice.

The elimination of gender and racial discrimination will require continuing global mobilization. Violence and injustice against women remain rampant. Pernicious practices such as honor killings and trafficking into slavery and prostitution are widespread. Education for girls is often disadvantaged. Women remain at the mercy of men. The world can never be content with this as a matter of simple justice for more than half of the global population. What is required is no less than a revolution as far as the human rights of women are concerned.

One is dealing here with entrenched biases and discriminations rooted in millennia of societal approaches and mores. What else can drive the movement for change if not the universal human rights idea and its championship of the rights of women? International human rights norms battle against social and cultural practices that adherents of cultural relativism choose to overlook. Take the practice of female genital mutilation, for example. When this problem was first brought up before the United Nations in the last quarter of the twentieth century, some governments raised arguments of cultural history and context. They no longer do so. Nonetheless, the problem has not disappeared. Its final disappearance will come with global education of people in the values of human rights. However, the practice is on the defensive, and the international human rights movement brought this about. The mission of human rights is to help change the world for the better.

Racial discrimination is another case in point. It is still widespread, and change will require continued pressure and mobilization nationally and internationally. What one is dealing with here are attitudes and prejudices rooted in human nature and history. International human rights law requires governments to have laws and institutions that will guard against discrimination in public policy and institutions, promote respect and tolerance, monitor prejudice and seek to combat it, and work constantly for better understanding of the UDHR's precept that all human beings are born free and equal. This is another example where the international human rights movement battles against ancient, innate prejudices and strives to make the world a better place. One can think of many other campaigns for equality that are similar, such as the fight for fair treatment for minorities, indigenous populations, and migrants. The international human rights movement is in the vanguard for change and justice. This is a pro-people agenda.

The future of human progress and prosperity will depend on the future march of the democracy idea. This is because of a simple truth, namely that in numerous countries across the globe, unrepresentative, inefficient, and corrupt governments are a blight on their own people. The rolling perspective of the history of the human rights idea has brought us to the stage where the UDHR proclaimed that the will of the people shall be the basis of authority of governments. The world conference in Vienna re-endorsed this precept. Debates rage about the definition of democracy and what gives some the right to preach democracy or impose democracy to others. Some of this is understandable, but this does not gainsay the fundamental point that while each country should choose its path to democracy, it is the will of the people that should decide. There should be no debate about this. Yet, in numerous countries, people have no say in how they are governed.

This must be pointed out and denounced wherever it happens. Who should do this? The people of each country, to be sure, but often they are not in a position to do so. Oppression and persecution may have them cowering for shelter and safety. Nevertheless, there are courageous voices for freedom. Nongovernmental organizations can help. International organizations can help. Democratic governments can also help. The community of democracies should help.

This is not an easy task, but it should be done as a matter of justice and efficiency. When the World Bank issued its 2007 report assessing the performance of different countries, it rode into a firestorm. However, it is a strong institution and has protective gear and good assets. It must not retreat. Future generations will thank it. The international human rights movement is also aiming at a global revolution in the way people are governed. The international human rights norms and jurisprudence help arbiter the pursuit of democracy globally.

The international human rights norms and jurisprudence also have a central role to play in the quest for poverty reduction and for development. What is involved is defining the content of governance. If the democracy idea means that the will of the people must decide, the right to development means that the mission of government must be to realize the basic economic, social, cultural, civil, and political rights of people. The right to development begins in each country, and then it moves across to the plane of international cooperation. The right to development means that governments must use available national resources efficiently and equitably in seeking to provide decent life chances for individuals and groups. The right to development means that economic, social, and cultural rights should be made judicially enforceable within each country. It means that each country should monitor itself and try to spot situations where poverty can be prevented. The concept of preventable poverty should take on a central role in anti-poverty reduction strategies.

The right to development means that countries should cooperate with one another in a fair, rules-based system of international economic relations. The internal and international dimensions of the right to development must go hand in hand. National implementation lays the basis for a dynamic approach to international implementation. National implementation of the right to development brings us back to the central mission of the human rights movement, namely to change the world so it becomes the mission of governments to respect, protect, and ensure the basic rights of their people. Democracy and good governance are essential for this.

The protection idea is, at heart, an expression of sentiments of shared humanity and solidarity among peoples across the globe. According to this idea, when human rights are violated, we should come to the aid and assistance of one another. Nearly 70 years after the UDHR was adopted, millions of people continue to be arbitrarily executed, tortured, enslaved, discriminated against, made to disappear, and to suffer the ravages of inequality. Despite lofty doctrines such as the responsibility to protect, protection is very hard to come by. The world is faced with a veritable crisis of protection.

When the wartime blueprints for the United Nations were developed by governments, civil society, academics, and thinkers, a central hope was that it should defend human rights. Writing for the International Law Association, Hersch Lauterpacht, the great jurist, advocated establishing an international bill of human rights.[2] Writing for the Institute of International Law, Charles de Visscher, another great jurist, called for the fundamental rights of human beings to be the basis for the restoration of international law in the post-war world.[3] Non-governmental organizations at the San Francisco conference pressed for the inclusion of the human rights provisions of the charter.

Conclusion   183

For six decades, the UN had to struggle with contending ideas of state sovereignty and international protection. State sovereignty is still predominant, but the UN has made significant strides in developing some institutions and procedures of protection.[4] Following the abolition of the CHR and its replacement by the new HRC, practically every aspect of the functioning and procedures of the commission had to be renegotiated. The principal result has been an emphasis by the majority at the UN that situations of human rights violations should be dealt with through procedures of cooperation and dialogue.

International cooperation in the field of human rights should proceed on the basis of three principles: respect, confidence building, and protection. Respect means that even when one is dealing with a government that has given cause for concern, engagement must be carried out in a manner that facilitates communications and dialogue.

Confidence building means that consensus must be built up around a set of ground rules for identifying situations of concern. The GA, ECOSOC, and the CHR articulated such ground rules on different occasions. The criteria used included the following: a situation involving *a consistent pattern of gross violations of human rights* (ECOSOC); a situation of *mass and flagrant violations of human rights* (GA); a *situation of widespread international concern* (CHR); a *criminal violation* of human rights (statute of the ICC); and a *prohibited practice* such as arbitrary and summary executions, torture, enforced or involuntary disappearances, violence against women, religious persecution.

Protection means that when it has been determined that there is a situation of gross violations of human rights, the UN is entitled to *discuss* it, adopt *resolutions* or *statements* about it, order *fact-finding* into it, make *recommendations* about it, launch a *dialogue* with the government about it, *condemn* the violations if necessary, send UN *peacekeepers* or *observers* if possible, and *refer the situation to the prosecutor of the ICC or to the UNSC* if necessary.

The idea of protection means that every state should have an adequate and effective national protection system that is capable of spreading a culture of human rights and stepping in where protection is necessary. When protection fails, the international community is entitled to step in and supplement the national protection system or substitute for it if necessary.

The human rights movement is at an historic crossroads. What is at stake is whether the international community will stand up to protect those whose rights are being violated or whether it will engage in weak processes of diplomacy, cooperation, and dialogue. There are international laws to be followed in dealing with these challenges. Dialogue and cooperation, for example, have specific content, as has been shown in this book. Dialogue and cooperation must serve to protect victims, rather than shield perpetrators.

The ideas of justice, remedy, and reparation are meant to galvanize world attention to the fact that human rights violations are unacceptable, must be remedied, and that those who have suffered grievous violations of human rights are entitled to redress and compensation. The GA's guidelines on redress and compensation are meant to heighten governmental and popular consciousness about the need to work for justice, redress, and compensation in the world.

Contemporary human rights ideas can help take us forward toward a world of greater human dignity, freedom, and respect for the basic rights of the individual. The challenge at hand is to implement the norms of international human rights law. Contemporary human rights ideas have a strategic mission: to rally the world around the belief that human rights are enabling and empowering, that human rights ideas are creative and foster development, that equality, development, and democracy can help build a better future, that gross violations of human rights sap the creative energies of humankind and impoverish us all, and that we must stand up to protect victims, for justice for all, and for the universal validity of the human rights idea. Whatever governments may do, people will stand up for these ideas; people will vindicate them through struggle. The human rights idea will win in the end because this is the will of the people. In his Nobel Prize-winning poem *Gitanjali*, Rabindranath Tagore expressed the shared values of humankind:

> The same stream of life that runs through my veins night and day runs through the world and dances in rhythmic measures.
> It is the same life that shoots in joy through the dust of the earth in numberless blades of grass and breaks into tumultuous waves of leaves and flowers.
> It is the same life that is rocked in the ocean-cradle of birth and of death, in ebb and flow.
> I feel my limbs are made glorious by the touch of this world of life. And my pride is from the life-throb of ages dancing in my blood this moment.[5]

His plea for freedom and human rights was stirring:

> Where the mind is without fear and the head is held high;
> Where knowledge is free;

Where the world has not been broken up into fragments by narrow domestic walls;
Where words come out from the depth of truth;
Where tireless striving stretches its arms towards perfection;
Where the clear stream of reason has not lost its way into the dreary desert sand of dead habit;
Where the mind is led forward by thee into ever-widening thought and action—
Into that heaven of freedom, my Father, let my country awake.
This is my prayer to thee, my lord, strike, strike at the root of penury in my heart.
Give me the strength lightly to bear my joys and sorrows.
Give me the strength to make my love fruitful in service.
Give me the strength never to disown the poor or bend my knees before insolent might.[6]

Notes

1 Thomas G. Weiss and David A. Korn, *Internal Displacement: Conceptualization and its Consequences* (London and New York: Routledge, 2006).
2 Hersch Lauterpacht, "Human Rights, the Charter of the United Nations, and the International Bill of the Rights of Man," *Report of the Forty-third Conference of the International Law Association* (1948): 80.
3 Charles de Visscher, "Les droits fondamentaux de l'homme, base d'une restauration du Droit International—Rapport," *Annuaire de l'Institut de Droit International* (1947): 9.
4 See Bertrand G. Ramcharan, *The Quest for Protection: A Human Rights Journey at the United Nations* (Geneva, Switzerland: Human Rights Observatory, 2005).
5 Rabindranath Tagore, *Gitanjali* (New York: Macmillan, 1971), 85.
6 Tagore, *Gitanjali*, 50–51.

Select bibliography

Agonito, Rosemary, ed., *History of Ideas on Woman: A Source Book* (New York: Putnam, 1977). A valuable collection of historical approaches on the rights, or non-rights, of women.

Beetham, David, *Democracy and Human Rights* (Cambridge, Mass.: Polity Press, 1999). A useful introductory text that discusses the conditions for democracy and the relationship between democracy and human rights.

Clapham, Andrew, *Human Rights: A Very Short Introduction* (Oxford: Oxford University Press, 2007). A helpful introductory text that looks at the idea of rights, the historical development of international human rights and the role of the United Nations.

Dalton, Dennis Gilmore, *The Indian Idea of Freedom: Political Thought of Swami Vivekananda, Aurobindo Ghose, Mahatma Gandhi and Rabindranath Tagore* (London: Cooperjal, 1982). A rare discussion of the idea of freedom from ancient times in India.

Davis, R.W., *The Origins of Modern Freedom in the West* (Redwood City, Calif.: Stanford University Press, 1995). A helpful discussion of the Western rights tradition.

Dershowitz, Alan, *Rights from Wrongs: A Secular Theory of the Origins of Rights* (New York: Basic Books, 2004). A serious account of the empirical development of human rights.

Drinan, Robert, *Cry of the Oppressed: The History and Hope of the Human Rights Revolution* (San Francisco, Calif.: Harper and Row, 1978). An introductory text, written with heart, that discusses the universal cry for human rights, the role of the United Nations, human rights advocacy around the world, and US human rights policy.

Foner, Eric, *The American Story of Freedom* (New York: W.W. Norton & Company, 1998). A superb historical discussion of the idea of freedom and its development in the United States.

Foner, Eric, *Give me Liberty: An American History* (New York: W.W. Norton & Company, 2012). A valuable discussion of the political struggles of rights in the United States.

Forsythe, David, *Human Rights in International Relations* (Cambridge: Cambridge University Press, 2006). A helpful introductory book that sets the human rights idea within the context of theories and the practice of international relations, and draws on the author's long years of teaching and reflection on human rights.

Fukuyama, Francis, *The Origins of Political Order: From Prehuman Times to the French Revolution* (New York: Farrar, Straus and Giroux, 2011). A superb discussion of the origins of political institutions and of the ideas of law and justice in ancient civilizations.

Hanski, Raija and Markku Suksi, *An Introduction to the International Protection of Human Rights*, 2nd edn (Abo/Turku, Finland: Institute for Human Rights, Abo Akademi University, 1999). A useful introductory text focusing on human rights at the United Nations, the specialized agencies, and regional organizations; it also discusses the role of NGOs.

Henkin, Louis, *The Age of Right* (New York: Columbia University Press, 1990). A superbly argued presentation of the history of the human rights idea and of the contemporary challenges of protection.

Hunt, Lynn, *Inventing Human Rights: A History* (New York and London: W.W. Norton & Company, 2007). An intriguing account of the spread of the notion of human dignity in European literature and its contribution to development of the human rights idea.

Ishay, Micheline, *The History of Human Rights: From Ancient Times to the Globalization Era* (Berkeley: University of California Press, 2004). An introductory background work on early ethical contributions to human rights, human rights and the Enlightenment, human rights and the industrial age, and during the period since the United Nations was established.

Lauren, Paul Gordon, *The Evolution of International Human Rights: Visions Seen* (Philadelphia: University of Pennsylvania Press, 2003). A helpful historical work, written with feeling, and presenting historical and contemporary visions of human rights. Solid background reading.

Mertus, Julie, *The United Nations and Human Rights: A Guide for a New Era* (London and New York: Routledge, 2005). A helpful introductory text presenting the different facets of the United Nations and its work for human rights. It has useful details and tables.

Morsink, Johannes, *The Universal Declaration of Human Rights: Origins, Drafting and Intent* (Philadelphia: University of Pennsylvania Press, 1999). Explores the drafting process and the ideas that went into the Universal Declaration of Human Rights.

Seidentop, Larry, *Inventing the Individual: The Origins of Western Liberalism* (London: Allen Lane/Penguin, 2014). This work traces the discovery of freedom from the first century AD and challenges the reader to consider the roots of liberalism and individualism in the Middle Ages, which the author argues were pioneered by early Christian thinkers.

Taylor, Robert, ed., *The Idea of Freedom in Asia and Africa* (Redwood City, Calif.: Stanford University Press, 2002). A helpful discussion of the rights traditions in the Afro-Asian world.

Van Kley, Dale, ed., *The French Idea of Freedom: The Old Regime and the Declaration of Rights of 1789* (Redwood City, Calif.: Stanford University Press, 1995). Contains useful information on French historical debates on the emergence of human rights.

Vickery, Amanda, *Women, Privilege and Power: British Politics, 1750 to the Present* (Redwood City, Calif.: Stanford University Press, 2001). A valuable discussion of the struggle for women's rights in England from the eighteenth century.

Zakaria, Fareed, *The Future of Freedom: Illiberal Democracy at Home and Abroad* (New York and London: W.W. Norton & Company, 2003). An intense presentation of the idea of freedom, contemporary challenges, and future prospects.

Index

Abi-Saab, Georges 150–51
Adler, Mortimer 26–27, 87
African Charter of Human and People's Rights 18, 68, 126
African Commission on Human and People's Rights 42, 109–11, 123, *145, 146*
African Peer Review Mechanism (APRM) 125–26
African peoples: campaign by descendants of slaves 166; customary humanitarian law 137; as victims of racism and slavery 3, 81
African states: approach to right to development 99; leaders' objections to human rights norms 62
African Union (AU) 54, 90; Economic, Social and Cultural Council 126; summit, Durban (2002) 125–26, *see also* Organization of African Unity
Aga Khan, Prince Sadruddin 129–30
agrarian systems: development 101
Albania 77
Alexander, Charles 137
Allende, Salvador 165
American Commission on Human Rights 141
American Constitution 26
American Convention on Human Rights 68, 142
American Declaration of Independence (1776) 4, 24, 26
Amin Dada, Idi 47
Amnesty International 44–45, 143

ancient civilizations: ideas of law and human rights 2–3, 11–15; law codes providing protection 136–37
Annan, Kofi 62–63
apartheid 3
Aquinas, Thomas *see* Thomas Aquinas, Saint
Arab Charter on Human Rights 68
Arab Commission on Human Rights *146*
arbitrary detention 128
Arbour, Louise 55, 129
Argentina 85
armed conflicts: obligations under ICCPR 57; protection of civilians 156–57; protection of victims by ICRC 148–50; reference in Millennium Declaration 105
Asia: arguments against universal human rights 64; historic protection of foreigners 137; influence on UDHR's opening article 66
Asian peoples: discrimination/ racism against 81
asylum role of UNHCR 154–55
asylum seekers 81
atrocities 1, 47–48
Augustine of Hippo, Saint 22
Australia 100
authoritarian/repressive governments: arguments against universal human rights 2, 64

Babylon 3
barbarism 136

Barcelona Traction case 136
belief *see* religion or belief
Bello, Emmanuel 137
Bentham, Jeremy 24, 25
Binaisa, Godfrey 47–48
biotechnology 177
Blackstone, Sir William 15
Boutros-Ghali, Boutros 35, 86–87
Boven, Theodore van 34, 141–42
Brahimi Report (2000) 159–60
Brownlie, Ian 60
Buddhism 15–16, 17
Burke, Edmund 24
business 125
Bwallia, Peter Chiko 84

Cairo Islamic Declaration on Human Rights 68
Cambodia 143, 169
Canada: in debates on right to development 100; *Lovelace* case about tribal rights and equality 50, 72
Cassese, Antonio 86
Cassin, Rene 66
Catholicism 16, 22
Chang, P.C. 67
Charter of Cyrus 2–3, 15
child mortality: in Millenium Development Goals *106*
children: exploitation of 97, 177; issues in UN Aide Memoire 156; refugees 155; UN report on children and armed conflict (CAAC) 157–58; violence against 42
Chile 67, 77; Pinochet's crimes 165
China 67, 85
Chorzow Factory case 59–60
Christianity 15–16, 17
civil rights 26–27, 91, 128, 182
civil society 92, 105
civilizations 39
Clinton, President Bill 93
Code of Hammurabi 2, 3, 14
Coke, Sir Edward 15
Cold War 1
colonialism 3
Committee Against Torture (CAT) 122, *145*
Committee on Economic, Social and Cultural Rights 109, *144*
Committee on the Elimination of Discrimination Against Women *144*
Committee on the Elimination of Racial Discrimination 143, *144*
Committee on the Rights of all Migrant Workers and Members of their Families *145*
Committee on the Rights of the Child *145*
Commonwealth of Independent States (CIS) 130
compensation: victims of human rights violations 166–67, 169, 174, 184
Compilation of International Instruments on Human Rights (UN) 54, 60
Conference on Security and Cooperation in Europe (CSCE) 54
conflicts 1, 86, 95, 136, *see also* armed conflicts
Confucianism 17
Congress of Vienna (1815) 137
constitution: in national human rights protection 37
constitutional rights 26–27
Convention against Enforced and Involuntary Disappearances 54
Convention on Elimination of All Forms of Discrimination Against Women (1979) 159
Convention on the Rights of the Child (1989) 159
cooperation 39, 183–84; in bringing to justice those guilty of crimes 121; in economic relations 182; in Human Rights Council 120, 156; with human rights mechanisms and procedures 121; principle of 115, 131; resolutions adopted by CHR 121, 122; states' obligations regarding remedy and reparation 171; UN's growing emphasis on 115; World Conference on Human Rights 118–19
corporations 41
Council of Europe 54, 142, 143
country engagement: Commissioner's emphasis on 129; UN human rights special procedures 128, 179

Cranston, Maurice 20
crimes against humanity 60, 121, 141, 161, 167
crimes against peace 161
Cuba 67
cultural development 91, 101, 104
cultural diversity 1–2, 64, *see also* diversity
cultural relativism: debates 4, 63, 180
cultural rights 91, 101, 182
cultures: debate and dialogues 39

Dalai Lama 17
Dante Piandiong et al. v. The Philippines 120
Darfur 46, 115, 143, 169
debt 99, 108
Declaration on Decolonization 18
Declaration on Freedom of Religion or Belief 68
Declaration on the Elimination of Violence Against Women 79, 80
Declaration on the Principles of International Law Concerning Friendly Relations and Cooperation Among States 116–17, 121
Declaration on the Right to Development 79, 98, 99, 100, 102–4, 118
declarations of human rights: historic process 4
decolonization 33, 85
democracy 84, 181; content 90–93; democratic legitimacy 86–90; in governance 91, 93, 94, 95; and human rights 88, 91; promotion of as human right 91–95, 92–95; self-determination 85–86, *see also* elections
Democratic Republic of the Congo 169
deportations/extradition: obligations against under ICCPR 57; states' obligations regarding remedy and reparation 171
Dershowitz, Alan 19, 27
developing countries: debates on right to development 99–100; involvement in drafting of UDHR 67; justifications for authoritarianism 64; Millennium Development Goals *106–7*, 108; post-colonial state of poverty 97–98
development: debates on rights-based approaches to 98, 99–100, 111–12; Declaration on the Right to Development 102–4; global partnership for 122; in ICESCR 100–101; link with democracy 94, 182; in Millennium Development Goals *106–7*, 108; and poverty indicators *106–7*; World Conference on Human Rights 118
dialogue *see* human rights dialogue
dictatorships: issues regarding states of emergency 88–89
diplomacy: ICRC 149
diplomatic and consular practice protection 137–38, 139
disadvantaged groups 76–77
discrimination 1, 180; addressed in ICCPR 74–79; addressed in UDHR 67; versus distinction 75–76, *see also* gender discrimination; racial discrimination
displaced persons 156, 159, 177; fleeing Uganda under Amin 47–48
diversity: in democracy 93, *see also* cultural diversity
drugs: access and affordability referred to in MDGs 108
Durban Declaration *see* World Conference Against Racism, Racial Discrimination, Xenophobia and Related Intolerance
Dworkin, Ronald 21

Ebadi, Shirin 2
economic development: as condition for democracy 91; Declaration on the Right to Development 104; ICESCU 101; used as justification for authoritarianism 64
economic freedom 40
economic rights 27, 46, 67, 91, 92, 128, 182
education: about human rights 39, 47, 119, 180; in democratic society 92; gender discrimination 180; International Covenant on Economic, Social and Cultural Rights

192 Index

101; reference in Millennium Declaration 105, *106*; role of Human Rights Council 155
Egypt: ancient rights 2, 3, 11; input into drafting of UDHR 67
elections 87, 91, 94, 130–31
Endorois community (Kenya) 109–11
enforced and involuntary disappearances: in Chile under Pinochet 165; obligations to investigate cases 59; UN human rights special procedures against 128
enfranchisement 27
English Civil War 3–4
English Declaration of Human Rights 4
English law 15
environment 1, 52
environmental sustainability: in Millenium Development Goals *107*
equal opportunities: Declaration on the Right to Development 102
equality 180; addressed in UDHR 67, 74; concept in international human rights law 72–73; Durban Declaration (2001) 81–82; fundamental meaning 73; principles of ICCPR 74–76, 74–79; religious rights in Treaty of Westphalia 137; World Conference on Women's Rights 79–81
ethnic cleansing 54, 119, 167
Europe: development of "protecting powers" 137
European Commission of Human Rights (now European Court of Human Rights) 88, 89, 122–23, 141
European Convention on Human Rights 68, 76, 88, 142
European Court of Human Rights (ECHR) 46; authority regarding states of emergency 89; on equality of treatmen and distinction 76; notions of democracy 88; protection of human rights 142, 143, *145, 146*
European Union: debates on right to development 99–100

extra-judicial killings 135; in Chile under Pinochet 165; obligations to investigate cases 59; UN human rights special procedures against 128
extradition *see* deportations/extradition

female genital mutilation 180
financial system: Millennium Development Goals 108
France: text for opening article of UDHR 66–67, *see also* French Declaration of the Rights of Man and the Citizen (1789); Napoleonic Codes
Freeden, Michael 23
freedom: and justice 11; political liberty 27
freedom of opinion and expression 92
French Declaration of the Rights of Man and the Citizen (1789) 4, 24

Gandhi, Mahatma 18
Garcia-Amador, Francisco V. 138
gender discrimination 72–73, 82, 156, 177, 180
gender equality: General Comment of HRC 78–79; in Millenium Development Goals *106*
general principles of law 5–6; in states' obligations to human rights norms 51, 59–60
Geneva Conventions 149, 150; protecting powers under 137, 150–51, 159
genocide 36, 119; as international crime 161, 167; reference in Millennium Declaration 105; world leaders' commitment to protection against 141
German Institute of Human Rights 123–24
Germany: early treaties for religious rights 137
Gettysburg Address 26
global partnership for development: in Millenium Development Goals *107*
global warming 177

globalization: Millennium Declaration's reference to 105; need for framework of human rights 34, 39–41, 47–48
Goodrich, Leland 117
Gore, island of (Senegal) 97–98
governance: democracy 90, 91, 93, 94, 95, 181–82; need for human rights framework 5, 34, 36; UNSC resolutions concerning democracy 89–90; World Bank judgments 85, 181
governments: dimensions of national protection system 36–39, 47; human rights obligations to international law 5; role in protection of human rights 26–27
Grahl-Madsen, Atle 139
Greece 89, 148
Greek philosophy 3, 21–22
Grotius, Hugo 22
Guiding Principles on Internal Displacement 159

Hambro, Edvard 117
Hart, H.L.A. 20–21
Henkin, Louis 53, 88
Hinduism 15–16
HIV/AIDS 105, *106–7*, 177
Hobbes, Thomas 23
honor killings 180
human rights: common struggle 19; debates 1–2, 4; distinctions with other moral rights 20; ideas from ancient civilizations 2–3, 11–15; strategic mission of contemporary ideas 184, *see also* universality of human rights
Human Rights Commission 46–47; drafting of UDHR 65–68
Human Rights Committee 50, 58, 60, 143; addressing of equality 73, 77–79; comment on human rights dialogue 122, 127–28; emphasis on cooperation 120; Mauritian women's case 72–73; on right to participate in public affairs 94; roles *144*; on states of emergency 88; Zambian democratic rights case 84

Human Rights Council (HRC) 143, 155–56, 183; dialogue with UNHCHR 129; emphasis on dialogue and cooperation 33, 115, 120, 123, 127–28, 156, 183; performance in international protection 156; principles to advance democratic legitimacy 87; problems with Sudan over Darfur conflict 115; role in preventive/protective action 36, 46–47, 155, 161; roles *144*; special procedures 42, 43, 46, 127–28, 141, 156, 179; Special Rapporteur on Extreme Poverty 109; universal periodic review process 179
human rights dialogue 122–23, 131, 183–84; African Peer Review Mechanism 125–26; bilateral 123–24; with business 125; and cooperation 39, 115; in Human Rights Council 120, 156; with human rights treaty bodies 127; with non-state actors 124; with OSCE High Commissioner on National Minorities 130; and promotion of democracy 130–31; with UN human rights special procedures 127–28; with UNHCR 129–30
human rights treaties *see* treaties
human rights treaty bodies: dialogue 127, *see also under names of Committees*
human rights violations 1, 33, 34; as challenge to universality of human rights 63–64, 69–70; challenges for international protection 41–46, 47, 161; children afflicted by armed conflict (CAAC) 158; CHR's emphasis on international cooperation in prevention of 122, 183; condemnation at World Conference on Human Rights 119; criteria for situations of concern 183; definition of victims 171–72; ideas of justice, remedy and reparation for victims 166–76, 184; need for preventive strategies 35–36, 141–42; role of Human

Rights Council 155; in Second American Restatement of the Foreign Relations Law of the US 52–53; showing ongoing need for protection 135–36, 182; states' obligations to investigate 59; UN Aide Memoire on the Protection of Civilians in Armed Conflict 156–57; UNSC's role in international protection 143, 183; vitiation of development 119

Human Rights Watch 45, 134, 143

human trafficking 177; UN human rights special procedures against 42–43, 128; victims' need for international protection 136; women as victims of 97, 180

humanitarian assistance 156

humanitarian intervention 137

humanitarian workers: protection of civilians against abuse by 156, 157

humanity, principle of 60

immigration laws: gender inequalities 78

impunity 161

India 67, 77; ancient codes 2, 15; emphasis on individual's duties to the community 18

indigenous peoples 136, 166, 177

indigenous rights 19, 128

individual duties to community 17–19

injustice 19

institutions: in democratic government 91, 93; in national human rights protection system 36, 38

instruments *see under names of Conventions and Declarations*

insurrectionists 124

Inter-American Commission and Court of Human Rights 46, 111, 123, 142, 143, *145, 146*

Inter-Parliamentary Union (IPU) 90, 95

International Association of Democratic Lawyers 143

International Commission of Jurists 143

International Commission on Intervention and State Sovereignty 36, 140

International Committee of the Red Cross (ICRC): cooperation and dialogue with governments 122; protection functions 140, 142, 143, 148–50

International Conference on Human Rights, Tehran (1968) 115

International Conference on New and Restored Democracies 89, 94

international consensus 34, 39; and legislation 28; on universality 63

International Convention Against Torture 54

International Convention on the Elimination of All Forms of Discrimination Against Women 54, 77, 79

International Convention on the Elimination of All Forms of Racial Discrimination 54

International Convention on the Human Rights of Migrant Workers and their Families 35, 54

International Convention on the Rights of the Child 54, 79, 178

International Court of Justice (ICJ) 52, 74, 136

International Covenant on Civil and Political Rights (ICCPR) 18, 36, 54, 68, 142; on conduct of public affairs 94; international legal obligations under 55–59, 60; Optional Protocol to 84, 142, *146*; principles and promotion of democracy 87, 88, 130–31; principles of equality 74–76, 76–77

International Covenant on Economic, Social and Cultural Rights (ICESCR) 36, 54; addressing of equality 74, 75; on aspects of development 98, 100–101, 104; statement on poverty 109

international crimes 161, 167; prosecution and trial of persons accused of 168–69

International Criminal Court (ICC) 46, 47, 143, 167, 176, 183; prosecutions 169; roles *144*; Rome Statute on crimes against humanity 59, 159, 169

international criminal tribunals 46, 143
international customary law 28; concept of international protection 136; states' obligations to human rights norms 47–48, 51, 52, 54–55, 60; universality 65
international human rights institutions: performance of protection system 156; roles *144–45*, *see also under names of institutions*
international human rights law: beginnings 3; concept of equality 72–73; gross violations of 169–75
international human rights norms 51, 52; African leaders' objections to 62; arbitration of pursuit of democracy 181–82; need to further increase 178; need to implement 184; universality 65–68
international humanitarian law: and human rights dialogues 139–40; ICRC's role in developing 148–50
International Institute for Democracy and Electoral Assistance (IDEA), Stockholm 94–95
International Institute of Human Rights, Strasbourg 98
International Labor Organization (ILO) 122, 142, 143, 147–48
international law: core of human rights ideas within 4; diplomatic protection 138; general principles 5–6, 51–52; governments' obligations under 50–51, 178–79; and international cooperation in prevention of violations 122; peremptory norm 5, 52; Princeton Principles of Universal Jurisdiction (2000) 161; requirements of national judiciary 37–38; role of Human Rights Council 155; treaties 37, *see also* international customary law; international humanitarian law
International League for Human Rights 143
international obligation 5, 50–51, 60, 178–79; acceptance and implementation of contemporary human rights ideas *51*; general principles of law and guidelines 51–52, 59–60; human rights treaties 51, 52, 55–59, 60; international customary law 51, 52, 54, 60; regarding justice, remedy and reparation 172–73; Second American Restatement of the Foreign Relations Law of the US 52–53; UN Charter 5, 53, 56, 60
International Protection of Minorities (UN report, 1947) 147
Iraq 43–44
Iraqi Security Forces (ISF) 43–44
Ireland v. The United Kingdom (1978) 89
Islam 15–16, 17
Islamic State in Iraq and Syria (ISIS) 43–44
Islamic State in Iraq and the Levant (ISIL) 43–44

Jews 137
Judaism 17
judiciary: institutions in democracy 92; international law's requirements of states 37–38; national systems 135–36; requirements of ICCPR 58; states' obligations regarding remedy and reparation 171, 172–73
jurisprudence: duty to international cooperation 120
justice: Adler on sovereignty of 167–68; codes in ancient civilizations 2, 11–15; entitlement of victims of human rights violations 166, 168, 176, 184; and freedom 11; issues in remedial and compensatory protection 142–43; need for democratic environment 87, 88; need for international human rights norms 34–35; two current campaigns by descendants of wronged peoples 166

Kant, Immanuel 25–26
Kennedy, Robert 10
Kenya 109–11

Laurens, Paul Gordon 16–17
Lauterpacht, Hersch 73, 182
law codes: ancient civilizations 2, 11–15
LAWASIA Statement of Basic Principles of Human Rights 68
Laws of Manu 3, 15
League of Arab States 143
League of Nations 54, 138, 147
legal positivism 20–21
legal rights 26–27; distinctions with moral rights 20
Liberia 169
Lipit-Ishtar 14
Locke, John 18, 23
Lovelace, Sandra 50, 72

Magna Carta 3, 15
malaria 105, *106–7*
Malik, Charles 66, 67
maternal health: in Millenium Development Goals *106*
maternal mortality 105
Mauritius 72–73
Mavrommatis Palestine Concession case 138
Mbaye, Keba 97–98
Mesopotamia: ancient rights 2, 14
Middle Ages: Catholic doctrine of natural law 22
migrants: Durban Declaration's condemnation of discrimination against 81; references in Millennium Declaration 105
migration 35, 155; economic 177
Mill, John Stuart 25
Milosevic, Slobodan 165
Minogue, Kenneth 3–4
minorities: ICCPR 18; inequalities 177; need for international protection 136; treaties to protect 54, 147; UN report on international protection of 147
minority rights 105, 128
monitoring: country-level 129; of elections 131; in national human rights protection system 36, 38
moral rights 20
Muller, Herbert 2, 11, 136–37

Napoleonic Codes 15
national charters 63
national human rights institutions: dialogue with high commissioners 129; performance in international protection 156
national legislation 37, 135–36
natural disasters 105
natural law 22–23
natural rights 21–27; Locke 18, 23
Neer case 138
neo-fascism/neo-nazism 82
Netherlands 77
New Partnership for Africa's Development (NEPAD) 123, 125
new technologies 108
Nobel Peace Prize (2003) 2
Non-Aligned Movement (NAM) 99, 100
non-governmental organizations (NGOs): concerns over HRC 156; human rights monitoring 36; input for UN Charter at San Francisco conference 183; reference in Millennium Declaration 105; role in cooperation and dialogue 118; role in protection of human rights 46, 142, 143
non-refoulement 154
non-state actors: dialogue 124
North-South divide 1
Nottebohm case 136

Obeid, Osman 67
Office for the Coordination of Humanitarian Affairs 143
Office of the High Commissioner for Human Rights (OHCHR) 41–44, 93, 129, 130–31, 135, *see also* UN High Commissioner for Human Rights
Ogoniland 111
Optional Protocol on the Procedure for Individual Communications 120
Organization for Security and Co-operation in Europe (OSCE): High Commissioner on National Minorities 123, 130

Organization of African Unity (OAU) (now African Union) 54, 68, 143; summit, Harare (June 1997) 62–63
Organization of American States (OAS) 54, 142, 143

Paine, Thomas 24–25
Pan-African Parliament 126
Panama 67
peace 91
Peace and Security Council 126
peace treaties 138
Peacebuilding Commission 36
peacemaking/peacekeeping operations: Brahimi Report (2000) 159–60; measures to prevent abuse of civilians by members of 156, 157; need for human rights components 34, 36; plans to increase support for human rights components of 129; reference in Millennium Declaration 105
Permanent Court of International Justice 138
petition systems 142, 146
Philippines 66–67
philosophical systems: influence on declarations of human rights 4; respect for shared humanity 15–17; view of individual's relationship with community 17–19
Pinochet, General Augusto 165
piracy: as international crime 161; against refugees 136
political development 104
political rights 27, 91, 128, 182
political struggles 4
positive rights 19–21
poverty 1, 41; addressed at World Conference on Human Rights 119; as factor in human trafficking and exploitation 97; as framework for African states' approach to development 99; indicators in developing countries *106–7*; issues and aims to prevent 123–24; Millennium Declaration and MDGs 105, *106*, 108; and right to development 182

prevention strategies 35–36, 141–43; guarantees of non-repetition of human rights violations 174–75; international protection 141–43; role of Human Rights Council 155
Princeton Principles of Universal Jurisdiction (2000) 161
private sector 105
promotion of human rights: difference with protection 139; role of Human Rights Council 155–56
prostitution 97, 180
protection of human rights 135, 161, 181=184; antecedents 136–39; anticipatory or preventive 141–42; Brahimi Report on peace operations 159–60; children in armed conflicts 157–58; civilians in armed conflicts 156–57; concept of responsibility to protect 140–41; continuing need for at international level 135–36; cooperation from individuals 121; curative 142; debates regarding responsibility for 4; direct and indirect 146; Geneva Conventions 150–51; internally displaced persons 159; International Committee of the Red Cross 148–50; International Labor Organization 147–48; international situations and international agencies 143; minorities 147; at national level 135, 183; performance in international system 156; protecting powers 137, 150–51, 159; real challenges of human rights violations 41–46; remedial and compensatory 142–43; responsibility of international community 34, 36, 46–47, 182; role of international cooperation and dialogue 122, 131; scholarly views 139–40; UN High Commissioner for Refugees 153–55; United Nations developments 151–53; universal criminal jurisdiction 161; women and girls 159
public accountability 92
public information 119

public policy: international norms 5, 52, 65; need for human rights framework 34; role in human rights 27–28
public reasoning 27

Quran 17

racial discrimination/racism 73, 119, 136, 177, 180–81; addressed in Durban Declaration 81–82; addressed in Milenniumn Declaration 105; addressed in UN Charter 60
racism 105, 119, 136
rape 119, 156, 159
Rawls, John 27
reconstruction assistance 142
Refugee Convention (1951) 159
refugees 136, 156; Durban Declaration's condemnation of intolerance against 81; fleeing Uganda under Amin 47–48; UNHCR protection 153–55
regional charters and instruments 63, 68
regional development banks/institutions 109
regional human rights organizations 35, 46
religion or belief: freedom of 65; historic treaties respecting rights 137; right to change 69
religious systems: respect for shared humanity 15–17; view of individual's relationship with community 17–19
religious tenets 63
remedy and reparation 166–67, 169–75, 184
Reparation case 136
resources: discrimination as cause of lack of access to 109
Rodney, Walter 87
Roman laws 22
Romulo, Carlos 66
Roth, Kenneth 45
Rousseau, Jean-Jacques 24
Russet, Bruce 86
Rwanda: international criminal tribunal 46, 143, 169

Santa Cruz, Hernán 66
Saramake people (Suriname) 111
Schuster, Edward James 17
Second American Restatement of the Foreign Relations Law of the US 47–48, 52–53, 54–55, 166–67
security: need for respect for human rights 34; reference in Millennium Declaration 105
segregation 3
self-determination 18, 85–86; considerations of humanity 60; reference in Declaration on the Right to Development 103
Sen, Amartya 27–28, 112
Senegal 97–98
sexual abuse/exploitation 97; committed by humanitarian/peace workers 156, 157; UNSC resolution on protection of women and girls 159
Sierra Leone 143, 169
Simma, Bruno 117
Simons, Anne 117
slavery: Africans 3; campaign for compensation by descendants 166; human rights norm interdicting 51; human trafficking of women into 97, 180; as international crime 161; treaties to protect people from 54; victims' need for international protection 136
slum-dwellers 105
social development 91, 101, 119
social rights 46, 67, 91, 128, 182
sovereignty 4, 183
Soviet Union: refugee situation following break-up of 130
Spain: attempt to extradite Pinochet 165
Spencer, Herbert 25
Sri Lanka 16
standard of living 100
states of emergency 88–89, 136
Stoics 21–22
Sub-Commission on Prevention of Discrimination 76
Sudan 115
Sumerians 2, 14
Suriname 111

Swiss Federal Department of Foreign Affairs 123–24
Switzerland: Federal Political Department 73–74; religious rights in Congress of Vienna (1815) 137
Syria 43–44, 46

Tagore, Rabindranath 184–85
Taylor, Charles 165
technology transfer 99
telecommunications technology 177
terrorism 1, 33, 150, 177; democratic legitimacy as key to prevention 88; need for security with respect for human rights 34–35; UN human rights special procedures on 128
Thomas Aquinas, Saint 22
Tittoni Report (1920) 147
torture: actions called for at World Conference on Human Rights 119; in Chile under Pinochet 165; as international crime 161, 167; obligations to investigate cases 59; UN special procedures against 128
trade 99, 108
transitional justice 168
treaties: historic use of 137; international cooperation 120; and national legislation 37; states' obligations regarding remedy and reparation 171; states' obligations to human rights norms 51, 52, 54–59, 60, 178–79, *see also under names of Conventions and Declarations*
Treaty of Westphalia (1648) 137
Trusteeship Council 131
Truth and Reconciliation Commissions 142–43
Turkey 137

Uganda 47–48, 169
UN Aide Memoire on the Protection of Civilians in Armed Conflict 156–57
UN Assistance Mission for Iraq (UNAMI) 43–44
UN Charter: on detection, arrest and extradition of war criminals 121; development and human rights 109, 182; emphasis on international cooperation and dialogue 115–17, 122; humanity principle 60; and international constitutional law 52; member states' legal obligations under 5, 53, 56, 60, 178; principle of universality 66; principles of equality 74, 76, 79, 82; promotion and protection of human rights 138; reaffirmations of commitment to 69, 105; San Francisco conference (1945) 151, 182; self-determination 18, 85
UN Commission on Human Rights (CHR) 34, 84, 98; adoption of resolutions on cooperation 121, 122; affirmation of democracy as fundamental human right 93; basics of right to remedy and reparation 169–75; consideration of issue of violations of human rights 151–52; criteria for situations of concern 183; performance in international protection *146*; practice of dialogue 123; replaced by UN Human Rights Council 183; special procedures 127–28
UN Conventions *see under names of Conventions*
UN Declarations *see under names of Declarations*
UN Democracy Fund 94
UN Department of Political Affairs, Division for Electoral Assistance 131
UN Development Program (UNDP) 94, 109, 135
UN Economic and Social Council (ECOSOC) 47, 123, 169; criteria for situations of concern 183; lack of action in human rights field 35; performance in international protection *146*; recommendations on violations of human rights 151–52; roles *144*
UN Educational, Scientific and Cultural Organization (UNESCO) 18, 39, 47, 142, 143
UN General Assembly (GA) 29, 35, 47, 68, 69; basic principles and guidelines on right to remedy and

reparation 166, 169, 184; criteria for situations of concern 183; Declaration on the Elimination of Violence Against Women 80; Declaration on the Principles of International Law Concerning Friendly Relations and Cooperation Among States 85, 116–17; Declaration on the Right to Development 102–4, 111; dialogue with UNHCHR 129; and monitoring of elections 131; monitoring of Millennium Declaration 105–8; on need for promotion and protection of human rights 151; performance in international protection *146*; political supervision by 139; resolution establishing Human Rights Council 120, 155; resolution on human rights dialogues 123; resolution on protection against human rights violations 152–53, 161; roles *144*; Third Committee (Social, Humanitarian and Cultural) 128

UN High Commissioner for Human Rights 47, 123; role of protection 135, 141, 142, 143, *146*, 153, 158; use of human rights dialogue 129

UN High Commissioner for Refugees (UNHCR): role of protection 143, 153–55; use of human rights dialogue 129–30

UN International Children's Emergency Fund (UNICEF) 39, 47

UN Millennium Declaration 1, 2, 4, 62, 69, 84, 104–5, 114

UN Millennium Development Goals (MDGs) 98, 100, *106–7*, 108

UN Secretary-General: role in protection of human rights 141, 153, *see also* Annan, Kofi

UN Security Council (UNSC) 33, 35, 47; performance in international protection *146*; resolutions referring to democracy 89–90; role in protection of human rights 141, 143, 152, 161, 183; roles *144*

UN Sub-Commission on the Promotion and Protection of Human Rights 46

UN Summit of World Leaders (2005) 69, 141

UN Treaty Bodies *see under names of Committees*

United Kingdom 165

United Nations: beginnings of international human rights law 3; Compilation as crucial in defining human rights for future 4; *Compilation of International Instruments on Human Rights* 54, 60; declarations, principles and guidelines 60; development of protection of human rights 151–53; events and programs on new and restored democracies 89; San Francisco conference (1945) 151, 183; seminar on democracy and human rights (2005) 91=94; 25th anniversary 85, *see also under names of bodies, Conventions, etc.*

United States (US) *see* American Commission on Human Rights, etc.; Clinton, President Bill; Second American Restatement of the Foreign Relations Law of the US

universal criminal jurisdiction 161, 171

Universal Declaration of Human Rights (UDHR) 2, 4, 10–11, 18, 34, 40, 46, 177, 179; on democracy 87, 93, 130; on governance 36; on individual's duties to community 18; member states' obligations to respect 52, 53, 109, 178; process of drafting 65–68; recognition of equality 74, 79, 82, 181; sixtieth anniversary 35

Universal Declaration on Democracy (Council of the Inter-Parliamentary Union) 90

universal values 1–2

universality of human rights 20, 40, 60, 179–80; bases 68–69; challenges of implementation 69–70; debates 4, 63; democratic test of 68, 70; as goal 65; instances of

reaffirmation of consensus over 67, 69; as normative concept 65–68; problem of arguments for cultural diversity 64; UN commitment to 65–68; World Conference on Human Rights 118
Uruguay 77

Vienna Convention on the Law of Treaties 56
Vienna Declaration *see* World Conference on Human Rights, Vienna (June 1993)
violence against children 42
violence against women 177, 180; addressed in UN Aide Memoire 156; reference in Millennium Declaration 105; UN human rights special procedures against 128; UNSC resolution on protection of women and girls 159
Virginia Declaration of Rights (1776) 24
Visscher, Charles de 182

war: reference in Millennium Declaration 105; systematic rape of women 119, *see also* armed conflicts
war crimes 121, 141, 161, 167
Western-non-Western divide 1
Wilson, President Woodrow 85
Wolfrum, Rudiger 117
women: action called for at World Conference on Human Rights 119; HRC's guidance on non-discrimination for ICCPR 77; issues in UN Aide Memoire 156; refugees 155; relief brought by concept of equality in international law 50, 72–73; trafficking of 97, 180; UNSC resolution on protection of 159, *see also* gender discrimination; violence against women; World Conference on Women's Rights
Working Group on the Right to Development (2007) 99
World Bank: role in tackling poverty 109; *Worldwide Governance Indicators* (2007) 85, 181
World Conference Against Racism, Racial Discrimination, Xenophoboa and Related Intolerance, Durban (2001) 73, 81–82
World Conference on Human Rights, Vienna (June 1993) 2, 28–29, 34, 115, 118–19; concerns over lack of justice or reparation 166; on democracy, development and human rights 88, 181; endorsement of right to development 97, 98, 101, 111–12; on international obligations 50; reaffirmation of universality of human rights 67, 69, 177–78; Vienna Declaration and Program of Action 33, 50, 62, 72, 84, 97, 118, 134, 165, 178
World Conference on Women's Rights, Beijing (September 1995) 73, 79–81
World Conference to Combat Racism and Racial Discrimination (August 1978) 73
World Court 59
world order 5, 28–29, 34–36, 47–48
World War I 138

xenophobia 81–82, 105, 119

youth 108
Yugoslavia (Former): international criminal tribunal 46, 143, 169

Zambia 84
Zeid Ra'ad Al Hussein 43

Routledge Global Institutions Series

106 The North Atlantic Treaty Organization (2nd edition, 2015)
by Julian Lindley-French *(National Defense University)*

105 The African Union (2nd edition, 2015)
by Samuel M. Makinda *(Murdoch University)*,
F. Wafula Okumu *(The Borders Institute)*,
David Mickler *(University of Western Australia)*

104 Governing Climate Change (2nd edition, 2015)
by Harriet Bulkeley *(Durham University)* and
Peter Newell *(University of Sussex)*

103 The Organization of Islamic Cooperation (2015)
Politics, problems, and potential
by Turan Kayaoglu *(University of Washington, Tacoma)*

102 Contemporary Human Rights Ideas (2nd edition, 2015)
by Bertrand G. Ramcharan

101 The Politics of International Organizations (2015)
Views from insiders
edited by Patrick Weller *(Griffith University)* and
Xu Yi-chong *(Griffith University)*

100 Global Poverty (2nd edition, 2015)
Global governance and poor people in the post-2015 era
by David Hulme *(University of Manchester)*

99 Global Corporations in Global Governance (2015)
by Christopher May *(Lancaster University)*

98 The United Nations Centre on Transnational Corporations (2015)
Corporate conduct and the public interest
by Khalil Hamdani and Lorraine Ruffing

97 The Challenges of Constructing Legitimacy in Peacebuilding (2015)
Afghanistan, Iraq, Sierra Leone, and East Timor
by Daisaku Higashi (University of Tokyo)

96 The European Union and Environmental Governance (2015)
*by Henrik Selin (Boston University) and
Stacy D. VanDeveer (University of New Hampshire)*

95 Rising Powers, Global Governance, and Global Ethics (2015)
edited by Jamie Gaskarth (Plymouth University)

94 Wartime Origins and the Future United Nations (2015)
*edited by Dan Plesch (SOAS, University of London) and
Thomas G. Weiss (CUNY Graduate Center)*

93 International Judicial Institutions (2nd edition, 2015)
The architecture of international justice at home and abroad
*by Richard J. Goldstone (Retired Justice of the Constitutional
Court of South Africa) and Adam M. Smith (International Lawyer,
Washington, DC)*

92 The NGO Challenge for International Relations Theory (2014)
*edited by William E. DeMars (Wofford College) and
Dennis Dijkzeul (Ruhr University Bochum)*

91 21st Century Democracy Promotion in the Americas (2014)
Standing up for the Polity
*by Jorge Heine (Wilfrid Laurier University) and
Brigitte Weiffen (University of Konstanz)*

90 BRICS and Coexistence (2014)
An alternative vision of world order
*edited by Cedric de Coning (Norwegian Institute of International
Affairs), Thomas Mandrup (Royal Danish Defence College), and
Liselotte Odgaard (Royal Danish Defence College)*

89 IBSA (2014)
The rise of the Global South?
by Oliver Stuenkel (Getulio Vargas Foundation)

88 Making Global Institutions Work (2014)
edited by Kate Brennan

87 Post-2015 UN Development (2014))
Making change happen
*edited by Stephen Browne (FUNDS Project) and
Thomas G. Weiss (CUNY Graduate Center)*

86 Who Participates in Global Governance? (2014)
States, bureaucracies, and NGOs in the United Nations
by Molly Ruhlman (Towson University)

85 The Security Council as Global Legislator (2014)
*edited by Vesselin Popovski (United Nations University) and
Trudy Fraser (United Nations University)*

84 UNICEF (2014)
Global governance that works
by Richard Jolly (University of Sussex)

83 The Society for Worldwide Interbank Financial Telecommunication (SWIFT) (2014)
Cooperative governance for network innovation, standards, and community
*by Susan V. Scott (London School of Economics and Political Science)
and Markos Zachariadis (University of Cambridge)*

82 The International Politics of Human Rights (2014)
Rallying to the R2P cause?
*edited by Monica Serrano (Colegio de Mexico) and
Thomas G. Weiss (The CUNY Graduate Center)*

81 Private Foundations and Development Partnerships (2014)
American philanthropy and global development agendas
by Michael Moran (Swinburne University of Technology)

80 Nongovernmental Development Organizations and the Poverty Reduction Agenda (2014)
The moral crusaders
by Jonathan J. Makuwira (*Royal Melbourne Institute of Technology University*)

79 Corporate Social Responsibility (2014)
The role of business in sustainable development
by Oliver F. Williams (*University of Notre Dame*)

78 Reducing Armed Violence with NGO Governance (2014)
edited by Rodney Bruce Hall (*Oxford University*)

77 Transformations in Trade Politics (2014)
Participatory trade politics in West Africa
Silke Trommer (*Murdoch University*)

76 Committing to the Court (2013)
Rules, politics, and the International Criminal Court
by Yvonne M. Dutton (*Indiana University*)

75 Global Institutions of Religion (2013)
Ancient movers, modern shakers
by Katherine Marshall (*Georgetown University*)

74 Crisis of Global Sustainability (2013)
by Tapio Kanninen

73 The Group of Twenty (G20) (2013)
by Andrew F. Cooper (*University of Waterloo*) and Ramesh Thakur (*Australian National University*)

72 Peacebuilding (2013)
From concept to commission
by Rob Jenkins (*Hunter College, CUNY*)

71 Human Rights and Humanitarian Norms, Strategic Framing, and Intervention (2013)
Lessons for the Responsibility to Protect
by Melissa Labonte (*Fordham University*)

70 Feminist Strategies in International Governance (2013)
edited by Gülay Caglar (Humboldt University, Berlin),
Elisabeth Prügl (the Graduate Institute of International and
Development Studies, Geneva), and Susanne Zwingel (the State
University of New York, Potsdam)

**69 The Migration Industry and the Commercialization of
International Migration (2013)**
edited by Thomas Gammeltoft-Hansen (Danish Institute for
International Studies) and Ninna Nyberg Sørensen (Danish Institute for
International Studies)

68 Integrating Africa (2013)
Decolonization's legacies, sovereignty, and
the African Union
by Martin Welz (University of Konstanz)

67 Trade, Poverty, Development (2013)
Getting beyond the WTO's Doha deadlock
edited by Rorden Wilkinson (University of Manchester) and
James Scott (University of Manchester)

**66 The United Nations Industrial Development Organization (UNIDO)
(2012)**
Industrial solutions for a sustainable future
by Stephen Browne (FUNDS Project)

65 The Millennium Development Goals and Beyond (2012)
Global development after 2015
edited by Rorden Wilkinson (University of Manchester) and
David Hulme (University of Manchester)

64 International Organizations as Self-Directed Actors (2012)
A framework for analysis
edited by Joel E. Oestreich (Drexel University)

63 Maritime Piracy (2012)
by Robert Haywood (One Earth Future Foundation) and
Roberta Spivak (One Earth Future Foundation)

62 United Nations High Commissioner for Refugees (UNHCR) (2nd edition, 2012)
by Gil Loescher (University of Oxford), Alexander Betts (University of Oxford), and James Milner (University of Toronto)

61 International Law, International Relations, and Global Governance (2012)
by Charlotte Ku (University of Illinois)

60 Global Health Governance (2012)
by Sophie Harman (City University, London)

59 The Council of Europe (2012)
by Martyn Bond (University of London)

58 The Security Governance of Regional Organizations (2011)
edited by Emil J. Kirchner (University of Essex) and Roberto Domínguez (Suffolk University)

57 The United Nations Development Programme and System (2011)
by Stephen Browne (FUNDS Project)

56 The South Asian Association for Regional Cooperation (2011)
An emerging collaboration architecture
by Lawrence Sáez (University of London)

55 The UN Human Rights Council (2011)
by Bertrand G. Ramcharan (Geneva Graduate Institute of International and Development Studies)

54 Responsibility to Protect (2011)
Cultural perspectives in the Global South
edited by Rama Mani (University of Oxford) and Thomas G. Weiss (The CUNY Graduate Center)

53 The International Trade Centre (2011)
Promoting exports for development
by Stephen Browne (FUNDS Project) and Sam Laird (University of Nottingham)

52 The Idea of World Government (2011)
From ancient times to the twenty-first century
by James A. Yunker (Western Illinois University)

51 Humanitarianism Contested (2011)
Where angels fear to tread
by Michael Barnett (George Washington University) and Thomas G. Weiss (The CUNY Graduate Center)

50 The Organization of American States (2011)
Global governance away from the media
by Monica Herz (Catholic University, Rio de Janeiro)

49 Non-Governmental Organizations in World Politics (2011)
The construction of global governance
by Peter Willetts (City University, London)

48 The Forum on China-Africa Cooperation (FOCAC) (2011)
by Ian Taylor (University of St. Andrews)

47 Global Think Tanks (2011)
Policy networks and governance
by James G. McGann (University of Pennsylvania) with Richard Sabatini

46 United Nations Educational, Scientific and Cultural Organization (UNESCO) (2011)
Creating norms for a complex world
by J.P. Singh (Georgetown University)

45 The International Labour Organization (2011)
Coming in from the cold
by Steve Hughes (Newcastle University) and Nigel Haworth (University of Auckland)

44 Global Poverty (2010)
How global governance is failing the poor
by David Hulme (University of Manchester)

43 Global Governance, Poverty, and Inequality (2010)
edited by Jennifer Clapp (University of Waterloo) and Rorden Wilkinson (University of Manchester)

42 Multilateral Counter-Terrorism (2010)
The global politics of cooperation and contestation
by Peter Romaniuk (John Jay College of Criminal Justice, CUNY)

41 Governing Climate Change (2010)
by Peter Newell (University of East Anglia) and Harriet A. Bulkeley (Durham University)

40 The UN Secretary-General and Secretariat (2nd edition, 2010)
by Leon Gordenker (Princeton University)

39 Preventive Human Rights Strategies (2010)
by Bertrand G. Ramcharan (Geneva Graduate Institute of International and Development Studies)

38 African Economic Institutions (2010)
by Kwame Akonor (Seton Hall University)

37 Global Institutions and the HIV/AIDS Epidemic (2010)
Responding to an international crisis
by Franklyn Lisk (University of Warwick)

36 Regional Security (2010)
The capacity of international organizations
by Rodrigo Tavares (United Nations University)

35 The Organisation for Economic Co-operation and Development (2009)
by Richard Woodward (University of Hull)

34 Transnational Organized Crime (2009)
by Frank Madsen (University of Cambridge)

33 The United Nations and Human Rights (2nd edition, 2009)
A guide for a new era
by Julie A. Mertus (American University)

32 The International Organization for Standardization (2009)
Global governance through voluntary consensus
by Craig N. Murphy (Wellesley College) and JoAnne Yates (Massachusetts Institute of Technology)

31 Shaping the Humanitarian World (2009)
by Peter Walker (Tufts University) and
Daniel G. Maxwell (Tufts University)

30 Global Food and Agricultural Institutions (2009)
by John Shaw

29 Institutions of the Global South (2009)
by Jacqueline Anne Braveboy-Wagner (City College of New York, CUNY)

28 International Judicial Institutions (2009)
The architecture of international justice at home and abroad
by Richard J. Goldstone (Retired Justice of the Constitutional Court of South Africa) and Adam M. Smith (Harvard University)

27 The International Olympic Committee (2009)
The governance of the Olympic system
by Jean-Loup Chappelet (IDHEAP Swiss Graduate School of Public Administration) and Brenda Kübler-Mabbott

26 The World Health Organization (2009)
by Kelley Lee (London School of Hygiene and Tropical Medicine)

25 Internet Governance (2009)
The new frontier of global institutions
by John Mathiason (Syracuse University)

24 Institutions of the Asia-Pacific (2009)
ASEAN, APEC, and beyond
by Mark Beeson (University of Birmingham)

23 United Nations High Commissioner for Refugees (UNHCR) (2008)
The politics and practice of refugee protection into the twenty-first century
by Gil Loescher (University of Oxford), Alexander Betts (University of Oxford), and James Milner (University of Toronto)

22 Contemporary Human Rights Ideas (2008)
by Bertrand G. Ramcharan (Geneva Graduate Institute of International and Development Studies)

21 The World Bank (2008)
From reconstruction to development to equity
by Katherine Marshall (Georgetown University)

20 The European Union (2008)
by Clive Archer (Manchester Metropolitan University)

19 The African Union (2008)
Challenges of globalization, security, and governance
*by Samuel M. Makinda (Murdoch University) and
F. Wafula Okumu (McMaster University)*

18 Commonwealth (2008)
Inter- and non-state contributions to global governance
by Timothy M. Shaw (Royal Roads University)

17 The World Trade Organization (2007)
Law, economics, and politics
*by Bernard M. Hoekman (World Bank) and
Petros C. Mavroidis (Columbia University)*

16 A Crisis of Global Institutions? (2007)
Multilateralism and international security
by Edward Newman (University of Birmingham)

15 UN Conference on Trade and Development (2007)
*by Ian Taylor (University of St. Andrews) and
Karen Smith (University of Stellenbosch)*

**14 The Organization for Security and
Co-operation in Europe (2007)**
by David J. Galbreath (University of Aberdeen)

13 The International Committee of the Red Cross (2007)
A neutral humanitarian actor
*by David P. Forsythe (University of Nebraska) and
Barbara Ann Rieffer-Flanagan (Central Washington University)*

12 The World Economic Forum (2007)
A multi-stakeholder approach to global governance
by Geoffrey Allen Pigman (Bennington College)

11 The Group of 7/8 (2007)
by Hugo Dobson (*University of Sheffield*)

10 The International Monetary Fund (2007)
Politics of conditional lending
by James Raymond Vreeland (*Georgetown University*)

9 The North Atlantic Treaty Organization (2007)
The enduring alliance
by Julian Lindley-French (*Center for Applied Policy, University of Munich*)

8 The World Intellectual Property Organization (2006)
Resurgence and the development agenda
by Chris May (*University of the West of England*)

7 The UN Security Council (2006)
Practice and promise
by Edward C. Luck (*Columbia University*)

6 Global Environmental Institutions (2006)
by Elizabeth R. DeSombre (*Wellesley College*)

5 Internal Displacement (2006)
Conceptualization and its consequences
by Thomas G. Weiss (*The CUNY Graduate Center*) and David A. Korn

4 The UN General Assembly (2005)
by M. J. Peterson (*University of Massachusetts, Amherst*)

3 United Nations Global Conferences (2005)
by Michael G. Schechter (*Michigan State University*)

2 The UN Secretary-General and Secretariat (2005)
by Leon Gordenker (*Princeton University*)

1 The United Nations and Human Rights (2005)
A guide for a new era
by Julie A. Mertus (*American University*)

Books currently under contract include:

The Regional Development Banks
Lending with a regional flavor
by Jonathan R. Strand (University of Nevada)

Millennium Development Goals (MDGs)
For a people-centered development agenda?
by Sakiko Fukada-Parr (The New School)

The Bank for International Settlements
The politics of global financial supervision in the age of high finance
by Kevin Ozgercin (SUNY College at Old Westbury)

International Migration
by Khalid Koser (Geneva Centre for Security Policy)

Human Development
by Richard Ponzio

The International Monetary Fund (2nd edition)
Politics of conditional lending
by James Raymond Vreeland (Georgetown University)

The UN Global Compact
by Catia Gregoratti (Lund University)

Institutions for Women's Rights
*by Charlotte Patton (York College, CUNY) and
Carolyn Stephenson (University of Hawaii)*

International Aid
by Paul Mosley (University of Sheffield)

Global Consumer Policy
by Karsten Ronit (University of Copenhagen)

The Changing Political Map of Global Governance
*by Anthony Payne (University of Sheffield) and
Stephen Robert Buzdugan (Manchester Metropolitan University)*

Coping with Nuclear Weapons
by W. Pal Sidhu

Global Governance and China
The dragon's learning curve
edited by Scott Kennedy (Indiana University)

The Politics of Global Economic Surveillance
by Martin S. Edwards (Seton Hall University)

Mercy and Mercenaries
Humanitarian agencies and private security companies
by Peter Hoffman

Regional Organizations in the Middle East
by James Worrall (University of Leeds)

Reforming the UN Development System
The Politics of Incrementalism
by Silke Weinlich (Duisburg-Essen University)

The United Nations as a Knowledge Organization
by Nanette Svenson (Tulane University)

The International Criminal Court
The Politics and practice of prosecuting atrocity crimes
by Martin Mennecke (University of Copenhagen)

BRICS
by João Pontes Nogueira (Catholic University, Rio de Janeiro) and Monica Herz (Catholic University, Rio de Janeiro)

Expert Knowledge in Global Trade
edited by Erin Hannah (University of Western Ontario), James Scott (University of Manchester), and Silke Trommer (Murdoch University)

The European Union (2nd edition)
by Clive Archer (Manchester Metropolitan University)

Governing Climate Change (2nd edition)
by Peter Newell (University of East Anglia) and Harriet A. Bulkeley (Durham University)

Protecting the Internally Displaced
Rhetoric and reality
by Phil Orchard (University of Queensland)

The Arctic Council
Within the far north
by Douglas C. Nord (Umea University)

For further information regarding the series, please contact:

Nicola Parkin, Editor, Politics & International Studies
Taylor & Francis
2 Park Square, Milton Park, Abingdon
Oxford OX14 4RN, UK
Nicola.parkin@tandf.co.uk
www.routledge.com

eBooks
from Taylor & Francis

Helping you to choose the right eBooks for your Library

Add to your library's digital collection today with Taylor & Francis eBooks. We have over 50,000 eBooks in the Humanities, Social Sciences, Behavioural Sciences, Built Environment and Law, from leading imprints, including Routledge, Focal Press and Psychology Press.

Choose from a range of subject packages or create your own!

Benefits for you
- Free MARC records
- COUNTER-compliant usage statistics
- Flexible purchase and pricing options
- 70% approx of our eBooks are now DRM-free.

Benefits for your user
- Off-site, anytime access via Athens or referring URL
- Print or copy pages or chapters
- Full content search
- Bookmark, highlight and annotate text
- Access to thousands of pages of quality research at the click of a button.

ORDER YOUR FREE INSTITUTIONAL TRIAL TODAY

Free Trials Available

We offer free trials to qualifying academic, corporate and government customers.

eCollections
Choose from 20 different subject eCollections, including:

- Asian Studies
- Economics
- Health Studies
- Law
- Middle East Studies

eFocus
We have 16 cutting-edge interdisciplinary collections, including:

- Development Studies
- The Environment
- Islam
- Korea
- Urban Studies

For more information, pricing enquiries or to order a free trial, please contact your local sales team:

UK/Rest of World: **online.sales@tandf.co.uk**
USA/Canada/Latin America: **e-reference@taylorandfrancis.com**
East/Southeast Asia: **martin.jack@tandf.com.sg**
India: **journalsales@tandfindia.com**

www.tandfebooks.com